Experiential Learning in Sport Management

Internships and Beyond

Susan Brown Foster, PhD
Saint Leo University

John E. Dollar, PhD
Northwestern State University of Louisiana

FiT

Fitness Information Technology
A Division of the International Center
for Performance Excellence
West Virginia University
262 Coliseum, WVU-CPASS
PO Box 6116
Morgantown, WV 26506-6116

Library of Congress Card Catalog Number: 2010926359

ISBN: 978-1-935412-15-1

Cover Design: Bellerophon Productions

Cover Photo: © Sportgraphic | Courtesy of Dreamstime

Typesetter: Bellerophon Productions

Production Editors: Matt Brann and Aaron Geiger

Copyeditor: Berkeley Bentley

Proofreader: Maria E. denBoer

Indexer: Maria E. denBoer

Printed by Sheridan Books, Inc.

10 9 8 7 6 5 4 3 2 1

Fitness Information Technology
A Division of the International Center for Performance Excellence
West Virginia University
262 Coliseum, WVU-CPASS
PO Box 6116
Morgantown, WV 26506-6116
800.477.4348 (toll free)
304.293.6888 (phone)
304.293.6658 (fax)
Email: fitcustomerservice@mail.wvu.edu
Website: www.fitinfotech.com

Experiential Learning
in Sport Management:
Internships and Beyond

Titles in the Sport Management Library

Contents

Dedications

To my husband, Joe, who supported the idea of a full year sabbatical to undertake this project and who was extraordinarily understanding of the time dedicated throughout the year it took to complete the book.

—SF

To my wife, Janet, for her love, understanding, and support of the time and efforts required to complete this project, and to my loving Grandmother for her guidance and encouragement many years ago to provide education to the needy.

—JD

Foreword

We are all in search of happiness in our lives and, for most Americans, happiness stems from a fascination or some affiliation with sports. We choose to completely surround ourselves with an aura of sport shows, themes, décor, sport apparel and billboards, game summaries, and scores. According to many, our number one sporting event of the year is the Super Bowl, and we only want to see the very best teams in the contest, playing the very best game of the year, with at least one overtime, before the final buzzer. And we always hope that it will be the greatest extravaganza and sport spectacle ever, even more so than last year! Because sport garners so much attention and is so much a part of anyone's life in the United States—from supporting your local pro or college team or engaging in online fantasy sports leagues, to actually participating in interscholastic or summer recreational activities—it is not uncommon for many of us to think a job in sports will provide us with lifelong happiness. "I want to *play!*"

According to a 2007–2008 high school athletics participation survey conducted by the National Federation of State High School Associations, nearly 7.5 million boys and girls participated on an interscholastic sports team. According to the NCAA, a membership-led nonprofit association of colleges and universities committed to supporting academic and athletic opportunities, there are over 380,000 student-athletes participating in intercollegiate sports activities each year. Yet for the nearly 8 million participants, there are not enough job opportunities within the four major leagues (NFL, MLB, NBA, and NHL), nor when combining the large number of minor league teams and facilities, to provide all of those participants a business career in sports. "I *still* want to *play!*"

You know the NCAA commercial, "There are over 380 thousand student-athletes in the NCAA and just about all of them will be going pro in something *other* than sports." Well, they may be referring to suiting up and *playing* professional sports, but many of these participants will wear the other kind of suit and their courts/fields will be in the business offices of sport. "May I *play* here?"

Years ago, it used to be that you could only get a job in sports if you were related to a team's owner or knew the owner or his relatives. Though networking is still a necessary procedure for anyone to be "recruited" or "discovered," our company, TeamWork Online, has encouraged most all of the major sports organizations to open their positions to the public. We have provided an online recruiting network to make those positions public to you. "Maybe I can *play!*?"

Much like one's opportunities to *play* professional sports, both the numbers of jobs are few and the competition for those jobs is fierce. In 2009, nearly 600 sport organizations including a majority of the major league sport organizations such as the New York Yankees, Boston Red Sox, Pittsburgh Penguins, Detroit Red Wings, Cleveland Cavaliers, Los Angeles Lakers, Houston Texans, and Chicago Bears, as well as tracks owned by International Speedway Corporation, tournaments on the ATP and WTA Tours and the LPGA, posted only about 7,500 job opportunities. Fortunately for some, over two-thirds were for entry level, part-time, or internship positions. However, in response to a recent posting for a Public Relations Assistant position with an NFL Team, over 1,000 people applied in eight days, so overwhelming the network that the team had to shut down the posting early. "OK, so I CAN *play!*"

Rest assured, there will be over 50,000 volunteer opportunities for the London Olympic Games. There are typically hundreds of volunteer positions available to raise money for a charitable organization by selling food and beverages at many outdoor venues. There are hundreds of volunteers needed at each professional golf tournament. "I want to *volunteer!*"

The purpose of a volunteer position or an internship in sport business is for you to test the water: to figure out whether or not the sport business industry will make you happy and demonstrate your skills as a "player" to a potential employer. How do I compare to the other players? Professional athletes try out for teams at "training camp." Business people get a chance to try out for teams as well; we call that an "internship." Maybe we should call it "training camp, too!" "I want to *make* the team!"

When most people do get a chance to "attend training camp," they make the mistake of going through the motions of a task for an internship, and then seem surprised when nothing comes from the internship. This is similar to attending season long swim practices with a varsity team, swimming in one meet and not scoring any points, and subsequently being surprised to not receive a college swim scholarship, let alone a varsity letter. Make your experience count. "I want to SCORE!!"

Will a career in the business of sport make you happy? Are you prepared to demonstrate your best efforts to the industry? I encourage you to read, *Experiential Learning in Sport Management: Internships and Beyond* and prepare to not only serve in the industry, but, most importantly, to be prepared to learn how to suit up and make the team through the exciting and rewarding experiential learning opportunities outlined in this book, including full-time internships. *Experiential Learning in Sport Management: Internships and Beyond* may be even better than an early signing bonus! Then you can say, "Whew, I MADE the team!"

—Buffy G. Filippell
President
Teamworkonline.com and Teamwork Consulting, Inc.
22550 McCauley Road
Shaker Heights, Ohio 44122
216.360.1790
Fax: 216.292.9265
Email: buffy@teamworkonline.com
www.teamworkonline.com

Preface

Experiential learning is a seriously important factor in the educational landscape in American education. Collectively, we have more than 40 years of experience in supervising students in field experiences. We have seen what might be characterized as the good, the bad, and the ugly. Trial and error has taught us that the more organized the entire experience is from the managerial side, the better the resulting internship experience is for the student.

We first discussed co-authoring some type of internship book in the late 1990s. Our thoughts and perceptions about internships, in general, were extremely parallel. We ran into each other at a sport law conference in 2009 and, immediately, the discussion turned toward resurrecting the idea; the contract for the book was signed one month later.

Many textbooks of this type include chapters in which the student may not have much interest. Sample internship affiliation agreements, information about developing the working relationship between the educational institution and the internship site, and institutional oversight bear very little interest for the student. This book is different! Because both of us believe in working very closely with the student in the internship and other experiential learning processes, we wanted to write the book . . . to the student . . . for the student. Faculty information appears in an online supplement.

We hope this book will become a great reference for you and one that will be kept throughout your educational career and beyond. It is intended to be a program-required text. In other words, it can be purchased in your freshman introductory sport management class and be just as valuable when preparing students for a practicum, senior internship, or graduate level experience. As a student, we hope you will be exposed to it as soon as you arrive on campus or as soon as you know you wish to pursue a career in the sport business industry. Whether that will be in high school, during your undergraduate education, or while pursuing a graduate degree, we believe it will provide information and tips for an extended period of time as you search for your dream career position.

We are passionate about quality experiential learning. The book provides information from industry professionals employed in a variety of positions within the sport industry with perspectives on their own career paths, their insights, and their comments on particular topics. We have tried not to date the book. In other words, it has been written in a manner by which the information will remain relevant for years to come.

The Foster Five-Step Experiential Learning Model in Chapter 1 was not developed just for this textbook. It was conceived after years of experimentation with experiential learning concepts regarding what worked the best in helping students explore various career paths. We both believe the more opportunities an individual has to learn about an industry segment, the earlier they will discover a comfortable career choice—one for which they can become passionate in its pursuit.

We realize that many professors approach experiential learning differently. However, three common threads were discovered after collecting internship syllabi from numerous sport management colleagues, pouring over entire sport management curricula, and discussing the internship process. First, and foremost, is an early introduction—the earlier, the better—to the sport industry through volunteering, activities sponsored by a sport management major's club, class assignments, or an early formal experiential learning encounter. Most sport management programs provide one or more of these experiential learning activities. A second thread was the appearance of a culminating internship where a student worked full-time for an extended period of time without interruption. The third commonality discovered was the existence of a full semester pre-internship class. All of these seemed to be the most direct path for full and complete preparation of a student intern, especially at the undergraduate level. But experiential learning is important at any level, so the concepts of the book are applicable from high school (see Chapter 10) through graduate school.

We have also purposively reached out to the students who are contemplating graduate school including those attempting to make a decision about the pursuit of a doctoral degree. Thus, we have included the sport management professor as an intentional career path in Chapter 10 and provide several interviews of sport management professors and educators.

Enjoy!

Acknowledgments

We would like to acknowledge the assistance of several individuals who supported our passion for this project and kept us sane and laughing. To all of the individuals who graciously gave of their time in the development of the chapter practitioner comments, Time Out Interviews, and the end-of-chapter experiential learning examples—without your assistance, this book would not have been possible.

To the following Northwestern State University of Louisiana Graduate Assistants: Steven Tjaden, N. Garrison Burton, and Nathan Dunams, for assistance with references, e-mail correspondence, and Internet research.

To the following from Saint Leo University: Deirdre Selwyn, whose consistent quality and prompt assistance in Interlibrary Loan truly made research for this book much faster and easier; to Molly-Dodd Adams, Communications Manager in the Office of Public Relations, who went above the call of duty in the selection of some photographs for the book; to Michael Gradisher, Legal Counsel, who provided recommendations and forms; and to the more than 2,000 apprentices, practicum students, and interns we have had the pleasure of supervising, past and present, whose dedication to performing quality work played a role in building the sport management programs at the institutions at which we have taught. Your work and belief that quality placement is as much about hard work and personal sacrifices as it is about willingness to accept a mentor's guidance was a significant building block in the writing of this textbook.

To the administrators and colleagues who believed in our background knowledge of the sport business industry and our confidence in building quality programs, and who understood the experiential learning program was a key factor to becoming a top sport management program—your support when we made positive curriculum and program changes will never be forgotten.

And finally, to the many internship site supervisors and organizations that have provided experiential and career opportunities for our students, thank you.

1

Introduction to Experiential Learning

"Your students are go-getters that understand the overall picture. They are clearly more prepared than their peers . . . your students understand personal sacrifice, can be trusted with more than ordinary tasks, and they truly represent our organization and yours in a first class manner."

—Buck Rogers
General Manager, Huntsville Stars (AA—Milwaukee Brewers)

THE WARM UP

Sport as an industry dominates the economy. Leagues, teams, and sporting events on both the professional and amateur stages will always be a primary staple of North American society. Internationally, sport is growing as evidenced in one sector when new countries participate at each Olympic Games. Many countries are realizing the importance of grassroots sport programs to improve the quality of life and foster a strong interest and desire in youth to become athletes who will then represent their countries well in international competitions. Many foreign students desire an education in the United States, but prefer to intern or work in another country, perhaps their home country. Whatever the venue, there will always be a need for qualified sport managers and sport organizations willing to design quality internship positions that will allow the hard-working individual to gain experience through a variety of experiential learning opportunities.

Due to the glamour of the sport business industry, many may believe it is difficult, if not impossible, to get their foot in the door. Dismal pictures have been painted in key newspaper articles. In a *Wall Street Journal* article, Helyar (2006) questioned if sport management programs were "the tickets to great sport jobs" (p. R5). Belson (2009) similarly stated in a *New York Times* article that individuals would stay in "low-paying, unglamorous jobs like selling ads, tickets, and concessions" (para. 1). While these types of jobs are typical for an entry level individual starting a career in professional sport, careers in the sport industry extend far beyond this one segment of the industry. Yes, as with other industries, the recession hit the sport business industry hard in 2008 and jobs were lost. Even storied sport management programs with a strong track record for graduate job placement experienced problems (King, 2009). But as the economy rebuilds, so, too, will an industry and sport that has traditionally been known to do better than others in difficult times.

What this dismal publicity does not explain to the aspiring sport career professional is that there will always be excellent opportunities, for those who are motivated and patient, to work their way up a career ladder just as in any other industry. Very few start in the sport business industry, or any industry, in a top position which is the level to which many sport management majors aspire. Sport seems glamorous to many, but beyond the glitter and glitz, very good careers exist with good salaries. And, as one works in sport, the glitter and glitz one perceives decreases. However, sport managers typically love their careers and experience a variety of daily scenarios far different than the everyday doldrums of many jobs. Even the seasoned veteran rallies with excitement when their team, event, or business "hits a home run!" Thus, the negative publicity sport management programs receive fuels the already passionate desire of the authors to drive sport management students across geographical regions toward a clear understanding that a career in sport business is more than possible. Indeed, careers in this field are extremely desirable, fun, exciting, rewarding, and many are very financially rewarding. Six figure salaries exist in numerous segments of the industry.

Is the path to obtaining a full-time career easy? Absolutely not! But neither were the on-field practices or days in the weight room that some athletes endured in their little league, high school, or collegiate playing days. We are sure you have heard the saying, "Practice makes perfect, but only when it is perfect practice!"

Another perspective the newspaper articles do not print are the successes even in the smallest of programs. Any professor at any academic level and practicing sport management professionals throughout the sport business industry understand the key ingredient for gaining entry is gaining experience—early and often. Getting involved in the sport management associations and taking on leadership roles are great starting points. Attending conferences and participating in student competitions such as the ones hosted by the Sport Marketing Association (SMA), the Sport and Recreation Law Association (SRLA), and the North American Society for Sport Management (NASSM) can be important. Students who often win these competitions have absolutely no problem getting noticed and landing full-time positions. In several chapters of this book, we present Time Out Interviews of industry professionals. Please take note of their college degrees and the institutions from which they received their degrees. This is proof positive that student success is not relegated to graduates of a few programs or only those with master's degrees. Many of these programs get a lot of the press for educating sport business leaders of tomorrow simply because of their size or name recognition. If you are attending a school with a quality curriculum and quality faculty and get experience early, then you too can hold a position in sport business and climb those industry ladders.

This book has many purposes. First and foremost, it is to tell a story. It is written to the student and for the student as a handbook for understanding how getting an early start to gaining experience can assist you, the student, in gaining full-time employment by graduation day! It will help you develop a pre-career timeline and provide valuable tips for getting your foot into the industry as well as avoiding pitfalls which will sabotage your chance of realizing your dream.

UNDERSTANDING THE SPORT BUSINESS INDUSTRY

The sport business industry is large and complex. In 1995, from a financial perspective, it was reported to be a $152 billion industry (Lambrecht & Kraft, 2009) in the United States and in 2008, the *Sports Business Journal* reported it to be "more than $225 billion—far more than twice the size of the U.S. auto industry and seven times the size of the movie industry" (p. 29). PricewaterhouseCoopers reported the British sports industry grew by 23% between 2006 and 2007 and the global sports market (non-U.S.) was expected to increase to more than $140 billion by 2012 (Strong Growth, 2008).

Sport crosses other industries in a manner that is most difficult to describe. Figure 1.1 portrays a Sport Employment Model that encompasses the athlete or consumer, the two drivers of the sport industry. Included in the model are ten components that encompass the breadth of possible employment opportunities in sport. While many will not take you to the ballpark every day, an entry level position in any of them could lead to contract deals with top athletes, a position where services provided touch each athlete, or to an eventual transfer to an organization where sport is the main product. Subsequent chapters in this book will investigate many of the core components. Thus, this chapter will only serve to explain the model and provide initial insight into the scope of the industry.

In Figure 1.1, the oval on the left depicts the athlete and consumer. This is the very heart of sport. The athlete, whether professional, collegiate, recreational, young, or old, is the core ingredient for an event to happen. The consumer may be the spectator or the individual purchasing merchandise or tickets. Regardless, the entire sport industry would collapse without the athlete and the consumer.

Professional sport, at the top of the model, is a prime employment destination for many. We are using government to explain all non-educational programs or departments sponsored by a branch of a city, county, state, or national government. Examples include city recreation departments and sports commissions or authorities. Non-profit is being used to capture any non-profit sport related foundation or private organization. YMCAs, Boys and Girls Clubs, Little League Baseball, a private foundation that sponsors golf tournaments for fundraising purposes, or an organization such as Special Olympics would fall into this category. Education, of course, would encompass college athletic and recreational sport management departments and any kindergarten through 12th grade sponsored sport program. This model would put all of the college bowl games, the National Collegiate Athletic Association, all high school athletic association offices, and collegiate sport athletic conferences under this umbrella. Arguably, some of these organizations can very appropriately fall under the label of non-profit, but we chose to place them in this category because the central component of all of these events is the athlete participating from an educational setting.

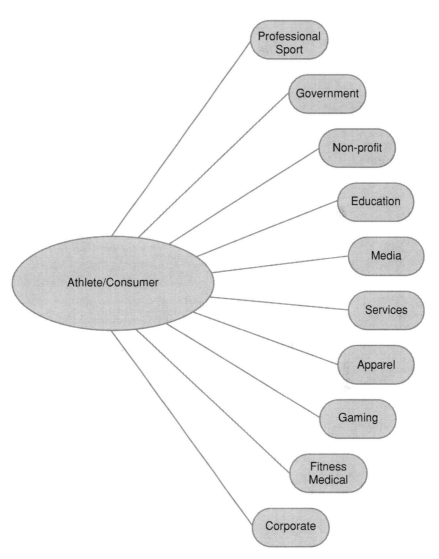

Figure 1.1. Sport Employment Model: The entire sport industry would collapse without the athlete and the consumer.

Media—newspapers, magazines, television or radio, and Internet related websites tied to sport—create numerous positions that we would label as working in sport. Whether one is covering a live event or working in a paid position tied to fantasy sports, the employee may be living out their passion through their connection to sport. Services

Students learn how to use current technology through internships at an on-site location. (Courtesy of Susan Foster)

or support businesses are large components. Companies that specialize in food, security, event and facility management, marketing, media, and sporting goods that also provide services to or operate a sporting event, large or small, are categorized under this label. This includes all entrepreneurs who own their own sport related firm. **Apparel** needs little explanation but does include shoes, fitness clothing, and merchandise needed for participation, linked to a sport or a team, or purchased because of an athlete's endorsement.

Gaming includes the popular games tied to sport and played on systems such as Wii and Xbox. Shaun White is involved in decisions made regarding his snowboarding games. Thus, extreme sport enthusiasts may seek out this type of employment. This component could include poker, horse and greyhound racing. Purists who subscribe to the most basic definition of sport and believe a "sport" must have a fitness component, including the authors, would not include poker as a sport. Since ESPN chooses to cover these events that are extremely popular, however, we felt it important to mention them in this category.

Fitness and medical must be included in this model. Certainly, the fitness of an athlete is of utmost importance at any level especially to prevent the athlete from having to seek out medical services. Athletic and fitness trainers and team doctors play extremely important roles in sport from preventative and rehabilitative perspectives. However, this text will not delve into careers falling into this category.

To complete the model, **corporate** is defined as any organization that uses sport to market their non-sport product. Companies like Coca-

Cola and Bank of America have long been corporate sponsors of sport and have several individuals within their companies whose positions are very closely tied to large and small sporting events and facilities.

COMMON SAYINGS: MYTH OR REALITY?

There are several sayings you may hear relating to getting your foot in the door of the sport business industry. Some are part myth, but all are based in reality. The first saying that needs discussion is, "It's not what you know, but who you know." This may be true in some pockets of the industry and someone influential might be able to help you land your first position, or a new position once you are firmly entrenched within the industry's walls. However, two alternate sayings portray a better reality and an introductory strategy for everyone.

First, "It's not who you know, but who knows you." Inviting guest speakers to a college campus is a great way to start, but getting beyond the walls of a specific class or outside the college by meeting people—"networking"—is equally important. Attending conferences, volunteering to work sporting events, or meeting influential individuals and starting a personal network of professional contacts are all paramount to career success. There are positive steps a student can take that will draw the sport business professional into the student's personal network where that individual will know and, hopefully, remember the student. Examples include thank you notes, a student business card, and an offer to volunteer at the next event. All initiatives, when properly planned and executed by the student, can reap future benefits in ways that may not immediately be revealed. Lindy Brown, Associate Sports Information Director at Duke University, began his career by working for five years as a student in the sports information office at Western Carolina University. During that time, he met the Sports Information Director (SID) from Duke, stayed in touch with him, and four years after graduation, a position opened at Duke and Lindy was hired. It was all about networking and experience. Of course, Lindy had over eight years of experience by the age of 26; he had also attended his first sport management conference as a college freshman!

The second saying, "It's not who you know, but what you know that keeps you in the industry," provides important food for thought. While a friend or relative might be able to get you in the door, without the prerequisite knowledge to handle the responsibilities, your stay may be short-lived.

A great example of this is the appointment of Michael Brown by President George W. Bush to lead the Federal Emergency Management Agency (FEMA) and Brown's subsequent resignation two weeks after Hurricane Katrina hit New Orleans in 2005. He certainly had connections to get appointed, but keeping the position proved difficult. According to a *Time* news article, Brown's only experience in emergency management was three years serving as an assistant to the city manager of Edmond, Oklahoma, who oversaw the emergency services division. Brown had no responsibility for anyone and did not personally oversee any aspect of the division (Fonda & Healy, 2005).

FROM INTERNSHIPS TO FULL-TIME POSITIONS

Many believe getting into the sport industry is nearly impossible. This statement is untrue. There are internships, paid and unpaid, as well as a wealth of positions in this industry. The truth in this statement lies in one's definition of the industry and personal preparation to establish a strong résumé. One must go beyond the major professional leagues and college athletic departments to comprehend the breadth of the industry. While working in one of the four major professional leagues may be an ultimate employment goal, the number of minor leagues and teams in professional sport is ever-changing. Positions exist within governing bodies at all levels (e.g., USA Basketball, International Softball Federation, or the Women's Basketball Coaches Association [WBCA]), college recreational sport programs (e.g., Ohio State and its multi-million dollar budget and $125 million dollar facility), major sporting events (e.g., professional golf tournaments or the Paralympic Games), major sporting facilities (e.g., the St. Pete Times Forum and Raymond James Stadium in Tampa, FL), and more. Professional associations and foundations such as the National Intramural-Recreational Sports Association (NIRSA) or the Women's Sport Foundation offer additional employment options. Many larger cities and counties now have sports commissions or authorities which exist solely for securing major sporting events within their borders. Private sport marketing and event management firms can be found in the pages of the *Sports Business Journal* or the local yellow pages. Sporting goods stores exist in just about every town in the United States where middle and upper level management positions bring in above average salaries. YMCAs have large budgets and run sport programs which qualify them as a sport business. While the scope of the industry will be examined in greater depth in Chapters 3 through 5, employment is highly probable for those who carefully execute a well-developed plan for gaining experience in all facets of the industry.

If professors were given $100 for every student that comes into their program indicating they want to be an agent for the next Michael Jordan or the general manager for their favorite professional sport team, sport management professors would retire wealthy. Reality dictates, however, that there is only a certain number of professional sport positions with the title of general manager. Looking at the larger picture provides clarity; there are plenty of doors available for opening. Rising to the top level in sport is no different than in any business. General managers are usually appointed due to their experience, knowledge, and work ethic, and not simply because they knew someone. Becoming a top agent generally occurs after law school, perhaps after several years of working for an athlete representation firm, or working as a runner for an agent or a law firm specializing in athlete representation. While the path to any top position in sport is not always garnered in the same manner, careful study will generally reveal the achievement ladder climbed often began with an internship that provided entry into the field.

In summary, the number of full-time positions available in what can be considered the sport business industry cannot, realistically, be counted. There are simply too many organizations, large and small, that provide employment in positions related to sport. Even if astute entrepreneurs create their own niche and start their own sport business, often their history will reveal they served an internship, volunteered at numerous sporting events, or worked part-time in an entry-level position (e.g., ushers or ticket takers) which gave them insight into the industry.

IMPORTANCE AND DEFINITIONS OF EXPERIENTIAL LEARNING

Experiential learning can typically take several forms such as part-time/full-time work experiences or a classroom assignment. Volunteering is even a form of experiential learning, although often in a very informal format. Thus, it is important to define terms that will be used in this textbook. Internships can be defined in many ways. Individuals can volunteer and someone will call it an internship. However, gaining experience is the focus of this book and having a general understanding of how the industry is organized can be important. Experiential learning can be categorized in many

ways and often has one of many labels such as volunteering, an apprenticeship, a practicum, an internship, cooperative education, service learning,
and a graduate assistantship are the more common ones. Recently, service
learning has gained a great deal of publishing ink as a form of internship.
The federal government also has official definitions that include student
learner and learner (Employment, 2005). Regardless of the label, the individual is generally working or volunteering for an organization in order to
gain on-the-job experience in their preferred field of work before graduation
from an academic program. However, some organizations will hire "interns"
even if they are not formally part of an academic program or curriculum.
Throughout this book, when referring to specific types of field placements,
they will be called by the appropriate name as defined below. When referring to all types of experiences, the terms **field experience** or **experiential
learning** will be utilized. The experiential learning model explained later in
this chapter involves five steps. Thus, we will explain different experiential
learning terms in a sequential order, from lower levels of involvement
through intense forms of field experiences. Additionally, a graduate assistantship will be defined because this type of position is certainly an advanced
form of experiential learning.

> **Volunteerism** probably does not need any formal introductions, but for
> the purpose of this book, we will define it as any unstructured experience
> where one willingly provides hours of their time without academic credit
> or financial reward in order to gain experience in some area of the sport
> management field. This is often where many get hooked on working in
> sport or get their start. From a legal standpoint, the federal government
> defines a volunteer as "an individual who performs hours of service for a
> *public* agency for civic, charitable, or humanitarian reasons, without
> promise, expectation, or receipt of compensation for services rendered"
> and their services must be "offered freely and without pressure or coer-
> cion, direct or implied, from an employer" (Application, 2007, 1). While
> the government's definition does not fit most learning experiences in
> sport, it does provide a framework for understanding the legal aspects of
> any acceptance of a paid or unpaid learning experience.
>
> A **practicum** or **apprenticeship** will be used to define a part-time posi-
> tion that can last anywhere from 5–15 hours per week for a semester or
> be used to explain a cumulative hourly requirement (e.g., 100 hours) es-
> tablished by some institutions. While it may seem odd to leave out those

working 16–19 hours, it would be difficult to find an institution that defined their requirements using this type of work load. **Practicum** is the more recognized term and is derived from the word practice which certainly defines the experience. One is "practicing" on the job and learning a skill or becoming more proficient in industry practices.

Some institutions use **apprenticeship** and, when operationally defined, this term fits within an experiential learning model. Formal definitions of an apprentice in Webster's online dictionary (Apprentice, 2010) include "one who is learning by practical experience under skilled workers" and "an inexperienced person." Certainly, these definitions describe a sport management student that is just beginning to build their skill set.

Cooperative Education is typically defined as an experience that combines skills and components learned on the job while integrated with a classroom experience. While many sport management programs do not directly utilize this definition, a university office may classify all experiential learning as cooperative education on their individual campus. Some students will take time away from campus and classes and work full-time for an organization and this is often labeled as a cooperative learning program by the organization.

Service learning is defined by the Learn and Serve America's National Service-Learning Clearinghouse as "a teaching and learning approach that integrates community service with academic study to enrich learning, teach civic responsibility, and strengthen communities" (2004, slide 2). In the educational environment, sport management classes can become involved in sport related activities and events that fulfill this definition. This form of experiential learning has recently been gaining momentum at universities and in the media even though its conceptual theory in education has been around for quite awhile (Bennett, Henson, & Drane, 2003).

Graduate Assistantships are part-time work related positions for graduate students pursuing either a master's or doctoral degree. We hesitate to use the word employed to define the experience because some courts and some states choose not to classify a graduate student as an employee. Regardless of how an individual entity may define an assistantship, this type of position is typically offered to qualified individuals by colleges to provide experience for 20 hours per week in a position that assists the institution in completing necessary projects or fills employment vacancies. In exchange, the student usually provides a service for anywhere from one to three years depending upon the time it will take them to complete their graduate degree. These positions are an excellent way to obtain an advanced degree while gaining experience in the college environment as an assistant coach or athletic department assistant. One can also serve as a teaching or research assistant to a college professor. These latter positions are generally offered for those pursuing a doctoral degree with hopes of entering the college teaching profession. Often a graduate assistantship takes the place of a culminating internship or other required work experience while attending graduate school. More information on graduate assistantships appears in Chapter 10.

It is important to be aware that many organizations refer to all volunteers and students as interns. While this can be very confusing, any individual seeking an experience should be very clear regarding institutional established requirements and guidelines. This can prevent misunderstandings and avoid loss of academic credit. An educational institution should have established policy guidelines for all students required to work in the industry.

The term **internship** will be defined as a 20- to 40-hour per week work-related experience that lasts for a minimum of ten weeks. While many institutions require interns to work the duration of an academic semester, some organizations may require an intern to work an entire sport season or academic year. The pros and cons of working in a 40-hour per week experience as compared to a 20-hour per week placement as well as the discernment over the acceptance of a paid or unpaid placement, are extremely important. Both of these topics will be discussed at greater length in Chapter 3.

THE FOSTER FIVE-STEP MODEL: EXPERIENTIAL LEARNING TO THE NTH DEGREE

The learning theory behind the Foster Five-Step Experiential Learning Model (Figure 1.2) has been used for many years. It was developed by the textbook's lead author as a way of getting students involved in the classroom, through student major clubs, in formal supervised learning experiences in the sport industry, or by simply volunteering for a local event sponsored in an individual's home town. Many institutions probably use segments of the model in one format or another. Overall, it is a method for prompting, encouraging, and requiring sport management students to gain experience in

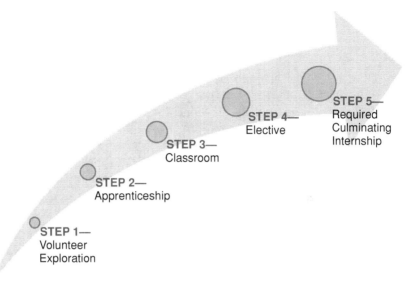

Figure 1.2. Foster Five-Step Experiential Learning Model.

the sport industry before applying for the first full-time position. With vigorous application in the early steps, one can be very-well qualified for many industry internships that are capstone experiences for undergraduate or master's degrees. Some individuals can even qualify for a full-time position and use this as an internship if the sponsoring organization is in agreement.

Support for the development of formal experiential learning practices can be found throughout the literature (Bridgstock, 2009; Cunningham & Sagas, 2004; Dewey, 1938; Higdon, 2004; Marx, Walker, & Weaver, 2009; Pacheco, 2007; Southall, Nagel, LeGrande, & Han, 2003; Spence, Hess, McDonald, & Sheehan, 2009; Stratta, 2004; Thiel & Hartley, 1997; Wehmeyer et al., 2003; Young & Baker, 2004). In fact, Parkhouse (1987) reported research results over 20 years ago that undeniably claimed field experiences to be extremely important. Kelley, DeSensi, Beitel, and Blanton (1989) presented a research based undergraduate curricular model describing practica and internships as a "series of professionally related work experiences that should move from general to very specific" (p. 24). Furthermore, they indicated the internship should be a "one semester full-time applied work experience directly focused toward each student's professional sport management outcome objective, and should be the culminating experience" (p. 24). The research of Kelley et al., also described the necessity of a

graduate internship as a culminating semester-long full-time work experience. The Foster Model supports this research, but takes practical experiences much further spreading experiential learning across the entire post
secondary academic experience. It encompasses informal and formal, student and professor initiated experiences from matriculation to graduation.
The following sections explain the Model in detail.

Step 1: Volunteer Exploration. This step can begin as soon as the student
steps foot on a college campus, into a high school that supports formalized industry learning, or begins a graduate assistantship. The purpose of
Step 1 is to introduce the student to the industry as soon as possible. For
college freshman and graduate students, this can involve membership in
the sport management major's association and volunteering to work an
on-campus sporting or recreation event or concert. The faculty advisor
should be able to assist the student in finding industry related part-time
paid positions with a local sport organization or a work study position in
an athletic or intramural sport department or public relations office.
Many sport organizations will accept all types of volunteers, and first
year students can certainly become involved in this manner during the
first semester. Examples of experiences may include working/volunteer-
ing as a parking attendant at a college football game, serving as an usher,
or working in the concession stand for a professional sport organization.
Large metropolitan areas obviously offer a variety of opportunities, but if
someone is isolated in a smaller geographical location, opportunities to
volunteer and obtain that first experience can always be found. Non-
profit organizations or foundations often look to sport to raise money.
This often happens through golf tournaments, sport memorabilia auc-
tions, or road races. Regardless of the role an individual may accept in
any one of these initiatives, just getting started is important. While beginning to build the résumé is a main objective for Step 1, learning basic
skills and observing sport managers in action rounds out the overall learning objective for this step.

Many individuals want to start as an assistant to a high level administrator. This is often possible and presented to some. When offered even
the slightest chance to participate, jump on it. Why? The number one
reason is your foot is now in the door and good professors often tell students they must learn to sweep the floor. While one may not literally undertake a maintenance position, we want student learners to focus on

learning the basics. If one learns the very basic operations of an organization, that individual will be a better manager because they know the foundations. You have learned what it is like to be an usher, to work in a concession stand, or to understand the questions consumers pose when they call the organization and you are answering the phone. You will have a clearer understanding, and perhaps more empathy, for lower wage earners and their tasks. As you climb the ladder, you will learn the organization inside and out. This will be beneficial when you reach the management level and especially true in smaller organizations where climbing the corporate ladder may be swift. Larger organizations may present a challenge for an individual wanting to learn the entire organization as departmentalization is common place.

Step 2: Apprenticeship. The second step of the experiential learning model is the apprenticeship or other formalized entry level work experience. The purpose of this step is to get some formal learning experience early in your academic career, preferably in your freshman or sophomore year if you are an undergraduate. If graduate students are entering a sport business master's level program and do not have an undergraduate degree in a field related to sport, this will be the starting point as well. When starting early in gaining experience, one of two things will happen.

First, you discover the experience is not what you believed it would be. It is very good to learn this early on when it is not too late to change your industry segment focus. One thing that should be considered is taking on a second or even a third apprenticeship in a different segment of the industry. Finding what you like early will assist you in focusing all future experiences and perhaps class assignments/projects on a preferred industry segment.

Second, You discover you absolutely love your apprenticeship and believe it is the area of sport you wish to pursue. Move forward without hesitation; you are well on your way! Find as many opportunities as you can to build your résumé in the chosen area. Summer jobs, community events, certifications, and leadership positions will all boost your employability in the future.

When choosing an apprenticeship, seek out a great opportunity. Your college may allow you to select an apprenticeship during any academic semester, but many students will select this opportunity during the summer. This is especially true for college athletes due to practice schedules during the regular academic year. Your main goal is to select an organization that is most closely aligned to your career aspirations. If you want to work in professional sport, finding a professional sport organization that will accept you is your best route. The old saying that practice makes perfect only when it is perfect practice is right. If you wish to work for a professional sport team and select an apprenticeship in a YMCA—well, ask yourself, "Am I going to learn or get a feel for what it is like to work for a professional baseball team, if that is where I perceive my chosen career to be, working at a YMCA?" Absolutely not! Professors have had students who wait until their senior internship to obtain their first experience in what they believe to be their dream job only to find out, they do not like it. Also, selecting what is easy or convenient because you can live at home, or you have a friend or relative that can get you inside the organization, may not assist you in making an early decision and actually prevents an individual from practicing networking skills. Work with your academic advisor or program chair in finding a position that best fits *you*. Maybe you volunteered for an organization under Step 1 and you really liked it. Perhaps contacting the organization again to formalize an entry work experience for you will be a starting point.

The overall guidelines for this level are to identify a sport organization that will allow you to volunteer at least one day a week for them. This should be a minimum of five hours a week during an entire semester. Remember, the key here is that the organization is accommodating you. Showing up on time, maintaining a regular schedule each week, and being reliable is extremely important. You want to come out of this experience with a strong positive recommendation from the individual who supervised you. This will add to your professional network of individuals that know you. Some organizations will find it difficult to fill four to five hours in one day. It also may be difficult to obtain a class schedule that gives you a block of time on one day. Thus, the minimum work schedule you may want to establish is two hours per day, two days a week, at the same time each week. Most class schedules and organizations can accommodate this format.

Typical assignments one may encounter in an apprenticeship certainly can vary. You may encounter a different project each week. Other organizations will use an apprentice to prepare for upcoming events. Be prepared to assume the role of a data entry clerk in positions where you may assist a college athletics compliance coordinator or an organization's finance office. Be flexible in accepting assignments. While an organization appreciates your ability to show up on time for work on a regular pre-established schedule, they may ask if you can work an event on a weekend. Whenever possible, work the events in addition to your weekly schedule. This will exhibit to a supervisor that you will do whatever it takes to get your foot in the door. Yes, volunteering means without pay, and this can be difficult to do with bills to pay. But this formal first experience can make or break your career.

Some institutions require a student to work a number of hours, let's say 50, to get their first experience. A student takes this to heart and obtains an assignment that allows the student to work three weeks in a college athletic department at night and on weekends. This is certainly possible at a large university that has major college football and men's and women's basketball programs. "Fifty hours. Great, I'm done!" Have you established a strong relationship with one person who would vouch for your work ethic? Was your working relationship strong enough where one person supervised you for the entire 50 hours and will remember you next year when you need a recommendation? Regardless of the institution's requirement, take it upon yourself to view the requirement not as an academic credit to fulfill, but your first position in the industry! Make the most of it and come away with a strong personal recommendation from at least one person that can attest to your reliability and work ethic.

It is intended for the apprenticeship to be a work opportunity coupled with a classroom component—much like the definition of a cooperative education experience. Institutions may assign anywhere from one to three credits for this classroom experience. Many institutions today may limit the number of credits required for a major. A one-credit class is usually easy for you to fit into your class load and just as easy for the sport management faculty to fit into a total credit hour count. Some institutions may allow you to repeat the apprenticeship more than once. Consider this opportunity if afforded to you. This is explained more thoroughly in Step 4.

Apprenticeships can also be easy to find if your institution is only concerned with you getting that first experience regardless of the responsibilities. During spring break, find out in advance if you can interview for an usher or a concessionaire position at a sport facility or team somewhere close to where you will be living for the summer. While you may not meet the top personnel, if you display your strongest work ethic, you will be remembered and your foot is in the door! Summer apprenticeships away from campus can fulfill a classroom component using today's technology. Weekly assignments or work logs can still be submitted and weekly discussions conducted when designed using the variety of available online educational platforms. Even if your institution does not normally offer courses online, this is easily accommodated in the described format or perhaps as an independent study supervised by a faculty member.

Step 3: The Classroom. Aw, the classroom! Homework! This step asks you, the student, to be passionate about your classroom learning. This step really starts as soon as you take your first college course, whether it is sport related or not, but certainly, in your first sport management class. This step was simply put into the middle of the model because it can happen anywhere during the college experience. Many universities do not allow students to start courses in their major until their sophomore or junior year. Hopefully, yours permits you to start earlier.

Step 3 allows faculty to be extremely creative and develop assignments that are meaningful while learning more about the industry. Service learning projects can also be incorporated in this step. Guest speakers, role-playing, and even term papers can open doors. Exposure to all types of elements that exist in the industry can be the end result of an in-class team assignment. You can come away with a great personal project; in a job interview, you can provide an outline of the completed project to the interviewer or submit as part of a professional portfolio. A project well done can set you apart from other candidates where you become the only contender for hire. Get fired up about one of the possible assignments your professor may require in a list of sample classes provided below.

- *Introduction to Sport Management.* A web assignment asks you to find ten jobs in ten different industry segments. The purpose is to help you understand the breadth of the industry. Do you know the differences or similarities between college sports information, professional sport public relations, and community relations segments of the industry? This assignment can help you focus on choices you may wish to pursue in an apprenticeship or in Step 4.
- *Event Management.* Develop an individual sport small event from start to finish by applying tournament scheduling. Consider that you are

required to develop a double elimination tournament for your class-mates using any sport related computer game or by developing something as simple as a horseshoe tournament on one of the recreation fields. Your classmates are divided into groups and you must run the tournament all within one 80-minute class period for one group. Each group has ten members. Develop the rules and draw the tournament chart. Conduct the tournament and award prizes! This was done in an actual class and one student went so far as to obtain a sponsor and the sponsor provided the prize and drinks for all contestants. This is homework? C'mon!

- *Risk Management in Sport.* Write a risk management plan for an on-campus facility incorporating guidelines provided. While this assignment may not sound as much fun as the previous class—well, after all, this is school, one can learn a great deal and apply this in a future internship or job. Picture a job announcement that describes assisting an organization's risk manager in developing a safety conscious work environment and a risk management plan. You are the only applicant that has had this experience and you have the completed project to prove it! Provided that you approached the assignment with the same awesome attitude you have brought to every homework assignment, you are a shoo-in for the position. In a tight economy when positions for event managers and market researchers are scarce, you want to do everything possible to increase your positioning. It may not be your dream job, but you are now in the door!

- *Sport Marketing.* Your class is visiting a local professional sport team and the Vice-President (VP) of Sales will teach you how to work their ticketing software. The VP offers each one of the class members the opportunity to sell a certain number of tickets and if the entire group sells at least 500 tickets, the class receives a one-on-one half day meeting and luncheon with the team owner. The top seller within the class receives eight prime seat tickets for another upcoming game. Of course, you are going to be the top seller with your awesome attitude toward homework!

Picture this favorite story that started with a class assignment involving a sophomore who was looking to work in college athletics. Kerryann Cook approached her advisor and asked if she believed that Pat Head Summitt, the successful head women's basketball coach at the University of Tennessee, would grant her an interview for a class assignment. It was suggested that she call her. Coach Summitt not only granted the interview, but spent approximately 90 minutes with her. Kerryann ended up driving two hours one way on a weekly basis to perform an apprenticeship with the Tennessee Women's Athletic Department, after which, she was offered a full-time internship and graduate assistantship! True Story! Kerryann has been practicing law and is a partner in a new sport agency MK Sports & Entertainment Group, LLC, thanks to the start she got from one interview and her own motivation.

The above examples display just a few assignments that can actually give a student additional insight into the corporate sport business world. Of course, as much as we would like it, not every student approaches every assignment with their best work ethic. This is what sets apart those who get the job and those who do not. Perhaps this is the exact work ethic that got Theo Epstein the Boston Red Sox's General Manager's position at the youthful age of 28. He began as a summer media relations intern for the Baltimore Orioles at the age of 18. He had not been a star athlete and had no relative in baseball making calls for him as he was promoted through the ranks (Riordan, 2002). Jon Daniels was 28-years old when he was appointed general manager for the Texas Rangers. He also started as an intern with the Colorado Rockies (Fisher, 2005).

Part of Step 3 can also involve taking advantage of opportunities professors mention in class. At some point, a college professor probably mentions student membership in professional organizations. Jump on it! For example, several facility management professional organizations have student memberships and scholarships. These scholarships take many forms. Some are actual scholarships that will pay part of your tuition. Some offer scholarships that will pay for your attendance to a state, regional, or national conference. At the very least, you can meet and network with top industry professionals that are more than willing to assist students who show the initiative to join their professional organization. Check out www.iaam.org, www.floridafacilities.com, www.stadiummanagers.org, www.cosida.org, and www.nirsa.org as examples of organizations with student memberships.

Step 4: Practicum Elective. The purpose of this step is to gain additional experience. Some institutions will offer formal junior level or graduate student for-credit opportunities and some may require them. Some universities require a student to take a certain number of electives. This is where you can possibly repeat a one-hour apprenticeship and select another sport organization or jump to a three-credit hour requirement where you may have to work between ten and twenty hours a week. Some organizations prefer ten hours versus five anyway. Regardless, the purpose of this step is to simply get more experience with different responsibilities in an organization in which you have already worked or to find another organization in a different industry segment. As mentioned earlier, maybe you were not thrilled with the experience you had during your apprenticeship where you worked 60 hours per week and got paid for 40 while receiving minimum wage with the minor league team in your home town. Perhaps professional golf has always been a passion of yours and you can get involved in the planning of a major professional men's or women's golf tournament that is hosted near your university. Find the right contact. Call them and offer to send your polished résumé via e-mail or propose to drop it off at the end of the day. The latter suggestion is better because it creates an actual face-to-face networking opportunity; just make sure you dress appropriately. Your goal is to learn about another industry segment because you are not quite sure where you want to intern during your senior year or in meeting a graduate level internship requirement. The moral to the story is never put off investigating career interests. There are plenty of opportunities to volunteer and learn how professional golf tournaments are run without waiting to gain academic credit for the experience. Going back to Step 1 on a regular basis gives you more opportunities to examine career interests. The Professional Golf Association (PGA) and the Ladies Professional Golf Association (LPGA) Tours have internship opportunities that are extremely competitive. Having already worked in the planning of a professional golf event as a volunteer or apprentice may make you a top candidate for the internship as described below in Step 5.

Step 5: The Required Culminating Internship. Bell and Countiss (1993) described the internship as the cornerstone of a student's academic preparation and Sutton (1989) called it a core component. In our model, the internship is designed as a full-time internship after all course work is completed. Two main reasons exist for this. First, when a student does a great job, the possibilities are increased for being offered a full-time position. If the internship is performed prior to this time, students have to make a choice. Do you accept, thus not completing your academic degree, or is the position turned down and you return to campus? An organization may state they will hold a position, but often another intern comes in and does as good a job, if not better, and is immediately available to begin work on a full-time basis. The organization might also realize they need a full-time position filled immediately and cannot delay another year.

The second primary reason for requiring a culminating internship is because course work is completed and students have been exposed to the entire curriculum. Most institutions have several courses with critical sport business concept knowledge toward the end of the degree program. Performing an internship before these important courses are completed may diminish the optimum performance level of the student. For example, if a sport marketing course is one of these courses, a student in a sales or marketing position may not have learned information beyond the four or five P's of marketing. The staff may determine that the student was inadequately prepared to accept the position. Not only has the supervisor formed a less than optimum opinion of the intern's work knowledge, other interns from the same institution may not be offered future positions. This is especially true if interns from other organizations are performing a culminating internship and have already been exposed to the requisite information in their course work.

The culminating internship is the time to shine! Don't be a **clock watcher**! The clock watcher arrives just before starting time with only seconds to spare and is the first out the door as the clock strikes 5:00. Projects are left uncompleted; sometimes others are held up in their work because the clock watcher was more interested in leaving than in the overall goals or needs of the work place.

Yes, we all know that many sport organizations do not operate on an 8:00 to 5:00 work schedule, though some do. Private sport marketing firms may be one that does unless an important meeting is coming with a potential sponsorship client and final work must be done on a proposal or additional research needs to be conducted. The intern who is truly interested in making it in the sport business world arrives early, is ready to start, or has already started work on assigned projects, and puts in enough quality time to complete a project needed very early the next day by another individual in the organization. Even if a deadline is not looming, completing work ahead of schedule is recognized as a good time management skill. However, caution must be taken. One should not rush into finishing a project without proofreading one's work, reviewing the project to see if any holes exist, and perhaps without conducting additional research or gathering more information that may make the work even better. An example of this in one's course work is when a student asks, "How many pages does it HAVE to be?" While some professors may provide a page requirement, one's goal should be to make it the best possible paper with quality work and research done in advance. Waiting until a week or two before a paper is due is not the prime way to approach an assignment nor is it a good way to approach work assigned by your internship supervisor. If unexpected things come up at the last minute such as illness, your work is not done and either someone else has to pick up the slack or has to wait for you to return. If sufficient time was provided to complete the project, weak time management skills have been exposed to the organization.

If your position happens to be in professional sport, let's say baseball, during the season, ten-day home stands and 70- to 80-hour work weeks are common. While one may be sleep deprived, take the extra effort to do the little things that completes your job before you leave. For example, you are assigned to your team's merchandising efforts. Rearranging products on the store shelves exhibits pride in your position and advance work for the next day. Of course, some assigned tasks can be left when you come in earlier than other interns the next day in preparation for the incoming spectators.

Another way to shine in one's internship is offering to help someone else who might be falling behind. Perhaps your site supervisor has had to leave the office to take a child to the doctor's office or has been asked by their supervisor to take on additional responsibilities. By finishing your tasks ahead of time, you may have some free time or can stay a little later to assist if possible.

Some individuals have the misconception that doing things in advance, offering to help others, or staying late to help the boss is "brown nosing" or "kissing up" to the supervisor or organization. Your goal is to be the best possible intern. What you do not want to do is become boisterous or arrogant about being recognized by the organization if complimented or given additional responsibilities. Just go about the work in the best possible way using great time management skills. If one is concerned about the perceptions of others, in some positions, you can take work home. Nobody has to know how you spend your evenings or what time you awake to get a head start in the morning before leaving for the office. Just stay ahead of the game and do not be one that is constantly running behind. Meet all deadlines!

The culminating internship may be one's first full-time opportunity to work with a sport organization and you want to be there to see the entire operations from sunrise to sunset. Some internships may be seasonal such as those existing in collegiate athletics. The organization may want you to begin in mid to late summer to prepare for football season and stay until the last pitch in the baseball College World Series in June (if your internship institution's team should make it). This could mean an intended nine-month internship is stretched to 10 months. You can do this because you have completed your course work; you have done an outstanding job in this collegiate internship and have made yourself indispensable. You now are offered a full-time position! You have skipped the entire process of having to send out résumés, submitting job applications, waiting for organizations to respond, and those nerve-wracking interviews! How much better can it get?

SUMMARIZING THE MODEL

Williams (2002) reported that institutions recommend students perform multiple "internships." The Foster Model has many advantages, as described, to facilitate these opportunities formally or informally (Steps 2, 4, and 5). Implementing the entire model on one's own, or within a sport business program, provides a very manageable road map through the maze of preparation, planning, and networking that can lead to full-time employment. A major advantage the model implies is that varying levels of academic credit should be available because sport organizations will require an intern to be enrolled for credit even if the institution does not require it or only requires one internship. This is where a one or three-credit experience such as the apprenticeship and practicum (Steps 2 and 4) assists the students from a financial perspective. Paying tuition for a one-credit opportunity on an elective basis is much better than requiring the student to pay for a full six or twelve credit internship for an additional elective opportunity. Many organizations do not care what the course is called as long as the interns are enrolled at the institution for academic credit while participating in any experiential learning opportunity with the organization. This fact is not presented in this matter to trivialize academic credit. Written work should be a part of any experiential learning opportunity for credit even if it is an elective. Managerial participation on the part of the internship site and the host institution ensures an increase in the level of learning, thus justifying academic credibility. Jowdy, McDonald, and Spence (2004) very clearly presented an in-depth approach to internships by applying the Wilber's All Quadrant, All Level Theory of Everything (TOE) that included the faculty member's role in assisting a student in making sense of all elements of their self-development. Therefore, one should expect a faculty advisor to monitor/require assignments that assist the student in applying theory to their experiential learning opportunities.

STUDENT MOTIVATION TO BECOMING SUCCESSFUL

The Foster Five-Step process described in this chapter can be formally and informally applied. Most institutions likely apply at least three of the steps (e.g., classroom assignments, events identified as volunteering, and work experiences). You, the student, can be self-motivated to find events in the area or in your home town for which to volunteer. Finding summer positions that very closely align with one's intended career path is recommended.

This first chapter has utilized an experiential model that is time-tested. Students at six institutions where the authors have worked have been exposed to all or parts of the model to advance their careers. It works! However, self-motivation is part of the process. One can minimally meet requirements or go above and beyond to be at the top of the game. Alumni of the process are team and business owners, vice-presidents, sports information directors, athletic directors, coaches, facility and event managers, and consultants in all types of sport organizations.

Does everyone make it? Of course not, but the experience of the authors working with students has elicited patterns of employment. Motivated individuals who are not concerned initially with salary, location, or work hours will succeed in the sport business industry. Others may as well; it might just take them longer to get their foot in the door and climb the ladder. Patience and persistence is crucial. An academic program can provide background knowledge, the sport business network to get you started, and tips and tools to enhance your employability, but a student's desire to be the best at every stage completes the proven formula for success.

Learning how business applies to the sport industry is crucial for success.
(Courtesy of Dreamstime)

POSITION AVAILABLITY IN THE SPORT INDUSTRY

Many critics of sport management programs claim that not enough internship or full-time positions exist for the number of students graduating from
programs in the United States. There are approximately 240 collegiate institutions offering either bachelor's or master's degrees that prepare students
for the sport business industry (Foster, Gillentine, Pinsky-Newman, & Fay,
2003). However, if sport is defined very broadly using the Sport Employment Model previously discussed, the industry is enormous.

Positions are available in all of the following:

- the professional major, minor, and independent leagues in numerous
  team sports;
- local organizing bodies that plan and manage professional golf or ten-
  nis tournaments;
- over 100 amateur and professional national governing bodies in the
  United States alone such as USA Basketball (USAbasketball.org), the
  United States Table Tennis Association (USATT.org), the United States
  Association of Blind Athletes (usaba.org), and the Ladies Professional
  Golf Association (lpga.com);
- professional organization governing bodies such as the Florida Facility
  Manager's Association (FFMA) or the National Intramural-
  Recreational Sports Association (nirsa.org);

- over 1,000 colleges (two and four year) with athletic and campus recreation departments;
- high schools where a sport management degree may be acceptable to fill physical education teaching, coaching, and athletic director positions;
- private and public recreational programs and facilities such as county recreation departments or YMCAs;
- sports foundations established by teams and individual athletes;
- collegiate and high school conference offices such as the Atlantic Coast Conference (ACC) or the Florida High School Activities Association (FHSAA);
- large and small private and public facilities that host sporting events such as the Red Bull Arena in Secaucus, New Jersey, or the Asheville Civic Center in Asheville, North Carolina;
- large sport management facility firms such as Comcast-Spectacor;
- local sport commissions or sports authorities such as the Tampa Bay Sports Commission and the Tampa Sports Authority;
- state games and senior games such as the Georgia State Games and the North Carolina Senior Games;
- publications and websites reporting and supporting sport and sport media;
- television and radio stations that broadcast sports;
- youth league organizations, both local and national, such as Little League Baseball;
- Disney Sports;
- private sport agencies such as marketing, event management, athlete representation firms, and even athlete concierge services;
- local organizing committees for Olympic and Paralympic games and events; and
- all of the sporting events and organizations that exist outside of the United States.

Whew! There are probably even a few possibilities that have been missed. In summary, the number of positions to be counted would take a great deal of time to mention. In fact, a full-time position could possibly be created just to count and keep track of the number of positions available in sport. Thus, employment and internships ARE available. Individuals get side-tracked when limiting themselves to a specific team, sport, or position. Get your foot in the door and then target specific positions as you climb the employment ladders.

WHY A DEGREE IN SPORT MANAGEMENT AND NOT A GENERAL BUSINESS DEGREE?

A common question asked by parents and academic administrators is why should an individual seek a degree in the field of sport management versus a general business or physical education degree in order to pursue a sport business career? Additionally, why would we address this topical area in a chapter discussing experiential learning? The answers are simple. First, a sport management degree has some very unique components and among these is the experiential learning opportunities provided to students. Many degree programs in general business do not even require an internship.

Unique parameters of the sport industry itself have been addressed by many introductory and sport marketing texts for the past 30 years. But probably one of the first authors to highlight the uniqueness was Dr. Bernie Mullin (1980), who held early positions as a professor of sport management and then elected to seek key top level practitioner positions in sport. He has worked in professional basketball, baseball, and hockey, has been a college athletic director, and formed his own consulting business in 2008 called the Aspire Group with the Cleveland Indians and the National Hockey League (NHL) signed as two of the company's first clients (Mansasso, 2008).

The authors believe there are at least seven unique parameters of the sport industry and include the following concepts.

1. *Ancillary revenue:* The majority of revenue in sport is not made from the main product—i.e., the game. While revenue is realized from the sale of tickets for the event, the majority of revenue is made from sponsorships, concessions, team wear and souvenirs, parking, and media contracts (Mullin, 1980). Compare this to a particular product large or small where revenue is only realized from the sale of the product. Thus, understanding how to write a sponsorship proposal or understanding spectator loyalty to a particular team and how that translates into team product sales even for a losing team is important. (Yes, a losing team requires the sales team to sell the worst product in the market!) This concept knowledge is taught in many sport management programs and a generic business school class does not typically address sport sponsorships, sport sales, and all the revenue opportunities available in sport.

2. *The product is pre-sold* and the consumer must wait often for months at a time to experience the product—the game. Ticket packages, group

tickets, ticket sales, and the ability to predict sales based on fan loyalty are learned concepts in a quality sport management curriculum.

3. *Marketing:* The sport marketer cannot predict the outcome of a sporting event (Mullin, 1980). Can you imagine a non-sport business company not promising the quality of their product? Basically, this is what a sport marketer can be up against, especially when the result of the content can be drastically affected by the starting pitcher getting injured in the first inning, the star running back fumbling the ball three times, or the favored figure skater falling twice in a routine. In essence, the sport marketer cannot guarantee the outcome of an event (the product) or the quality of play from day-to-day or year-to-year.

4. *Revenue sharing:* Most general businesses do not share revenue. For example, you would not catch two competing phone companies sharing revenue. However, in sport, it is not uncommon for professional sport teams to be required to share revenue realized from ticket sales or other income generating contracts. College athletic departments also share revenue when the National Collegiate Athletic Association (NCAA) issues checks to schools after one or more of a conference's teams participated in a bowl game or the Final Four. It is what keeps competition equal in many sports leagues.

5. *Power and influence of sport as a social institution:* Parks, Quarterman, and Thibault (2007) believe this is an additional unique parameter and the authors agree. Sport parallels, contributes to, and mirrors society. Sport is utilized to open lines of communication between political leaders (Olympic Games) as well as assist in the development of troubled minors (mid-night basketball leagues or games), and professional athletes establish foundations to assist with societal needs. Equal opportunity for all by providing participation opportunities that eliminates gender, handicapping medical conditions, or race as a means for participation is certainly a societal concern. Classes in sport sociology are necessary components of a sport business curriculum in order for the future sport business manager to effectively function.

6. *Sport law and risk management* are essential concept knowledge for a sport management student. While a business law class can include important generic legal vocabulary and information, it is important to learn how certain laws apply to the sport business world. For example, business law classes typically do not address Title IX, yet it is one of the most fundamental laws taught in most sport law courses; it is an

extremely important law to know and understand for those pursuing a career in high school or college athletics. Campus recreation programs are also affected by this law. There are many other statutes, constitutional amendments, and laws that have specific application to sport and anyone working in sport should have a clear understanding of this area of study. Sport, recreation, and physical education are highly litigated areas . Risk management in sport is all about keeping spectators safe and preventing lawsuits. Furthermore, sport facilities are now a terrorist target, so possessing an in-depth knowledge of risk mitigation methods is also crucial.

7. *Career paths:* Mullin (1980) advanced the thinking that career paths associated with sport management are not well defined. This still holds true today to some extent. The Foster Five-Step Experiential Learning Model explained earlier defines a system that can assist in predicting a more normal career path. Mullin's theory is supported when individuals gain degrees or experience in businesses unrelated to sport and then obtain a position in a sport business.

The rationalization for a sport management degree over a physical education degree is not as complicated. Quite frankly, in the opinion of the authors, it comes down to whether you wish to enter a position focusing on business knowledge or a coaching position. Coaches may have business-related responsibilities such as budgeting, but knowledge of physiology, kinesiology, and conditioning principles can contribute to a coach's success. These concepts are best learned in quality physical education or kinesiology degree programs. In fact, when you coach, you teach, so there are some distinct advantages to the physical education degree over sport management because many sport management degrees do not educate students in teaching methodology. Yes, some sport management programs are still housed in physical education departments and require some science related courses. However, the *Sport Management Program Standards and Review Protocol* (Sport Management Program Review Council, 2000) did not require sport management programs to offer course work in education or the sport sciences and the Commission on Sport Management Accreditation (2008) principles do not list any similar requirements in their Common Professional Components. Unless one works directly with an athlete in their physical or medical development, sport science courses are generally not put to good use in the majority of sport business positions.

THE FINAL BUZZER

The purpose and objectives of Chapter 1 were to provide an initial introduction to the scope of the sport business industry, the concept of experiential learning, and to describe The Foster Five-Step as a comprehensive experiential learning model that can be formally or informally applied by faculty and students. When vigorously applied by the student, the Foster Five-Step process provides a very successful pathway to employment. Furthermore, the intent was to dispel some myths regarding the sport business industry and provide some basic information about academic curricula in this field.

Classroom Experiential Learning Exercise

ROLE PLAYING

Students are assigned one team to manage for Women's Professional Soccer (WPS). Each group "pitches" their franchise to a potential sponsor. While one group represents the WPS franchise, the others act as the potential sponsor's marketing team. The WPS teams need to prove their fan base matches the target market of the sponsor company, whose marketing team will accept or deny the proposed relationship. Students take turns role playing as WPS franchise and company executives.

Submitted by Dr. Dina Gentile, Professor
Endicott College, Beverly, Massachusetts

Program Experiential Learning Example

GETTING INVOLVED EARLY

The University of Tennessee student organization is Partners in Sport. It organizes and manages four major events per year plus has many one-day professional development opportunities. The Sport Management program requires all students enrolled in their Introduction to Sport Management class to volunteer for at least one event. Sophomores get involved in the planning stages of the major events by being chosen to serve on a planning committee. In the junior and senior years, the students are asked to move into leadership positions. Students also have the opportunity for volunteering for other events held on campus and in the surrounding area.

Submitted by Dr. Robin Hardin, Associate Professor
Knoxville, TN

2

Selecting the Academic Program to Reach Professional Goals

"When choosing a sport management program, it is critical to align academic needs and wants with the strengths and opportunities offered through the program. In other words, make sure you are going to be a good fit and the program you are seeking to attend caters to your strengths and interests. By doing so, the likelihood that a program's faculty and curriculum will meet your expectations increases a great deal."

—Dr. Michael Sagas
Professor and Chair
Dept. of Tourism, Recreation and Sport Management
University of Florida

THE WARM UP

If you are reading this at present, perhaps you have not yet selected a post-secondary institution. Maybe you have already selected a university with a sport education program, but are still undecided on an academic major. Whether sport management, sport administration, or sport business has been selected, it can lead to a successful professional career. The respective program may be housed as an individual unit or listed as part of an academic program or department. The three programs are defined below in order to alleviate possible ambiguity.

SPORT MANAGEMENT/ADMINISTRATION/ BUSINESS DEFINED

Many individuals ask professors to define the difference between sport management, sport administration, and sport business. The formal answer to this question is really best provided by the educational institution offering the degree program. Sport business programs are usually tracks within a Business Department or College of Business within a University. Saint Leo University has a department of Sport Business and International Tourism within their School of Business. Flagler College in Saint Augustine, Florida, has a stand-alone Department of Sport Management. As programs develop standard curricula and grow student enrollments, many programs within a college or university are able to create a specific "department" centered around critical mass faculty. One may also find a sport related program, perhaps entitled "sport management" or "sport administration" housed under department headings such as Health and Human Performance (e.g., Northwestern State University of Louisiana), Kinesiology (e.g., Towson University of Maryland), or Physical Education (e.g., Valparaiso University). Other department titles may also include such labels as sport sciences or exercise science and may house a sport management major.

Many have used management and administration synonymously. An early definition by Mullin (1980), though, delineated the differences.

Sport business is a relatively new term that closely aligns with the sport industry today. In most situations, but not all, those in charge of sport are running a business. (Courtesy of iStockphoto Inc.)

Dr. Mullin explained sport management as a field where the top managers were responsible for all facets of the organization *including* finding the money to run the organization much as a small business would have to raise capital in order to operate. Mullin categorized this as a private sector organization. An athlete representation firm would be a good example of this.

A sport administrator was defined as an individual who was responsible for all facets of running the organization or a specific segment of an organization *excluding* having the responsibility for finding the money. Financing comes from tax dollars, grants, or perhaps student fees if within an educational setting. The budget is provided and all individuals within the organization have to stay within their budgeted allotment. The best example of this is a high school or college athletic director. Coaches in an educational setting generally fall under this category as well, and this type of organization is labeled a public sector organization. (Mullin, 1980)

Sport business is a relatively new term that closely aligns with the sport industry today. In most situations, but not all, those in charge of sport are running a business. This applies to professional sport, college athletics, and even to those in charge of running charitable foundations or national governing bodies. While not all individuals will be charged with raising the capital to operate, most often all are involved in improving the bottom line. This even applies to most college athletic directors today. While state dollars are provided to a public institution and an athletic director manages those dollars, fundraising and sponsorships are still an integral part of their role and for most in the sport industry. Simply put, sport is a business in today's world. For many, it is a multi-million dollar enterprise.

Thus, it might be said that all individuals working in sport are business managers even though responsibilities may differ. Even a coach with a sport science background must often wear the hat of managing or overseeing the business affairs of a team. When considering the supervision of such an academic degree, most programs identified as Sport Business programs are administered through a School/College of Business.

NATIONAL STANDARDS AND ACCREDITATION

A much more important factor in the program selection equation would be the recognition of authenticated curriculums. One of the requirements for employment may be that the student must have graduated from an "accredited" program or institution. How does one know if the chosen sport education program/curriculum is accredited or not? Fortunately, there is a professional organization to answer that very question for the prospective student. The North American Society for Sport Management (NASSM) is the umbrella organization for sport education in the United States and Canada, comprised of an international body of scholars and dedicated to the promotion and development of sport management through a broadly based scientific body of knowledge (Constitution, n.d.). One of its objectives is to protect the student seeking a sport education degree from fraudulent and innocuous academic fluff being offered at Ned's Auto Body Vocational Tech. Yes, several years ago a research study was being conducted by John Dollar and Bob Case regarding two and four-year curricula. An auto mechanic trade school that offered a sport management degree was discovered! Unless you plan on being a mechanic in NASCAR, this would not be the curriculum in which you want to enroll.

A task force of early pioneers in sport management academia, chaired by Dr. Stan Brassie from the University of Georgia and Dr. Brenda Pitts, now at Georgia State University, developed the first set of standards. The Sport Management Program Review Council (SMPRC) was then created to guide curriculum development for instructional programs in sport education for fourteen years (1993–2007). Called the "program approval" process, it served sport management administrators well during that time as program directors and faculty could follow an established and approved set of guidelines when setting up sport management curricula. "Approved Programs" still exist and, as of the printing of this book, still appeared on the NASSM website. Approved programs are listed with an "A" under the section of the website for sport management programs. Technically, some approved programs are scheduled to be recognized through 2014. This can be a starting point for those looking for quality programs educating individuals for future employment in the sport industry. For more information on approved programs, visit http://www.nassm.com/InfoAbout/SportMgmtPrograms.

In 2007, work began for the development of a new sport management accreditation process. The Commission on Sport Management Accreditation (COSMA) was developed and the first educational program went through site visitations in the fall of 2009. It will take a while for institutions to start obtaining the COSMA accreditation moniker. As this accreditation program moves forward, however, the number of accredited programs in sport management will increase and this will provide students, parents, and high school counselors with additional information on quality curricula. For more information on COSMA, visit http://www.aahperd .org/naspe/grants/accreditation/cosma.cfm.

Perhaps one of the more important decisions regarding sport management programs should be that of attending an approved or accredited program (Fielding, Pitts, & Miller, 1991). By doing so, a student is promised that course content and curriculum meets a national standard or guideline, whereby graduates have strong core concept knowledge upon which to build successful careers in the sport industry. One can now choose from sport business, sport management, or sport administration programs, but the institution chosen should be recognized by its approved or accredited curricula.

PARENTS

"But Mom, all of my friends go there!" Not all colleges are selected based upon sound rationale. Students often want to select a college because their friends are attending. Parents have a vested interest in the educational institution selection of their children. Parents will look at the broader scope of the college experience and, for the most part, make decisions based on sound economics, grade points, and transportation. In other words, common sense and the best education for their hard-earned dollar will be the determinants for the parents.

Parents tend to want what is best for their children and do not always understand that sport management can be a rigorous educational degree program with exceptional quality. If a son or daughter indicates that they wish to obtain a degree in this field, the parent may want a book report telling them what it is, what colleges offer the degree, and what one can do with it once a degree is conferred. Most parents would be very interested if the book report included some of the information in the preceding paragraphs and the rest of this textbook regarding program qualifications and accreditations. The bottom line is that if parents are interested enough in their child's education and are paying the bill, they usually want to have a say in the institution chosen. Knowing their children inside and out, they may feel qualified to indicate the academic fields in which the child may or may not be successful academically and socially. Their overall concern is one of success in the job market upon graduation.

STUDENTS

Hopefully, a sport management curriculum is not being pursued because of the perception that it might be an easy college degree! Preparing for college should be carefully planned by the prospective student and their parents or legal guardians. Well laid plans might begin at the junior or even sophomore level in high school. Nonetheless, being able to choose a career and then deciding which academic plan and curriculum will help you to achieve that plan can be a daunting assignment. "Can't I just do a book report instead?" C'mon! It's your life, YOUR future! The sport industry is much larger than Saturday and Sunday afternoon ball games on television. Career counseling is available at all educational levels. A career counselor or academic advisor that is knowledgeable about the sport management field can provide you with information to follow up on your interest and, perhaps, put you on the right track toward graduation and a satisfying career. You will have to make the final decision and then follow through with the curriculum plan. The key word here is PLAN, and if you choose not to plan for success, then chances are your success will be limited.

FACULTY OR PROGRAM SPECIALTIES

By nature of our species, we are social animals and seek company and companionship throughout our lives. Being a student in college does not exclude one from this social dilemma. In your search for people to help you pursue your career goals, do not overlook the possibility of a professor or instructor who may serve as a role model or mentor, share a common hobby or interest, or maybe even the same hometown. This instructor or professor may become your academic advisor and, thus, take a more personal interest in your program performance and success. Many professors and instructors enjoy working with students and take personal pride when that particular student excels academically. The educators in a sport education program are usually connected to the sport industry and, quite often, can provide expert advice on career options, access to professional contacts, and some may provide a letter of recommendation, as needed, if you perform well in the classroom.

Some universities also provide program specialties which enhance curriculums with specific career niches. In these program specialties, the aspiring student can find a specific topic of interest and get an in-depth focus on a specific athletic or sport topic of interest or concern. This is truer at the graduate level, because research professors often have a specific area of inter-

Selecting an internship based on the experience to be learned, and not the geographic location, should be a primary goal! (Courtesy of Susan Foster)

est for their research. More information on program specialties can be found in Chapter 10.

LOCATION: A HINDRANCE OR ADVANTAGE

Finding the best school for your undergraduate or graduate degree is now greatly facilitated by the World Wide Web and all of the information available on-line for making the final decision. While searching for the "perfect" degree program, if you were to determine the best program was in your hometown, would you be willing to travel to a lesser program? Will you be willing to travel to a better or best program? Remember, you are investing in your future!

Proximity to the program in which you choose to pursue your degree may be an advantage if you live in the same town as that number one program. You may have the advantage of living and eating at home, no transportation woes, being surrounded by family and friends, and generally not having to adjust to a new setting. You get to remain within your comfort zone. The only cost may be the tuition and books for the program. On the other hand, should you choose to attend school very far away from home, you would then have the added costs of room and board and travel-related expenses. Parents and teachers call this experience "growing up"! You would be cast outside of your comfort zone and have to adjust to a lot of new and different comforts. Selecting an internship away from both school and home would yet again throw you outside of your comfort zone. However, having moved to attend college away from home, another move for the internship may be less of a burden, especially if you and a roommate or fellow classmates were to intern at the same site. Sharing room and board as well as the burdens of moving again might seem to be a more manageable option. Seek input from those around you who may provide some educated and sage advice (Stier, 2002). Please see Chapter 6 for a brief discussion of location as part of a six-P formula for preparation for the internship and a more in-depth discussion in Chapter 7 as an important consideration for selection of an internship.

Because most quality sport management programs require an internship, information about the internship program ought to be part of the decision when selecting the educational institution you will attend (Kelley, 2004). The internship is a purposeful experience and some students would classify it as the most important part of their education. When aiming for a successful career, this is often true. Subsequently, when selecting the educational institution or making the decision to major in sport management, inquire about all experiential learning opportunities afforded the student.

The following chapters will help you understand how to make those decisions about the internship. If you make all of the right decisions for the right reasons, then sit back and be satisfied with your decision. You will most likely be satisfied with your institution of choice and the opportunities that will come your way.

THE FINAL BUZZER

In considering all that has been presented herein, the student should consider several parameters in the selection of the best-fit sport management program and how inquiries about experiential learning opportunities, especially the culminating internship, should be made at the same time. Be willing to invest time and review your options carefully to determine your best outcome. Ask for advice from trusted sources including professors and family. Select an internship that serves to your advantage. Do not be afraid to step outside of your comfort zone to take the challenge of new and rewarding experiences. C'mon, be adventurous!

As you read the learning examples below, think about whether the program in which you hope to enroll provides learning experiences such as the ones portrayed? Most quality sport management programs do!

Classroom Experiential Learning Exercise

PROJECT INVOLVEMENT WITH THE INDUSTRY

As in the business world, performance (grade) will depend on revenue/profit generated for the assigned projects. Students will have a role in determining target market, the promotions to reach that market, and the revenue goals set for each project. The sales project will involve selling Rice men's basketball or Houston Dynamo group packages.

This is a student-run project. Each student is expected to achieve an equal share of the minimum revenue goal. The goal for this project is $1,000 per student. Grades will be determined by individual performance. If a student is expected to generate $1,000 in total revenue and generates $1,000 or more, they would receive 100% for this project. If a student achieves $700 in revenue, their grade is 70% of the total possible credit. All students submit a detailed report of sales made. All payments are made by credit card or check and copies of these transactions are submitted with the order. Cash payments are not acceptable. Copies of checks/orders must be turned in with the designated individual's signature to receive credit.

At the conclusion of the project, students are asked to evaluate their performance based on target market sales achieved, sales volume, and customer experience. The class votes on the top three and additional points are awarded.

Submitted by Tom Stallings, Instructor
Rice University, Houston, Texas

Program Experiential Learning Example

ASSISTING UNDECIDED STUDENTS

Students at the University of Southern Maine who have an interest in Sport Management but are still undecided have several resources to assist in their decision-making. They are encouraged to join the Sport Management Club, participate in events sponsored by the organization, review the club's Facebook page, and are invited to Sport Management events. Students are also provided access to some sport management textbooks and encouraged to review sport career websites to see if the advertised career opportunities help them decide if Sport Management is the right major for them.

Submitted by Dr. Jo Williams, Associate Professor
Portland, Maine

3

Sport Business Industry Overview: Professional Sport

"A career in the sport business industry is an opportunity to take a unique business approach into a competitive and energy-filled atmosphere."

— Ryan Strickland
Manager, Sales/Ballpark Operations
St. Lucie Mets, Port St. Lucie, FL

THE WARM UP

In this chapter, we will begin a comprehensive review of the sport business/ management industry. This review will actually span over three chapters. This chapter discusses professional sport, both team and individual. The primary focus is on sport within the United States, although international professional sport is briefly examined. Chapter 4 is a comprehensive examination of Olympic and amateur sport while Chapter 5 will discuss areas of the industry that support the mainstream segments (e.g., event management and marketing) as well as entrepreneurial ventures in sport including small businesses started by individuals. Yes, there will be some overlap and this cannot be prevented. However, the three chapters combined will provide an in-depth look into this rather complicated industry.

Before we begin, it is necessary to discuss one important element as it applies to the business of sport and experiential learning, and that is the seasonality of some sport industry segments.

A SEASONAL INDUSTRY,
PLANNING CONSIDERATIONS

When one is planning for experiential learning opportunities, and more specifically, for the culminating academic internship experience, the seasonality of sport must be considered. For example, if one is pursuing their passion to work in baseball, the best internship experiences start in January. Many major and minor league teams recruit interns to start in January when the sales season is in full swing. While some sales take place for a baseball team from October through December, this is not really the time of year that most teams start interns and some new entry level start dates may also be delayed to January. It is, however, the hiring season. Many teams use Professional Baseball Employment Opportunities website to recruit, www .PBEO.com. The majority of minor and some major league teams will recruit via the Career Fair at the Baseball Winter Meetings™ generally held during the first or second week of December.

An internship beginning in January may not end until Labor Day weekend for those working in the baseball minor leagues. Major league internships generally end when the team's season ends. If an intern is fortunate to be working for any major league team advancing to the playoffs, the internship is often extended. Though this may upset future moves or employment plans, not many individuals would shun the chance to work for one of the two teams in the World Series. Often, divisional playoff and World Series teams offer additional incentives/perks to interns. How about a chance to earn a World Series ring? Wouldn't you want to stick around for that grand opportunity after having worked the entire season? There is no guarantee an intern would be awarded a ring, but just to have an internship end with such a spectacular event involving additional media hype and extra planning would be worth the extra month from an experiential learning perspective.

Seasonality is true for other team sport related internships. The prime hiring season for intern positions in the National Football League is April through July or August although some may start earlier. This is also true for the National Basketball Association (NBA), Major League Soccer (MLS), the National Hockey League (NHL), and other sport related leagues. It is our recommendation that students not approach a team for internships toward the end of a competition season unless there is an advertised position. Application materials may go unnoticed because the team will not be looking. Wait until after the season is over for that particular team; waiting until all playoffs have ceased for the entire league should also be considered. Post-season is often when a team will begin to assess the number of interns needed for the upcoming season. Sometimes a full-time employee may move on, and the team may decide to hire one or more interns to replace that individual. If you are enrolled in an academic program that allows you to accept full-time employment and use it to satisfy an internship requirement, you have earned your first bonus! However, the organization should be informed beforehand if this is your intention. Some will allow it; others will not. After all, if they can screen your abilities and pay you internship wages for three to nine months, this is a benefit to the sport organization. While some interns may be lucky and land a full-time position for an internship, it should not be expected, especially in tough economic times.

Yes, there are exceptions to the seasonality hiring cycle as described above. The Tampa Bay Rays is one professional sport team that hires interns during every academic semester, although they may hire more during the competition season. One suggestion is to maintain constant scrutiny on job or team websites. Sometimes an annual pattern for hiring can be recognized especially for larger organizations. If the team owns the facility lease and runs events unrelated to the sport season, such activity can explain the hiring of interns throughout the year, especially in event and facility management.

Quite often, positions not tied to a particular team or league are not seasonal. Organizations, such as IMG (discussed later in this chapter), operate on a twelve month cycle just as any other non-sport related business. Thus, there is no hiring season. This is true of marketing and event management firms; these areas will be discussed more fully in Chapter 5.

Our best recommendation is to look early and become familiar with the hiring seasons for teams or leagues of interest. It would not be too early to start this awareness process at the beginning of your post secondary academic career or during the first semester of a graduate degree. Become familiar with where all sport organizations post position openings. Some will post openings first on their own websites and these are often found under "careers," "job opportunities," "employment," or "human resources" tabs. If organizations are not successful in hiring someone through their own website or professional networking, they may post a position on one or more of the several sport related employment websites. Small organizations tend to use employment websites a great deal even for posting internships. For your convenience, a comprehensive, but never exhaustive, list of web addresses related to sport organizations and job information websites have been provided in Appendix A.

Exploring career and internship listings early, even if one is not ready to intern, gives the job seeker an additional advantage. As you progress through an academic degree, you can begin to cultivate a keen understanding of the skills and experience for which many organizations are searching simply by reading job announcements. If a particular area of the industry or even a particular team or sport is your employment objective, you may determine that many similar positions require a comparable set of skills. By utilizing the Foster Five-Step Model discussed in Chapter 1, specific events to work or targeted skills one hopes to acquire can be identified. The next section will explore various industry segments and provide a deeper understanding of the sport business industry.

In preparing for the internship, take advantage of all opportunities! As was indicated in the first chapter, some organizations call any volunteer experience an internship, though we clarified the differences. Regardless of the label, if you have a chance to learn ANYTHING about the operation of a sporting event or work in the offices of a sport organization, even if it means missing an important social event at your college campus, accept the opportunity. Answering the phone and filing still provides access to the people within the organization. These types of responsibilities are good for volunteer positions, part-time jobs, or apprenticeship learning opportunities. We do not recommend them as a sole responsibility for the culminating internship.

Another true story involving a student exemplifies this recommendation. An undergraduate transfer student came to campus to enroll in a sport management program. He quickly became involved in the sport management student association where the opportunity to work a variety of different sporting events was afforded him. He worked just about every event available and ended up leading the organization as president for two years. In the course of this experience, he took it upon himself to search out organizations and events which were as yet untapped and worked those events, and passed that information along to his peers. It did not matter if these opportunities were in amateur or professional sport or event or facility management. When he applied for his senior internship with an event management company, with only a phone interview and an e-mailed résumé, he was offered a full-time position with benefits and the promise of an eventual company car. While this is not a regular scenario even with the most involved individuals, it does represent what *can* happen if one takes advantage of every possible opportunity.

In the following sections and in Chapters 4 and 5, every attempt has been made to provide a wide scope of information on a broad range of sport industry segments. While we could not include information about every possible position, we have interviewed various individuals at different levels to provide as much information as possible to ponder while you search for an internship and a career in the sport business industry.

PROFESSIONAL SPORT SEGMENTS EXPLAINED AND EXPLORED

This section will explore the professional team and individual sport business industry. It is our recommendation students carefully explore all segments of the industry. While one may have a burning desire to be an agent or to work in a specific sport, experience has taught us that as one reads, investigates, and steps into an industry segment, the beliefs and perceptions an individual brings may change dramatically. How an organization actually works on the inside seven days a week can be drastically different from the fan's perception of how the organization works on competition day.

It would be impossible to list every position found in many of the sport industry segments. Visiting the website of an organization and viewing an organizational chart is the best way to gain a total understanding of the variety of positions and size of a department or organization. In fact, a well-defined organizational chart should be scrutinized before interviewing for a position within the organization. A chart provides insight into departmental divisions, names of key managers, how the organization is structured, and employees that may report to more than one individual. Be aware that some organizational charts may be outdated. Attempt to find a staff listing online and compare it to any chart you may find. By learning names of key employees, an individual enters an interview with great networking information.

PROFESSIONAL TEAM SPORT

Professional team sport is the industry segment where the majority of students hope to launch their sport business career. Listed below are many of the professional leagues and organizations that exist in the United States, but the list is not exhaustive. Thus, once again, it would be difficult to count the number of full-time or internship positions existing within professional sport. Some of the more notable leagues include:

- Major League Baseball (MLB), Minor League Baseball (MiLB), and independent league baseball;
- the National Basketball Association (NBA), the Women's National Basketball Association (WNBA), and the National Basketball Association Development League (NBA—D League);
- the National Football League (NFL) and Arena Football League (AFL);
- Major League Soccer (MLS);
- Major League Lacrosse (MLL—Outdoor) and National League Lacrosse (NLL—Indoor);
- the Association of Volleyball Professionals (AVP) with both its beach and indoor tours;

◆◆ TIME OUT INTERVIEW ◆◆

⁓ Professional Team Sport ⁓
MIKE STANFIELD

Position	Vice-President, Ticket and Suite Sales
Employer	New Orleans Saints
B.S. Degree	Saint Leo University—Sport Management
Career Path	• Vendor—Tampa Stadium, Four months • Cincinnati Reds, Spring Training, Four months • Assistant GM, Clinton Giants, Clinton, Iowa, One year • Ft. Lauderdale Strikers, Director of Marketing, Three years • Ft. Lauderdale Yankees, Director of Marketing/Sales. Two years • Florida Marlins, Ticket Sales, Two years • Miami Heat, Director of Ticket Sales, Two years • Detroit Vipers, Director of Sales, One year • Detroit Tigers, Director of Ticket Sales, Two years
Employment Recommendation	"Start in a position where you see how the entire team is run; see what all departments do. Examine your skill sets for the position you desire and then be willing to do anything it takes. There should not be anything 'under you' to do. Keep in mind there are 100 people trying to get your job. Become known for something; you must desire to be the best out there! You never know who might be able to help you."

- the National Hockey League (NHL) and seven professional minor leagues.
- National Pro Fastpitch Softball (NPF) which operated as a four-team league in 2010.

Internships in professional sport are not as hard to acquire as many people may believe. Minor league baseball or positions with a minor league in any sport, such as the National Basketball Development League (NBDL) or ice hockey leagues such as the Eastern Coast Hockey League (ECHL), are plentiful if one has built a résumé with several experiential learning opportuni-

◆ ◆ TIME OUT INTERVIEW ◆ ◆

― Professional Team Sport ―
TYRONE BROOKS

Position	Director of Baseball Operations
Employer	Pittsburgh Pirates
B.S. Degree	Accounting & Marketing, University of Maryland, College Park
Career Path	• Baseball Operations Trainee, Three months • Administrative Assistant/Scouting & Player Development, Three months • Baseball Operations Assistant, Three years • Midwest Area Scouting Supervisor, Three years • Assistant, Player Personnel, Two years • Director of Baseball Operations, Two years • Director of Baseball Administration, One year (All of the above positions were with the Atlanta Braves) • Pro Scout, Major and Minor league baseball Cleveland Indians, Three years
Employment Recommendation	"It is going to be very challenging to get into scouting or player development without a playing background (from college or the professional ranks), but not impossible. If you do not have a playing background, you must look at ways to separate yourself from the crowd. I, personally, did not have a great playing background, but I filled a need and provided value for my department based upon my skill set at the time. Just getting your foot in the door is the most important thing."

ties. Entry level positions are more difficult to find. Often the senior or graduate student internship is the optimum path to land an entry level position with a professional team.

Positions such as football or baseball operations are often not advertised and are filled from within. These positions are tied to player personnel, coaching, and scouting and often labeled as player development. Tyrone Brooks, one of our Time Out Interviewees for this chapter and Director of Baseball Operation for the Pittsburgh Pirates, indicated his job is to "work closely with the General Manager to oversee the entire operation, including handling the day-to-day running of the department, MLB rules compliance, roster management, budgeting, negotiating player and employee contracts, assisting with salary arbitration preparation, helping to oversee the pro scouting and non-Latin American international scouting staff, providing scouting judgments for possible trades and making internal evaluations within the minor league system."

Professional sport facilities offer a great learning laboratory for students.
(Courtesy of Saint Leo University)

To get into scouting, Mr. Brooks indicates, "the most logical route is by playing the game at some level, specifically college or pro. From the contacts made there, relationships are built and grown. The key is to see and be involved with as much of the sport as possible—at all levels. A scout needs to be able to differentiate the different levels of play and recognize ability and tools to play the game." (Personal communication, February 2, 2010)

Positions within professional sport can vary from organization to organization. However, typical position titles do exist. Most job seekers can find entry level positions within event or facility management and in sales. Pete Rozelle, former but long-time NFL commissioner, started his route to success through media relations with the Los Angeles Rams (Van Riper, 2008).

Game day operations is most closely associated with event and facility management. Events such as game day promotions are generally run by in-house staff. The operation of the facility will depend upon ownership and established leases. Some organizations may have an entire facility staff and manager of the facility even if they do not own the facility. But often a team will play in a publicly owned facility where all management and maintenance functions are under control of the local government. Chapter 5 more

◆◆ TIME OUT INTERVIEW ◆◆

~ Professional Sport ~
RICK NAFE

Current Position	Vice-President, Operations/Facilities
Employer	Tampa Bay Rays
B.S. Degree	Mass Communications, Florida State University
Career Path	• WCTV—Tallahassee, Assistant Sports Director, Two years • MacDonald Training Center for the Handicapped, PR Director, Three years • Tampa Sports Authority, Stadium Director, Twelve years; Executive Director, Five years
Employment Recommendation	"Be open to any possibility . . . take advantage of it . . . be enthusiastic . . . and treat every task as if it is the most important."

fully discusses event and facility management and marketing as entrepreneurial careers, but all of these areas can be pursued within professional team and individual sport. Chapters 4 and 5 both cover additional media related positions. This was necessary because of the differences between media positions within amateur and professional sport, and because an entrepreneurial career is not housed under either of these areas.

The media play an important role in professional sport and often rely on in-house personnel to support their efforts. The role of media personnel employed by the team may involve the development and publication of game programs, writing articles within those publications, writing press releases, assisting with game and player statistics, playing host to visiting media, and coordinating press conferences. Website development and maintenance may be an additional role, but some organizations will outsource this to a private company. One or more individuals may be assigned as a liaison between the organization and the television and radio media personnel. Oftentimes, one individual will be the main spokesperson for the team. Any of these specific areas may advertise entry level positions, but, in all probability, they will not be plentiful.

Media functions may fall under a separate department, but most often they will be housed under community or public relations. Community relations often involves foundations or fundraising functions of a team, but it also may include player appearances and other specialty programs. One such example is when a professional team sponsors a youth sport organization or develops an educational program with a local school district. All of these certainly involve public relations efforts, but some teams separate the community and public relations efforts into different departments. Others may house all of these functions under one department.

Marketing departments are structured differently throughout professional sport, but, often, individuals working in sales are promoted to a marketing position. In some organizations, sales and marketing may be housed in different departments. Regardless, both bring in revenue for the organization and any department that increases the bottom line often has more position openings. Both may involve ticket, sponsorship, group, and media sales. Thus, experiential learning opportunities should involve obtaining experience in all of the above if sales or marketing is the chosen specialized area of pursuit. If one chooses to pursue marketing, getting plenty of sales experience and obtaining marketing research skills are highly recommended.

◆◆ TIME OUT INTERVIEW ◆◆

— Professional Sport —
SEAN ARONSON

Current Position	Director of Broadcasting/Media Relations
Employer	St. Paul Saints Baseball Club
B.S. Degree	Journalism, University of Colorado, Boulder
Career Path	• Public Relations Assistant, Colorado Springs Sky Sox, Nine months • Director, Broadcasting/Media Relations Allentown Ambassadors, Two years • Director, Broadcasting/Media Relations Fort Myers Miracle, Four years
Employment Recommendation	"If you have aspirations of being a broadcaster, start off as a freshman and do any games you can. If you want to be a broadcaster in one sport, but all that's available are calling games in another, take it! It's all about getting comfortable behind the microphone. "It's an extremely competitive field. Do all you can to get a leg up on the competition and make your résumé as strong as possible. Listen to your tapes and let others listen to them as well. Take all the constructive criticism you can. "There is no one path that is right or wrong for getting into this field. Make sure the jobs you take are right for you."

Financial positions are also available and may include accountants and controllers. Individuals in these positions may have little or no sport related experience before being hired. According to Van Riper (2008), individuals filling these jobs are often hired from a team's or organization's auditing company. Thus, finding an entry level position may be difficult. Internships might be more likely found if you have a strong background with numbers. Good grades in general or sport related finance and accounting courses are a strong indicator of one's skills in this area.

Dependent upon an organization's structure and lease agreements, on any game day, there can be a wide variety of functions filled by volunteers.

Special events apart from the game surround the sport industry. (Courtesy of Susan Foster)

A position may exist for an individual solely responsible for selecting and supervising these volunteer groups. One of their functions may be the oversight of concession stands staffed by community organizations volunteering as a fundraising group and collecting a percentage of the income for their organization. However, this specific role may also be filled by an outsourced concessions company.

And the moral to the story? A variety of positions exist with a professional sport team. A larger professional sport team (e.g., in the MLB) may employ over 100 individuals on a year-round basis. But according to King (2008), professional sport franchises are considered "small to midsized business with fewer than 250 employees" (p. 3). Seasonal positions with teams are also available, but many are subcontracted to other organizations thus reducing the overall staff size. Looking for employment with the subcontractors creates additional opportunities.

PROFESSIONAL INDIVIDUAL SPORT

Working in the individual sport side of the industry can be very similar to a position aligned with professional or amateur team sport. Positions will exist in marketing, event management, public relations, and other analogous departments. However, working with an individual sport may actually be categorized as more exciting depending on one's point of view. In any segment of the sport industry, each day can present a different scenario with varied responsibilities. With individual sport, a new champion may be crowned weekly and event sites can change from year-to-year, so cris-crossing

North America or the world geographically may be a typical responsibility. For example, the LPGA's 2010 schedule started in Thailand and Singapore before hitting the United States mainland. The rest of the tour season was hosted in eight different states and six additional countries. A similar scenario can be experienced within the purview of other individual sport schedules. However, this does not mean every employee travels to every event. Individual responsibilities can dictate the travel schedule, if any travel is expected at all.

Professional golf tournaments are primarily staffed by a large corps of volunteers. In fact, professional golf or tennis tournament and other large individual sport events are excellent experiences where one can learn about the incredible amount of detail it takes to run a three- to four-day or longer affair and the number of different organizations involved. The student can get involved in the operation of a major event by volunteering to perform one or more functions. For example, professional golf recruits large corporations to sponsor their events. The tournament income pays the local organizing group's full-time employees, covers expenditures for running the event, and is the source of the prize money for the competitors. However, a great deal of the income also goes to numerous charities that have been identified as recipients.

In many individual sports, the event or tournament is owned/operated by someone else beyond the governing offices. Each event may have its own local event director and staff. The home office definitely consults and sends staff to work and control specific segments of the event, but entire office staffs and managers do not travel on a weekly basis. For example, the Transitions Championship is one of the PGA TOUR's annual events. Transitions Lenses is the title sponsor. Copperhead Charities owns the rights to this tour event and pays the PGA TOUR for these rights. The local staff running the event is paid through Copperhead Charities from sponsorship income (Doug Laseter, Personal communication, November 10, 2009).

Some of the more popular professional individual sports and their respective governing body websites are listed below.

- The Association of Tennis Professionals World Tour (ATP: http://www.atpworldtour.com/)
- Professional Bowler's Association (PBA: http://www.pba.com/);
- Professional Cycling Tour (PCT: http://www.procyclingtour.com/)
- Professional Golf Association TOUR (PGA: http://www.pgatour.com/)
- Ladies Professional Golf Association (LPGA: http://www.lpga.com/)

- United States Snowboarding Association (USSA: http://www.ussnow boarding.com/)
- United States Tennis Association (USTA: http://www.usta.com/Pro Tennis/USTAProCircuit.aspx)
- Women's Tennis Association (WTA: http://www.sonyericssonwta tour.com/)

◆◆ TIME OUT INTERVIEW ◆◆

⎯ Professional Individual Sport ⎯
MIKE COONEY

Position	Director, Human Resources
Employer	PGA TOUR
B.S. Degree	Valdosta State University, Business Administration
Certification Held	PHR, Professional in Human Resources; CCP, Certified Compensation Professional
Career Path	• Hoagies, Inc., General Manager, Six years • Langdale Forest Products, Valdosta, GA, Director of Personnel, Three years • Hawley Holdings, Atlanta, GA, Human Resources Specialist, Two years • Knowledgeware, Atlanta, GA, Human Resources Manager, Five years • RTM (Arby's franchisee), Atlanta, GA, Director of Human Resources, Three years • President Baking Company, Atlanta, GA, Senior Human Resources and Compensation Manager, Three years
Employment Recommendation	"The PGA TOUR hires from within and some entry level employees come from our large Diversity Internship program. However, if applying from the outside, create a profile in our on-line applicant tracking system and apply to positions as they come about. Networking is certainly the best way outside of our internship program. If you know someone at the TOUR, contact them to learn about the different opportunities. Start early and apply often. It may take several passes to get an interview."

Extreme or action sport is a segment of the industry where internships are not explored as often as other individual sports. Additionally, there is not complete agreement as to what constitutes an extreme sport. According to *Dictionary.com*, **extreme sport** is defined as any recreational activity that involves high risk, aggressive and spectacular stunts, and which appeal to the young" (Extreme Sports, 2010). Wikipedia defines it as an action or adventure sport involving high levels of inherent danger and counter-cultural (Extreme Sport, 2010). This segment of the industry is extremely popular with many students living or attending college in colder climates who may be interested in snowboarding or other winter action sports, but it does not preclude others from investigating possible internships with extreme sport governing bodies, tour hosts, or geographical regions where extreme sporting events are held. In 2010, the Dew Tour hosted six events featuring sports such as BMX, wakeboarding, snowboarding, and skateboarding. The Dew Tour is the main professional tour for extreme sports. The XGames, an ESPN created and owned event, involves a summer and winter televised event that is operated each year. Medals and prize money are awarded.

If you have a passion for sport in any of the industry segments listed above, there certainly are numerous positions. This is one area where it is quite easy to volunteer in order to learn first-hand how individual sporting events are run. A student living in an area where professional events are taking place could work events in successive years in different positions and gather a great deal of experience. When volunteering, one would have to focus on the responsibilities given, but it is very possible to meet key individuals and develop a network of contacts. For example, if you volunteered for the Transitions Championship mentioned above, you could possibly meet individuals from the PGA TOUR, Copperhead Charities, Suncoast Golf, Inc., Innisbrook Resort, their food concessions supplier, any one of a number of golf equipment suppliers, the Golf Channel, and more. Thus, volunteering and networking are probably the two most prominent ways to learn about individual professional sport. Does this sound familiar?

PROFESSIONAL MOTOR SPORTS

Motorsports truly go beyond the more notable professional car racing circuits. Powerboat racing, snowmobile racing—otherwise known as snocross—and ATV and truck racing all have professional circuits. However, this section will focus on car racing.

Several professional car racing circuits exist; this includes the more popular ones such as the National Association of Stock Car Racing (NASCAR), the IndyCar Series, the National Hot Rod Association (NHRA), and Formula One. NASCAR, the largest of these motor sports associations, is headquartered in Daytona Beach, Florida, with offices in four other states and two countries. Within the NASCAR family are the individual NASCAR teams. While there have been single and multiple car teams, the trend seems to be with multiple car teams where individual drivers sign with a team. For example, Joe Gibbs Racing (JGR) had, as of early 2010, four professional drivers in their organization ("The Team") and employed 450 individuals. Granted, many of these individuals are part of the maintenance crews for the drivers. However, marketing, licensing, sponsorship acquisition, and public relations are certainly mainstays of the organization. Several racing team websites were visited, and not one displayed a section for job opportunities or internships. An examination of the biographies of the six top executives on JGR's website revealed a closely networked group of individuals, only one having started as an intern (with "The Team"). Thus, the employment entry door is more tightly closed in this segment of motorsports. Checking with NASCAR and other parent organizations, contacting a marketing company that handles motor sport clients, and networking **are potential** paths for entry. Living in or near a hot bed for racing, such as the piedmont area of North Carolina, may also prove beneficial.

According to the Fédération Internationale de l'Automobile website, the governing body for world motor sport, there are 228 motoring organizations in 132 countries. So, the opportunity to work in motorsports is far reaching (2009, para. 2). Below is a list of several of the more popular automobile motorsports associations including international organizations.

- American Le Mans Series: http://www.americanlemans.com/
- Conference of Australian Motor Sport: http://www.cams.com.a/
- Federation International Association: http://www.fia.com/EN-GB/THE-FIA/Pages/Introduction.aspx
- Formula1: http://www.formula1.com/
- Indy Racing League: http://www.indycar.com/
- International Hot Rod Association: http://www.ihra.com/
- International Motor Sports Association: http://www.imsaracing.net/
- Motor Sports Association: http://www.msauk.org/custom/asp/home/default.asp

TIME OUT INTERVIEW

— Professional Motor Sports —
TIM RAMSBERGER

Current Positions	Vice-President and General Manager, Honda Grand Prix of St. Petersburg
Employers	• Andretti Green Promotions, LLC • University of South Florida—St. Petersburg, Adjunct Professor, College of Business, Business Law, Two years • Attorney, Timothy T. Ramsberger, P.A., St. Petersburg, FL, Ten Years
B.A. Degree	Business Administration, (Accounting Minor) Florida State University
J.D	Florida State University
M.B.A	Rollins College
Career Path	• Florida Supreme Court, Internship, Justice Ben Overton, Five months • Practicing Attorney, Orlando, FL, Six years • World Cup USA 1994, Inc., Deputy Venue Executive Director & Venue Operations Director, One and one half years • Atlanta Committee for the Olympic Games, Venue Management, Two years • Disney's Wide World of Sports, Orlando, Senior Manager, Event Programming & Business Affairs, Four years • Outback Sports, LLC—Tampa, FL, Vice-President, Three months • Dover Motorsports, Inc., St. Petersburg, FL, Two years (Previous owner of Grand Prix) • Champ Car World Series, LLC, Indianapolis, IN, Vice-President, Promoter Relations, Six months
Employment Recommendation	"Persist with as much professional courtesy as possible. Serving time as an intern is some of the best experience. Be varied in your approach and willing to work in areas where you have little experience. Don't be a 'big fan'; be a person interested in the business of the particular industry. Create opportunities for yourself and prepare for those opportunities."

- Score International Off-road Racing: http://www.score-interna
  tional.com/

ATHLETE REPRESENTATION FIRMS/SPORTS AGENTS

Becoming a sports agent is an early goal for a lot of sport management majors. The role of an agent can include many functions in today's sports landscape. While an agent is often viewed as the individual who negotiates a
player's or participant's contract, they are also referred to as contract advisors
or player representatives and can perform a variety of roles. These include,
but are certainly not limited to, providing legal advice, financial services,
insurance/tax planning, coordination of travel arrangements, handling personal errands or tasks, and more. An athlete may hire more than one representative given the broad range of roles listed. One of the main reasons an
athlete may sign with a large representation firm is because the firm may be
better equipped to handle a broad range of responsibilities.

The path to actually signing an athlete to a contract can be difficult and,
often, not well-defined. Different sports mandate different routes and different states have different certification requirements for agents. For example, in Florida, an agent requires certification and a thorough background
investigation is conducted by both the Florida Department of Law Enforce-
ment (FDLE) and the Federal Bureau of Investigation (FBI) (Morrison,
2008). The NFL requires an agent to have an advanced degree beyond the
bachelor's, but this is not true for all sports. Many agents got their start because a fraternity brother or college roommate was a scholarship athlete and
wanted a trusted friend as their agent. A solid business background and
knowledge of contracts are important credentials. Todd Crannell, owner of
Q2 Sports and Entertainment, indicates that he uses asset valuation techniques learned in his M.B.A. program to determine fair market value for
athlete services (Profile, 2007). Learning the art of negotiation is also a critical skill. For this type of career, a sport business curriculum can provide
good academic preparation because of the combination of business and
sport related courses. A master's of business administration (M.B.A.) can
provide advanced preparation as well. Some sport management programs
have faculty who also are attorneys/agents. If this is your desired career path,
finding one of these programs to obtain your master's degree would give you
great insight, possibly experience, and certainly a network. Chapter 10 discusses the selection of a graduate program.

◆◆ TIME OUT INTERVIEW ◆◆

— Sports Agency—Athlete Representation —
TODD CRANNELL

Current Position	President and Founder, Q2 Sports and Entertainment; NFL and Track & Field Agent
Employer	Q2 Sports and Entertainment, New York
B.S. Degree	Economics, Florida State University
M.B.A.	Oxford University, London, England
Career Path	• Economist, Bureau of Labor Statistics, Washington, D. C., Three years • Volunteer Assistant Track Coach, Georgetown University, Three years • Founder and Technology Developer, Global Sports Technology, One year • Director of Sports Division, Irene Management Group, Miami, FL, Two years • Intern, Irene Marie Management Group, Miami, FL, Three months
Employment Recommendation	"The key is to get experience and the best way is to secure several internships. It may take a little longer to break into the sport industry because of supply and demand. It can be done; it just takes time and patience."

As with all industry segments, getting your foot in the door is extremely important. This is perhaps more important in the area of athlete services, because actually signing an athlete may only happen after you have worked with experienced agents. Landing volunteer or part-time work experiences with an agent or a small law firm is a good place to start. Some agents hire and train runners. **Runners** are individuals hired as independent contractors or employed by an agent to make contacts with athletes in situations where an agent is not allowed. A runner can infiltrate a college campus and befriend an athlete (Willenbacher, 2004). In unethical situations, a runner is often the one that violates NCAA rules or the law, perhaps even unbeknownst to them. If this is the line of work you desire, educate yourself on the laws and NCAA's rules regarding runners and agents, and only accept a placement with an agent or agency that upholds the law and operates in an ethical manner.

Large athlete representation firms or sports agencies can be a great place to start a career as well. IMG World is the largest such firm in the United States and operates internationally. It has over 1,000 employees working in several different divisions. It is possible, but probably not realistic to believe that one could start in an agent's role with one of these firms as a first job out of college. As international as they are, IMG's agents do not represent athletes in all sports.

Internships are offered throughout the year at IMG with spring and summer internships of varying lengths in various cities where corporate offices exist. Some internships are eight weeks in length and often do not fit the academic requirements of many sport management programs, so this may pose a problem. Thus, obtaining this type of position in a summer leading up to a culminating senior internship, during graduate school, or immediately following graduation would be a recommendation. To be qualified for an agency internship, one should consider gaining experience in sales, marketing, event management, website development, or public relations, as different divisions of IMG include positions in these areas and more. Focusing law or graduate school studies on licensing and merchandising could create great content for an application and résumé. This could be a back door entry into athlete representation, because one could possibly meet and network with agents working with IMG.

Octagon is another large athlete representation firm that also specializes in sport marketing and event management. The organization owns many professional tennis and golf tournaments, as well as large marathons. Their website proclaims that they are the leading owner of professional tennis events at the global level (Octagon, 2009). Thus, the student is presented with another organization worth studying if athlete representation is the desired career. Once again, obtaining an internship or entry level position in event management could lead to an internal transfer to the athlete representation side of the firm.

Global Athletics & Marketing, Inc., founded in 1993, is an example of an athlete representation firm that specializes in running events, specifically operating track and field meets. It owns three of the top track and field events in the United States including the 100-year-old Millrose Games (About GA&M, 2010). While much smaller than IMG World or Octagon, this type of firm represents a firm with a specialization in a specific sport, and possibly event management employment opportunities which are discussed more fully in Chapter 5.

Many believe the life of an agent to be an easy route to wealth. While some agents make a great deal of money, particularly those that sign the first round draft picks each and every year, this does not represent a true lifestyle for most agents. Compensation varies for agents depending upon the sport. NFL player agents cannot make more than three to five percent of the athlete's contract. Professional baseball player agents are not as restricted, but compensation rules do apply. With individual sports, there are no player unions and the amount an agent makes depends on market forces, but is typically around 20% for marketing the athlete (Todd Crannell, Personal communication, October 12, 2009).

Finally, law school or obtaining a master's of business administration (M.B.A.) degree are the optimal routes to becoming an agent especially if one wants to represent NFL players. As of 2009, the NFL regulation for agents, called contract advisors, requires an undergraduate and postgraduate degree (master's or law) to apply for certification. There are provisions that allow an individual without an advanced degree to sit for the required examinations. These provisions usually ask for an individual to document experience to be considered in lieu of the advanced degree (NFL Players Association, 2007). Good information can be found at www.nflplayers.com.

The requirements for becoming a certified agent for other sports vary. For example, to represent a professional baseball player, the MLB simply requires an application, certification, attendance at required seminars, and payment of the appropriate fees. While the Major League Baseball Players Association (MLBPA) is the sole bargaining agent for all players, any player can select an individual to be their representative to negotiate or assist the player in negotiating a contract, but that individual must comply with all requirements for certification (MLBPA, 1997). An agent representing a professional baseball player must become certified if the player makes a 40-man major league roster (MLB.com, 2010). From an experiential background perspective, it is implied that the agent must simply have the necessary expertise, background, and skills to represent the player. However, a criminal background can prevent an individual from becoming certified as an agent in any sport.

Certified representation of professional basketball players in the National Basketball Association (NBA) and the Women's National Basketball Association (WNBA) is similar to that for baseball except the agent must possess a four-year degree or other qualifying experience (NBAPA ,1991; WNBAPA, 2000). The website, www.sportsagent411.com, provides a great deal of information about becoming an agent. In fact, the website provides, for reading purposes, the agent certification processes for many professional sports including international basketball, track and field, soccer, Canadian football, and hockey. Look for the Sports Agent Certification section.

The NCAA also has rules governing an athlete's relationship with an agent. Any agent should become very familiar with these rules, because a student-athlete could be ruled ineligible to participate in college athletics if these rules are violated. Familiarity with state laws or certification requirements is important as well. The Uniform Athlete Agents' Act (UAAA) allows an agent's certification to be valid in any state that has adopted the Act provided certain regulations are met. According to the NCAA website, 38 states, Washington, D.C, and the Virgin Islands have adopted this law and four other states have laws regulating agents or impending legislation (NCAA, 2009). The Sports Agent Responsibility and Trust Act (SPARTA), passed in 2004, is another federal law that was enacted to govern the conduct of sports agents. The law controls deceptive practices and is regulated by the Federal Trade Commission. A great deal of information about agents and professional sports leagues can be found on the NCAA website under Professional Sport Organizations.

Before accepting any position with a sports agency or agent, one should research the organization very carefully. Historically, there have been agents who violated NCAA rules and federal and state laws and landed in jail or became embroiled in lengthy lawsuits. Maintaining a strict ethical code should be a priority for any agent; the laws enacted for the governance of agents target ethical and illegal actions.

INTERNATIONAL OPPORTUNITIES

Professional sport in other countries has seen tremendous growth. Sport is being used as a national symbol of pride. The Beijing Olympics, while not considered a pure professional sporting event, was a prime example of a country using sport to boost its image and Schrag (2009) indicated that the media described the image boost as a logistical success. Manchester, England, increased its credentials in international sport when they hosted the 2002 Commonwealth Games and, subsequently, was awarded the World

2008 World Squash Championships. In January, 2010, Angola hosted the largest sporting event in its history when it hosted the African Cup of Nations soccer tournament (Africa, 2010). India hosted the Commonwealth Games, a 4,000+ athlete event, for the first time in 2010 (Commonwealth, 2010). Hoping to rival or surpass the NHL and to draw players from that league, Russia began the Kontinental Hockey League (KHL) in 2008 with several triple digit million dollar investors (Fraser, 2010). Middle Eastern states have also been heavily investing in sports (Fudger, 2010).

Leagues, traditionally confined to a single country, are increasingly crossing borders. England's Barclays Premier League (EPL) is now the top football league in Asia where it generates more than $350 million annually (Luer, 2010). We are all aware of the NFL's and the MLB's newer tradition of beginning their seasons overseas. The NBA and the NHL are drawing crowds as well (US Sports, 2010).

International professional sport can have a very different meaning in countries outside North America. Badminton, squash, and table tennis are wildly popular in many Asian countries and dominate television airwaves. In the U.S., one can find amateur tournaments, but rarely would they appear on television. Still, professional sport, however defined in a particular country, is growing. According to Luer (2010), "the next decade in Asia will be about local content, raising standards within the many leagues and events, developing local stars, and providing fertile grounds for careers in sport" (p. 17).

The World Baseball Classic is attempting to globalize professional baseball and neither the 2006 nor the 2009 events involved the U.S. team in the final game; both were won by Japan. Furthermore, playing sites for the 2009 Classic involved only two U.S. venues out of the seven total used for the event. This seems incongruous when the Classic was developed by Major League Baseball. Kelly (2007) claims baseball scholars refuse to label it a global sport. Regardless, professional baseball seems to be growing internationally, particularly in Central and South America. In terms of establishing a career in professional baseball management, this is a positive step, especially for bilingual students.

Dorscher reported in 2006 that the world had caught NBA fever and it was the number one sport in the Philippines. The same article declared that the NBA had over 100 international employees in nine offices and Germany and France were the largest markets for NBA apparel. The NBA has developed NBA China to grow its brand and the sport in that country ("China's

Market, 2009). Thibault (2009) recognized the NBA as an important role player in the "new sport world order" (p. 1).

Australian football may be quite confusing to a student studying in North America, because the Australian description of football does not relate to the NFL or Canadian football and the term could be used to describe rugby, soccer, or a combination thereof. Australia has four football "codes" better understood as "governing rules" and each involves professional, semi-professional, and development systems. Australian rules football (Aussie rules) sports the strongest financial support and Skinner, Zakus, and Edwards (2008) report the pure soccer code may be challenging the three other codes with the eventual pilfering of players, fans, and media attention because it has the highest participant rates even though it ranks fourth in popularity and resources.

Cricket, a professional sport non-existent in the United States, is fiercely popular in many countries including Australia, England, India, and New Zealand and has gained tremendous popularity in the Caribbean nations (Sinclair, 2005). According to Holden (2008), cricket's "sphere is currently being shaped . . . by tension between the routinisation of international cricket and a shift of wealth and power within the game towards India" (p. 337).

International professional sport in also governed differently than the professional sport system observed in the United States. Some countries, including those within the European Union, discuss sport within their national constitutions due to its sociological and societal importance; several governments provide financing while many believe in self-governance by sporting unions (Parrish, 2008) and financing through private grants or sponsorships. After Hong Kong's retrocession to China in 1997, the government abolished a Sports Development Board because of the board's use of venues and high salaries paid to directors (Scott, 2006).

Sport, professional or amateur, can be used as a political staging ground. Most countries have staunchly and outwardly claimed this is not the purpose behind their country's involvement in sport. But in an era of international political unrest, incidences to the contrary may be found. In an article published in early 2009, The United States Federal News Service stated that "athletics should unify people across cultural divides and international sporting events should not be used as venues for bigotry and prejudice"

◆◆ TIME OUT INTERVIEW ◆◆

— International Sport —
CATHY GRIFFIN

Current Position	CEO and Founder
Employer	Griffin Network
B.A. Degree	Business Marketing, Florida State University
Career Path	• Manager, Sports Promotions, Pepsi-Cola Company, Four years • Manager, Sports Merchandising, Sports Illustrated, Four years • Assistant to the Publisher, Sports Illustrated, Four years • Vice-President, Ticket Marketing, Soccer World Cup, Four years • Vice-President, Business Development, Zing Interactive TV, One year • Marketing Consultant, Nike, Two years • Vice President, AT Kearney Executive Search, One year • Vice-President/Partner, Korn/Ferry International, Four years
Employment Recommendation	"Get a basic understanding of business and marketing and get inside the business via television or consumer products such as footwear, apparel, or equipment."

(para. 2) when Dubai announced it was prohibiting the participation of an Israeli tennis champion in a Women's Tennis Association (WTA) tournament in its country. As a result of Dubai's actions, *The Wall Street Journal* pulled its sponsorship of the event. And, this discussion is but the tip of the iceberg regarding political and government involvement in professional sport.

Yes, there is no doubt professional sport is growing internationally (Emmett, 2010; Yang, Sparks, & Li, 2008). Thibault (2009) reminded us as of 2009, the Fédération Interationale de Football Association (FIFA) was larger than the United Nations with respect to member countries. However, neither this book nor this chapter can investigate international professional sport in the depth it deserves. Our main purpose in this section is to assist students who are contemplating a career in sport to understand that sport has a global landscape. Professional sport has existed in many countries for a long time; in others, it may just be developing. What is necessary to comprehend is that sport governance and structure can be very different from country to country, but many positions are available internationally and similar paths to internships and employment are possible when properly studied, planned, and pursued. In fact, Thibault (2009) proposes that international sport management has been inadequately examined by sport management professors.

Cathy Griffin, owner of The Griffin Network, an executive recruitment, marketing, and project management consulting firm, has extensive international experience and specializes in industries that cross sports and entertainment and sport and consumer products. Some of her clients have included Visa International, World Cup Soccer, ABC Sports, Scott Boras Corporation, ATP, The Global Sports Institute, the PGA TOUR, and the United States Olympic Committee.

Cathy's international career tied to sport began by accident when she was hired by Pepsi for a sport related marketing position. In order to get involved in international sport, Cathy recommends creating an opportunity to work in another country and that knowing the culture and learning the language is a definite asset (Personal communication, January 26, 2010). Cathy's Time Out Interview provides a snap shot of how she got involved with international sport even while living in the United States. Her current business ties her to international companies across the globe and her background is a wonderful example of how a career can be woven in and around sport, both in the United States and internationally.

In order to create an international opportunity, we recommend students begin by spending a minimum of one semester in a sport related study abroad program. Many sport management programs sponsor study abroad programs including ones in Germany, Greece, and Ireland. Commercially, GlobaLinks Learning Abroad offers programs in Europe, Asia, New Zealand, and Australia. (For more information, go to http://globalinksabroad .org/sport/.) By studying abroad, it is quite possible to make networking connections that could lead to international internships and employment.

International sport business conferences are on the rise as well. London plays hosts to several conferences a year and Monterrey, Mexico, Dubai, Paris, Monte Carlo, and Abu Dhabi are just a few international cities that have adopted the role of major conference host. All of these opportunities support the growing nature of professional sport on the global stage and the increasing possibilities for networking and employment in the sport industry.

THE FINAL BUZZER

The intent of this chapter was to expand a student's awareness to the seasonal nature of the team sport segment of the industry, provide some insight into gaining entry with a professional sport organization, and introduce the breadth of possible career opportunities in professional sport from a global perspective. By interviewing individuals in actual positions, researching organizational websites, and presenting information learned about the segments over the last twenty years, additional insight can be gained into careers and career paths. Just as each segment presents different employment responsibilities and foci, we felt the information presented should reflect the experiences of the individuals involved and highlight interesting information and aspects of the segment not found in many textbooks.

Classroom Experiential Learning Exercise

INDUSTRY EXPLORATION

Contact a current sport manager who works in the industry segment in which you hope to be employed. Set up a face-to-face interview meeting. Establish a set of questions to ask this individual to learn more about their career path and company. Communicate your desire to enter sport business. Please make it clear you are not asking for an apprenticeship, internship, or a job. However, bring a copy of your polished résumé in case the conversation leads in this direction. At the completion of the interview, immediately send a thank you letter. Submit a two- to four-page double-spaced summary of the interview including what you learned and whether the interview has led you to pursue an apprenticeship in this direction. The quality of questions asked and the written summary weigh heavily on the final grade.

Submitted by Dr. Susan B. Foster, Professor
Saint Leo University, Saint Leo, Florida

Program Experiential Learning Example

INVOLVING ALL STUDENTS WITH INVITED INDUSTRY PROFESSIONALS

York College of Pennsylvania has Professional Day as part of their senior professional development course. At the end of the semester, they invite people from different parts of the industry (including at least one alumnus) and they spend the day on campus doing mock interviews of the students in the class and conduct roundtable discussions with any sport management major that wants to attend. Students in the class are given the names of the individuals in advance; they are required to research the individuals' backgrounds. The students do not know who will be interviewing them so they have to prepare to interview with everyone on the panel. Each student must also prepare a résumé and cover letter to match the individual and the type of job for which they would be interviewing.

Submitted by Dr. Tim Newman, Associate Professor
York, Pennsylvania

4

Sport Business Industry Overview: Olympic and Amateur Sport

"My current position is one of the most challenging and rewarding I have ever held. I love sports and the sports culture. I love everything about athletics. Build a strong foundation of communication, organizational, and operation management skills. If you have these skills and passion, you will be successful."

— Sally Hanson
Assistant Director, JCC Maccabi Games

THE WARM UP

This chapter will explore industry segments that are generally considered Olympic or amateur in nature. For simplicity, sports that may not be included in the Olympics, but have a recognized national governing body are being collectively discussed in this category. We recognize that Olympic athletes receive compensation through endorsements and other competition prize money and may be more properly identified as professional athletes. But this book does not focus on the professional careers of the competing athlete. Instead, our focus is on the careers of the individuals creating, organizing, and conducting the events and managing the organizations. High

◈◈ TIME OUT INTERVIEW ◈◈

⌐ Sport Governing Bodies ⌐
KELLY SKINNER

Position	Team Leader, Sport Performance
Employer	United States Olympic Committee
B.S. Degree	Business, Western Michigan University
M.S. Degree	Sport Administration, Central Michigan University
Career Path	• Intern, USA Weightlifting, Five months • Director of Marketing, USA Weightlifting, Two years • Coordinator, Grants and Planning, USOC, One year • Vice-President, Marketing & Operations, North American Hockey League, One year • Manager, Grants and Planning, USOC, Fourteen months • Manager, Sports Partnerships, USOC, Four years • Director, Sports Partnerships, USOC, Six years
Employment Recommendation	"It is incredibly challenging to get an internship at the USOC. It is common to have in excess of 250 applications for 20–23 positions. The more that you have networked or demonstrated a true passion for what we do, the better off you will be. Use your time very wisely in school and get great experiences; learning a foreign language is also a great decision. What it comes down to is demonstrating your 'differential advantage' over the other 249+ applicants. Show that you have the passion to excel and that you can lead."

school and collegiate athletics and recreational sport also fall in to the category of amateur sport.

While some careers in this area may also see seasonal postings, positions not tied to a particular team, league, or competition season may be advertised at any time in a calendar year. These organizations operate on a twelve month cycle just as any other non-sport related business. Once again, as with the previous chapter, we are attempting to provide a wide scope of information but, of course, cannot explore every type of position that might be available.

National governing bodies for minor sports should be strongly considered for full-time positions and local Olympic organizing committees offer numerous temporary full-time employment possibilities. (Courtesy of Master Sergeant Lona Kollars/U.S. Army)

OLYMPIC AND AMATEUR SPORT SEGMENTS EXPLAINED AND EXPLORED

Governing Bodies

Sports falling under the umbrella of Olympic, Pan American, or Paralympic sport have a governing body that administers the affairs of the sports. A national governing body can be charged with coordinating competitions, fundraising, team selection processes, and management of national and international competitions. Grassroots (local) level branches or events tied to a particular sport may also be a responsibility. There are 45 Olympic and Pan American sports and 24 Paralympic sports with a recognized national governing body. Some sports share the same governing organization. Additionally, there are 51 United States Olympic Committee (USOC) Affilliated Organizations and ten Olympic/Paralympic Training sites (USOC Affiliated, 2010). The USOC alone employs over 55 individuals on its Executive and Management Teams (top-level administrators) exclusive of the other paid positions housed at their Colorado Springs national headquarters (teamusa.org, 2010b). All of these numbers reflect only national level organizations and the numbers are not all inclusive. Kelly Skinner, our highlighted professional in the Time Out Interview for this segment, estimates that there are over 1,000 positions in all of the national governing bodies listed on their website with around 150 at the disabled sport organizations (Personal communication, September 16, 2009). What a great testi-

mony to earlier comments that the number of positions in the sport industry cannot be counted! Another thought to contemplate is that some national governing bodies (NGBs) could have regional or state offices. A look
at just one sport and its governing bodies below further displays the endless
number of positions available.

The Amateur Softball Association (ASA), founded in 1933, is the official
governing body of softball in the United States and is one of the country's
largest sports organizations. Among its many roles is the regulation and
sanctioning of competition, ensurance of equal opportunity, sponsorship
procurement, equipment oversight, and rule development. With a membership of over three million, one can possibly understand that many jobs are
created by this one organization. Under the ASA alone, there are 80,000
youth teams and 170,000 adult teams playing both fast and slow pitch softball. According to Bill Plummer III, the Hall of Fame Manager at the ASA
Headquarters in Oklahoma City, Oklahoma, ASA employs approximately
29 full-time staff and generally hires two to three paid interns per year (Personal communication, August 5, 2009).

While these sport organizations will have numerous volunteers at the local level with some affiliation to the governing body, countless positions are
required at city and county recreation departments to manage the numerous local leagues and tournaments as well as playoffs and championships
held throughout the country.

To delve a little deeper into the governance of this one sport in the United
States, the ASA is not the only softball governing body. The International
Softball Federation located in Lakeland, Florida, is the international governing body for the sport and employs approximately eight individuals full-
time (ISF, 2009). The United States Fastpitch Softball Association (USFS)
sponsors girls fast pitch softball and is headquartered in Pensacola, Florida.
The Independent Softball Association (ISA) headquartered in Bartow,
Florida, was founded in 1984 and has two full-time employees. The organization sponsors league play and tournaments for amateur slow and fast
pitch softball and boasts 18,000 registered teams (http://www.isasoftball
.com/about/ August 17, 2009, and personal communication). The National
Softball Association (NSA), with headquarters located in Nicholasville,
Kentucky (http://www.playnsa.com/index.php), was founded in 1982 and
sponsors play for youth through adult teams. Finally, the United States Specialty Sports Association (USSSA) headquartered in Kissimmee, Florida,

◆◆ TIME OUT INTERVIEW ◆◆

⌐ College Athletic Administration ⌐
STEVE HORTON

Current Position	Associate Director of Athletics/Compliance
Employer	University of South Florida
B.A. Degree	University of Georgia, Journalism/Television
M. Ed	University of Georgia, Physical Education/Sports Administration
Other Certifications	Sports Management Institute Executive Program (Notre Dame and Southern Cal)
Career Path	• Honeywell, Marketing and Communications, Two years • University of Georgia, Public Relations & Advertising, Contract position for NASA, Six years • Graduate School & University of Georgia Athletic Ticket Office, Two years • NCAA, Legislative Assistant, Three years • Virginia Tech, Assistant Director of Athletics/Compliance, Seven years • Atlanta Olympics, Field of Play Supervisor, Eight months • University of Texas, El Paso, Compliance consultant, One year
Employment Recommendation	"Getting experience through internships, part-time positions, and volunteer work is the key to getting into the industry. The last open position we had, I had over 150 applicants, but because I was asking for one year of collegiate athletics experience, my qualified list was quickly pared to 15. Most people have an advanced degree; experience in athletics is what moves one to the 'front of the class.'"

was founded as the United States Slow Pitch Softball Association and changed its name in 2005. However, it still has a softball division that hosts world and national tournaments. In addition to the name change, it now sponsors events in nine other sports and employs approximately 13 full-time individuals (Personal communication, August 5, 2009).

By just looking at softball and further highlighting the concept introduced in Chapter 1, the number of full-time positions available in sport grows exponentially with each sport. It would be extremely difficult to count all of the governing bodies tied to sport in the United States and even more difficult to count the number of full-time positions.

Outside of the sport governing bodies, professional organizational governing bodies exist and may have large office staffs. The National Intramural-Sports Association (NIRSA) is one such organization. NIRSA employees oversee and work in departments such as marketing, conferences, membership recruitment, and more, and a very satisfying career can be found with these types of organizations. Entry level salaries in some of these organizations can be higher than those found in professional sport. See www.nirsa.org for more information on this type of organization.

Any sport governing body can be an excellent place for one to find internships or to volunteer in order to gain experience. Targeting a specific sport is possible and numerous doors can be opened to local administrative positions and exciting national and international involvement. Additional governing bodies will be highlighted as they pertain to some of the sections below.

COLLEGE ATHLETICS

Most people are very familiar with college athletics. However, understanding its depth is crucial to the prospective intern. While television gives one a first-row view of most major college programs, positions with smaller postsecondary institutions, as well as with conference offices, are available. Additionally, it is often easier to climb the ladder and rise to the top of your field within an organization when it is smaller. In fact, in hard economic times when states are cutting budgets, internships will often increase as a means of hiring interested and qualified individuals at a lower rate than would be offered to a full-time employee. In addition to the more than 1,085 member schools of the National Collegiate Athletic Association (NCAA), individuals interested in a career in this industry segment should also check for available positions with the following:

- National Christian College Athletic Association (NCCAA, http://www.thenccaa.org) and its 95+ member schools;
- the National Association of Intercollegiate Athletics (NAIA, http://naia.cstv.com) and its 285+ member schools;

◆◆ TIME OUT INTERVIEW ◆◆

— Collegiate Athletic Academic Advising —
SHAWN FAGAN

Position	Senior Athletic Academic Advisor
Employer	Temple University
B.S. Degree	Rehabilitation and Human Services, Pennsylvania State University
M.S.A.	Sport Administration, Belmont University
Career Path	• Academic Support Intern, Penn State, One year • Athletic/Academic Counselor, Vanderbilt University, Four years
Employment Recommendation	"Start as an intern in a university academic support center. Become familiar with the NCAA rules and regulations and undergraduate curricula. Attend NCAA conferences and/or join the National Association of Academic Advisors for Athletics (N4A). Network, network, network! This is a growing field that is all about building relationships and connecting with advising constituents which can eventually lead to employment. Gain a firm understanding of the daily challenges that student-athletes face by having to balance their academic, athletic, and social commitments. "Make a concerted effort to get a wide range of experience early. At a large school, individuals tend to be more specialized, whereas at smaller schools, responsibilities tend to be more of a collective and collaborative effort."

- the National Junior College Athletic Association (NJCAA, http://www.njcaa.org) and its 525 member schools; and
- the United States Collegiate Athletic Association (USCAA, http://www.theuscaa.com) and its 60+ member schools.

Within most governing bodies for college athletics, member schools are divided into divisions and the responsibilities of employees generally vary based on the size of the school. For example, the NCAA has traditionally divided its schools into three major divisions, with Division I housing the largest programs in two different subdivisions, Divisions I-A and I-AA. In 2006, for football, these subdivisions were renamed to the Football Bowl Subdivision (commonly known as the BCS) and the Football Championship Subdivision (NCAA, 2008).

Positions in college athletics vary widely especially at the larger schools. Individuals employed in this setting tend to work within one department with responsibilities focused solely in that area. It is recommended that an individual targeting this career field explores different niche areas as one does not start out as an athletic director. Climbing the ladder usually begins with a position in sports information, facility management, sales or marketing, compliance, athlete academic advising, or coaching. Gaining a graduate assistantship position (see Chapters 1 and 10) in one of these departments or with a team is often the best course to pursue.

Many aspire to become an athletics director (AD). According to Steve Horton, associate athletics director at the University of South Florida in Tampa, "being the athletics director at a Division I school can be both pres-

◆◆ TIME OUT INTERVIEW ◆◆

⁓ Collegiate Athletic Sports Information ⁓
LINDY BROWN

Current Position	Associate Sports Information Director
Employer	Duke University
B.S. Degree	Sport Management, Western Carolina University
Career Path	• Student worker, Sports Information, Five years • Internship, Marketing & Promotions, WCU—Three months • Director of Sports Information and Marketing/ Promotion Coordinator, University of South Carolina—Aiken, Three and one half years • Assistant SID, Duke University, Seven years
Employment Recommendation	"Get as much experience as possible while in college. Volunteer if you have to; the more experience you have, the easier it will be to get a job. Get to know people and stay in touch; often it is all about who you know."

tigious and financially rewarding. The responsibility of managing a complex department with daily issues in many areas keeps most ADs far removed from any interaction with student-athletes" (Personal communication, December 9, 2009). An AD at a Division I institution must accept the responsibilities of fundraising, public relations, facility development, a hefty travel schedule, and more. Thus, many may prefer holding other positions in college athletics and at smaller Division II and III institutions that keep individuals in touch with the athletes.

We have included a Time Out Interview in this chapter for a sports information director. This position, although specialized in the media area, may hold the title of an assistant or associate athletic director, as well. In the college athletic environment, the responsibilities are similar to those of a public relations director in professional sport, but most departments are labeled sports information instead of public relations. Often, sports information directors (SIDs) must be familiar with a wide variety of sports and computer programs, especially those involving game statistics. They will write press releases for newspapers and websites, particularly in smaller markets, and may not get credit for their writing in the print media. Many will contact home town newspapers of their institution's athletes and submit articles covering the athlete's college successes. And particularly in large athletic programs, they are also charged with protecting the student-athlete and coach from the outside media. Good writing and people skills are a must!

Many college athletic administrators would hire more female coaches and administrators if they simply applied. Obtaining a degree in sport management is a first step toward this career goal. (Courtesy of iStockphoto Inc.)

COLLEGE COACHING

Many aspire to enter college athletics through the coaching ranks. Entry strategies may vary depending upon the level of the institution. The best way to get your foot in the door of a Division I school is through a graduate assistantship (GA) which was defined in Chapter 1. Selecting a school in order to work under a specific coach and for the respective master's degrees offered is the first step. The NCAA publishes graduate assistant position offerings by member institutions at http://ncaamarket.ncaa.org/search.cfm.

Division II and III schools also offer graduate assistantships and, at some institutions, these positions are actual coaching positions. It is a less expensive way to hire head coaches, coaching assistants, and other staff members. At the same time, it is a great way to get a master's degree and experience at the same time. More information on graduate assistantships can be found in Chapter 10.

◆◆ TIME OUT INTERVIEW ◆◆

~ College Coaching ~
BRADLEY JORGENSEN

Current Position	Head Lacrosse Coach
Employer	Saint Leo University
B.S. Degree	Movement and Sport Science, Springfield College, Springfield, MA
M.B.A.	Saint Leo University, Saint Leo, FL
Career Path	• Head Lacrosse Coach; Director of Physical Education and Recreation, Wheaton College, Seven years • Defensive Coordinator (Graduate Assistant), Men's Lacrosse, Amherst College, Two years
Employment Recommendation	"Coaching is a career that starts with a lot more work than pay. The main compensation a young coach gets is experience. It is critical to view the experience as an apprenticeship and strive every day to collect as much knowledge as possible from your peers, coworkers, and direct supervisor."

At any institution, teaching may be part of a coach's responsibilities. Often a coach may teach sport skills classes, coaching theory courses, or other classes that fit their undergraduate degree. Some may be assigned teaching responsibilities for freshmen experience classes as well. Thus, anyone wishing to start a career in coaching may want to take a few education courses if there is room for electives within a sport business or business administration degree program. Of course, getting an education degree is a good option as well, but a physical education or kinesiology program is an excellent route for coaches. If one already has an undergraduate degree in one of these areas, a master's degree in sport management/business is a great compliment to round out the educational background.

Many believe that college playing experience is a pre-requisite for getting into coaching. There is no doubt that having been a collegiate athlete allows the individual an upfront and personal view of the pressures placed on athletes and the team environment. This experience also exposes them to a wide variety of game strategies and operations. However, according to Brad Jorgensen, Head Lacrosse Coach at Saint Leo University, playing experience means less and less the further one gets away from their playing days, but it might help one get that first coaching position. Playing experience only gets one so far. Coaches are evaluated on their current coaching abilities and professionalism, and this is what keeps one in the coaching profession (Personal communication, December 16, 2009).

At a smaller institution, coaches may wear many hats across traditional departmental boundaries. In addition to teaching, coaches may also hold responsibilities in areas such as facility maintenance or sports information, or in a fitness center or intramural sport programming. At any size school, it is not uncommon for a coach's educational minimum requirement to be a master's degree, particularly if teaching in the academic program is required.

The responsibilities of a college coach vary widely. A head coach, particularly for men's or women's basketball or football, is often delivering presentations, meeting with alumni groups, attending dinners, participating in golf or other sport related outings, traveling to meet with parents and recruits, and, of course, coaching. They are very much an organizational figurehead and an extension of an institution's public relations staff. A head coach of a major sport is also a manager of a sizeable staff, thus management and organizational skills and a people-friendly personality benefit one tremendously. They may also elect to teach. Jim Tressell, Ohio State University's

Head Football Coach, elects to do this. Jack Leggett, the Head Baseball Coach at Clemson University, who has had a long career coaching baseball, has also taught an exceptional baseball coaching class in his career.

While all coaches may have some budgetary accountability, a coach at a smaller institution is likely to have more hands-on responsibilities in this area, as well as other office duties, because their support staffs are not likely to be as large. They may drive the team van, organize races and meets, set-up their facility's venue, and even direct the maintenance crew. Thus, event management skills and knowledge of current facility technology, flooring, and field turf maintenance are necessary core skills. A coach at a smaller institution is very much a do-everything, know-everything type of person for their sport. The institution counts on them and their abilities to direct support staff in these areas.

HIGH SCHOOL ATHLETIC ADMINISTRATION

Individuals wishing to pursue a career as a high school's AD may elect sport management as their college degree field. Rising to this type of position usually begins with a coaching and/or teaching position. However, caution is warranted. Many states or school districts may require a specific degree in education with the appropriate teaching certifications. Some sport management programs are housed in an education department (i.e., physical education), but this alone may not qualify an individual to obtain teaching certifications in certain states. Additional education courses may be necessary. Private schools and certain school districts may have different requirements and may be able to hire an individual with a non-teaching sport management degree if they obtain a teaching certification in a designated number of years after being hired.

The responsibilities of a high school athletic director traditionally require accountability in a variety of areas including coaching, facility maintenance and management, eligibility compliance, game supervision, hiring and discharge of sport coaches, teaching, budget development, and management. Because a high school athletic director may supervise a large staff of coaches and other related personnel with little support staff, being an organized manager and a great people person are strong assets. A high school athletic director must also understand risk management. Creating a safe environment for athletes, coaches, and spectators and understanding the legal liabili-

◆◆ TIME OUT INTERVIEW ◆◆

― High School Athletics ―
ERIC TIMKO

Position	Athletic Director; Conference Chairman
Employer	North Fort Myers High School and Lee County Athletic Conference, North Fort Myers, FL
B.A. Degree	Michigan State University, Elementary Education
M.B.A Degree	Saint Leo University w/Concentration in Sport Business
Career Path	• Middle school social studies teacher, Two years concurrent with high school JV baseball coach, Five years • High school American History & Economics teacher, Two years; Football Coach, Four years; Basketball Coach, One season (Some positions concurrent)
Employment Recommendation	"To be a high school athletic director, you have to be involved in the system and have been a coach. Some large districts will have assistant athletic directors and this can be an early path to being an A.D., but rarely does one graduate from college and immediately become the athletic director. One needs good communication skills because you are the face of the athletic department."

ties involved in supervision of facilities and people are of utmost importance. ADs are often involved in the design and management of new sport facilities and all athletic directors are event managers. Many curricula in physical education do not have separate courses in any of these areas, so it is a strong recommendation that a student seeks out sport management courses on these topics if pursuing an education degree and teaching certification.

As with many positions in sport, a traditional 8 a.m. to 5 p.m. workday is not the norm. With teams playing in the evenings and on weekends, an AD must accept flexibility in their schedule, long hours, and time away from family. Because of the multitude of responsibilities of a high school athletic director, some schools/school districts may not allow an AD to hold a coaching position at the same time (Erik Timko, Personal communication, August 26, 2009).

RECREATIONAL SPORT MANAGEMENT

Careers in recreational sport management are often overlooked by those pursuing a sport management degree. Sometimes people believe a degree in recreation is best and others just simply have not explored this very satisfying employment area. This section is strictly devoted to recreational sport management and does not pertain to positions that may include such responsibilities as arts and crafts, story time, and other non-sport leisure pursuits.

COLLEGE RECREATIONAL SPORT

A comprehensive career in this industry segment can be found on most college campuses under the department of campus recreation. In today's higher education organizational structure, most campus recreation programs are aligned with a Division of Student Affairs. Several decades ago, the most likely place to find this type of department was under athletics and some institutions still operate in this manner.

Any quality campus recreation program houses a multitude of recreational pursuits and most relate to fitness or sport. A typical department will house intramural, extramural, club, fitness, and aquatic programming. Noncredit instructional programming such as aerobics, dance, martial arts, and basic sport skills development classes are customary. On large campuses, it is not uncommon to have a large (200,000 square feet or more) facility housing multiple team and individual sport courts, one or more areas dedicated to fitness, swimming pools, climbing walls, an outdoor equipment check-out station, and even athletic training and physical therapy facilities to treat and rehabilitate the recreational athlete. One of the newest collections of campus recreation facilities in the United States can be found at The Ohio State University. Five indoor recreational sport facilities and 70 acres of outdoor recreational space adorn this sprawling urban campus. First opened in 2005, the Recreation and Physical Activity Center (RPAC) cost $140 million and has a total square footage of 568,459. It houses five pools, a jogging track, three aerobics/multipurpose rooms, ten racquetball/squash courts, a wellness center, 25,000 square feet of weight and fitness areas, four gymnasiums, an indoor golf area with simulator, and putting and chipping areas, as well as ancillary support areas for lounging, babysitting, food serv-

◆ ◆ TIME OUT INTERVIEW ◆ ◆

⁓ Collegiate Recreational Sport Management ⁓
TIM McNEILLY

Position	Director of Campus Recreation
Employer	University of North Carolina, Wilmington
B.S. Degree	Sport Management, Western Carolina University
M.A. Degree	Sport Management, Appalachian State University
Career Path	• Graduate Assistant, Intramural Sports, Appalachian State—Two years • Store manager, Finish Line sporting goods store, Four years • Assistant Director & Associate Director, Campus Recreation, UNC—Wilmington, Nine years
Employment Recommendation	"Gain as much experience as you can during your undergraduate years. Work with intramurals, fitness, facility management, and more. You will prepare yourself for an opportunity to gain a graduate assistantship/internship. Plan on getting a master's degree to be on equal grounds against those with whom you will be competing for jobs."

ice, offices, locker rooms, massage areas, and a juice bar (Facilities, 2010).

Their $7.5 million dollar, 87,000 square foot Adventure Recreation Center houses indoor turf fields, basketball courts, a climbing center, a fitness center, and a rental equipment guest services counter. Outdoor facilities include a disc golf course; roller hockey rink; softball, flag football, lacrosse, and rugby fields; a jogging/bike path; basketball, tennis, and volleyball and sand volleyball courts; picnic areas and shelters; a children's play area; a winter sports hill; and a park support center. Most of the outdoor courts/fields are in numbers too numerous to mention here but sit on 83 acres (Facilities, 2010).

Why would we bother listing everything above? How many full-time positions would you believe are needed to run OSU's facilities and programs in campus recreation? Can you picture managing over 50 sport clubs, 800 basketball teams, 500 flag football teams, and countless more recreational sport teams along with several fitness centers? OSU also includes family activities and a strong philosophy that includes a wide array of programming and events for the physically challenged population. What would you imagine the operational and staff budget to be? Let us add to your understanding of the magnitude of this one department. Seventy-six full-time employees, 14 graduate administrative assistants (GAAs), and 850 students are employed. The annual operating budget is in excess of $18 million. Many graduate assistantships are available in this field and expect to see a master's degree as a preferred requirement for a full-time entry level position. According to J. Michael Dunn, long-time Director of Campus Recreation at Ohio State, the average starting salary for an entry level coordinator's position at Ohio State in 2009 was between $38,000 and $45,000. He recommends the following for anyone exploring a career in campus recreation (Personal communication, September 1, 2009).

- Join and be active in NIRSA by attending conferences, submitting presentations for any of NIRSA's conferences or workshops, and serving on committees.
- Get involved in conducting research with faculty or staff.
- Travel and visit other collegiate recreational sports programs in operation. Professionals working at NIRSA member institutions genuinely welcome individuals wanting to visit their campus with open arms.
- Begin looking for graduate schools as early as your junior year. One way to narrow your choice is to find institutions heavily involved in NIRSA and with a history of preparing and supporting young professionals.
- Maintain an undergraduate GPA of 3.0 or above.
- Meet and develop a professional relationship with a minimum of three to six mentors from other campuses that would support you in a mentee/mentor relationship.
- Develop a consciousness that is open to change. Adopt a forecasting mentality of possible changes in higher education and in recreational sport that will have a short- or long-term impact on your career. Reading the *Chronicle of Higher Education* on a regular basis can assist in the understanding of changes affecting higher education.

If you aren't lucky enough to be enrolled at a strong NIRSA institution for your undergraduate experience, or are not offered a graduate assistantship at one, work harder and smarter in other areas and take advantage of all opportunities (M. Dunn, Personal communication, August 31, 2009).

◆◼ TIME OUT INTERVIEW ◼◆

— City Recreational Sports —
FRANK GRIFFIN

Position	Director of Recreation and Parks
Employer	City of Natchitoches, Louisiana
B.GS. Degree	General Studies, Northwestern State University
M Ed. Degree	Sport Administration, Northwestern State University
Career Path	• Supervisor, Intramural Department, Northwestern State University of Louisiana, Five years • Intern, Lafayette Consolidated Government—Full-time, Nineteen months • City of Natchitoches, Assistant Director, Three years
Employment Recommendation	"Start working on the ground floor as an official, score-keeper, or day-camp worker. Having knowledge of how the entry level positions work is key. These are the people who are the face of your department and possessing hands-on knowledge of what they do is crucial."

Of course, finding an internship at a NIRSA member institution is highly recommended.

Recreational sport management positions can also be found within city and county recreation departments and non-profit organizations such as a YMCA. Some positions may be solely dedicated to the operation and management of sport leagues and tournaments and thus would fall under this employment category. Any municipal recreation department most likely has at least one full-time position dedicated to sport-related management. These other categories are explored more fully in the sections below.

CITY OR COUNTY RECREATIONAL SPORT

Working for a city or county recreation department can include an entire career involving sport programs of all types and for all ages. While men's, women's, and co-ed softball are extremely popular and well known, other sport leagues are offered. Of course, the sport offerings depend largely on available facilities and local or regional sport interests. Running tournaments is an exciting responsibility and some recreation departments are known for running numerous tournaments every year and submitting bids to host national championships. Thus, event and facility management combine to round out enormous responsibility under this employment umbrella.

MILITARY SPORT MANAGEMENT

Military sport is huge! Yet, most people are unaware of the extent of sport program offerings. Starting from the grassroots level, military bases have recreation and sport programs for service personnel. These programs usually fall under the Morale, Welfare, and Recreation (MWR) division. Some bases have begun to outsource these programs to fitness centers or civic recreation programs, but most bases still have formal MWR divisions. At Patrick Air Force Base in Satellite Beach, Florida, activities such as the Wing Sports Day Olympiad; a one-pitch softball tournament; an event entitled Peddle, Paddle, & Pant involving biking, canoeing, and a 1½-mile run; practices for the Air Force Women's Basketball team; and the Special Olympics State Championship have been hosted at the base. Family programming is also very much a part of MWR life. One does not have to be in a branch of the service to work for an MWR office. However, military individuals can head up or be assigned MWR positions and duties. For more information about Patrick's activities, visit http://www.patrick.af.mil/photos/mediagallery.asp?galleryID=2106.

Beyond individual base military programs is the Department of Defenses' Armed Forces Sports (AFS) programs where tournaments and events for a variety of different sports are hosted. Besides your typical team sport offerings, rugby, sailing, golf, parachuting, track and field, bowling, boxing, and several martial arts dot the AFS event calendar. Its purpose is to "provide an avenue for military service members to participate in national and international competitions" (Saty 2009, para. 1).

The U.S. Military All-Stars (baseball) operates a Red, White, and Blue Tour where off-duty military personnel play baseball and cover their own expenses. The tour visits about forty states and eight foreign countries making nearly 350 appearances annually to promote their mission of raising awareness of the sacrifices of the United States Armed Forces. The team travels annually and part of their tour includes games against major league teams in spring training. Several internships are available (T. Allvord, Personal communication, January 24, 2010) and full-time positions are also possible with this unique tour. For more information, check out http://www.heroesofthediamond.com/RedWhiteBlueTour/TourOverview.html.

On a larger scale, the best athletes in the United States military are selected to represent the United States in the Conseil International du Sport Militaire (CISM), founded in 1948. The purpose of CISM is to use "the playing field to unite Armed Forces of countries that may have previously confronted each other because of political and ideological difference" (Saty, 2009, para. 2). About 20 world championships are organized annually and, every four years, there is a CISM Military World Games. In 2010, the first CISM Winter Military World Games were hosted in Aosta Valley, Italy, and the 42nd Annual World Military Fencing Championships were hosted in Venezuela. For more information, visit http://www.cism-milsport.org/eng/001_HOME/001_homepage.asp.

All of these military programs represent the possibility of full-time positions working in amateur sport. When the U.S. military forces were first deployed to Iraq in Operation Desert Storm, job postings appeared for non-military individuals to run recreational sport programs for the troops in Iraq and Saudi Arabia. Furthermore, a creative programming idea was published in a NIRSA publication many years ago regarding the modified rules for playing softball on an aircraft carrier. Thus, regardless of where the U.S. Troops are located, the possibility exists for employment in recreational sport management via military sport programs.

OTHER NON-PROFITS AND PRIVATE RECREATIONAL SPORT PROGRAMMING

Local and national organizations exist that cater to communities through outreach programs and house fitness centers and sport leagues. The Young Men's Christian Association (YMCA) is the largest non-profit community service organization in America. The YMCA was actually founded in London, England, in 1844 to provide a place for rural men to live while working jobs in larger cities at the end of the Industrial Revolution. Bible study was incorporated as an alternative to life in the streets. The first YMCA in the United States was established in Boston in 1853. The 1880s saw a boom in the building of new and larger YMCAs and pools, gymnasiums, and bowling alleys were made part of the new YMCA environment. The sports of basketball, volleyball, and racquetball were started at YMCAs. There are claims that professional football also saw their early beginnings at YMCA's although the NFL claims a different story. By the close of World War II, many Ys were admitting women and soon people of all races and religions were welcomed. Housing men at the early Ys provided a great source of income and housing opportunities still exist for men and women at approximately 33 YMCAs in the United States. YMCAs exist in over 140 countries and, with over 2,600 YMCAs across the United States, it is logical to assume a large number of positions exist that fall under the recreational sport category (History of the YMCA, 2010). With a traditional focus on health and wellness, recreational sport has always formed a strong nucleus for many community programs involving individuals of all ages. The YMCA has strong professional training programs. Having held a job at a YMCA will give you an inside track to other YMCA positions throughout the world. Thus, unlike professional sport organizations where new ownership can result in immediate staffing changes in some departments, leaving previously very dedicated employees without jobs, the support network for finding full-time employment within the Y network is incredible. It is definitely a great place to establish a career that includes recreational sport management. Ys are known to heavily recruit from within. Every two weeks, alerts are sent to employees about position openings. For more information see http://www.ymca.net/about_the_ymca/history_of_the_ymca.html.

The Boys and Girls Clubs of America has also grown into a haven for youth to become involved in organized sport. It, too, has a long history with its first club organized by women in 1860. The Federated Boys Clubs began in 1906, eventually evolving into the Boys and Girls Clubs of America in 1990. Recreation has always been part of its core foundation (Our History, 2010). Some of its current programs include the "Reviving Baseball in Inner Cities (RBI)" and "Jr. RBI" programs sponsored by Major League Baseball, the NFL Youth Football program funded by the NFL Foundation, and Triple Play sponsored by Coca Cola that supports games, sports clubs, and social recreation initiatives. While no internships were listed on their website, internships can often be created by contacting a local club. More information can be found at http://www.bgca.org.

◆◆ TIME OUT INTERVIEW ◆◆

～ Recreational Sport Programming ～
CARLY HOUMAN

Position	Leagues Director
Employer	Tampa Bay Club Sport, Steinbrenner High School, Lutz, Florida
Position	Assistant Coach, Flag Football, Steinbrenner High School, Lutz, Florida
A.S. Degree	Business Administration, Saint Leo University, Saint Leo, Florida
B.A. Degree	Sport Management, Saint Leo University, Saint Leo, Florida
Career Path	• Event Support, Disney Wide World of Sports, Eight months • Assistant Event Director, Let it Fly (Flag Football Tournaments), Four months
Employment Recommendation	"Volunteer to find what you really like to do. Have a lot of patience. It takes a while to find a good fit for yourself and to get paid what you would prefer. Work hard in any position within a company. The bosses notice this and you will hopefully have more opportunities to move to another position you may prefer more. When you work with youth, you also work with parents. Customer service is a must!"

The Jewish Community Centers Association (JCC) is a well known and a very connected organization. With over 350 JCCs and camp sites in North America, the Association provides sport and recreation programs and has youth partnerships with the NFL, the NBA and WNBA, the Women's Sports Foundation, and Major League Soccer. Within their corporate structure, they house a Sports and Wellness Department and have established relationships with other organizations and their JCC fitness facilities. The JCC also hosts an annual JCC Maccabi Games which is the largest gathering for Jewish teens in North America. Competition is held in 13 different sports. This event celebrated its 25th anniversary during the summer of

2010 with 6,000 athletes participating. In recent years, this event has been
held at three to four host sites each year and has several major corporate
sponsors. For more information, see http://www.jcca.org/HPER.html and
http://www.jccmaccabi.org/.

Other private organizations provide sport programming for youth and
adults. The Amateur Athletic Union (AAU), headquartered in Orlando,

◆◆ TIME OUT INTERVIEW ◆◆

Youth Sport Programming
ERIN MCGAULEY

Position	Director, Super Y-League and Super-20 League Operations
Employer	United Soccer Leagues, Tampa, Florida
B.A. Degree	Sport Management, Flagler College, St. Augustine, FL
M.B.A.	Tiffin University, Tiffin, OH
Career Path	• Intern, St. Pete Times Forum, Tampa, FL, Three months • Intern, PSA/DNA Sports Authentication, Orwigsburg, PA, Three months • Major League Soccer, New York, Three months • Graduate Assistant, Women's Soccer, Tiffin University, Two years • Housing Coordinator, United Soccer Leagues, Six months
Employment Recommendation	"Working in youth sports is not a 9 a.m. to 5 p.m. job, nor does it involve sitting around watching sports all day. Being an athlete or playing a sport does not give you adequate experience; you need business experience and a familiarity with event management. Volunteer for various events in your area and gain insight of what goes on behind the scenes. Not only will you learn something new in each event, but you will also meet sport management professionals that may help you get a job. The most efficient way to get your foot in the door is to be pro-active."

Florida, has a long history and runs sports programming in over 20 sports. (Visit http://aausports.org.) I-9 Sports has over 100 locations and 200,000 members and uses the motto "Helping Kids Succeed through Sports." The website featured mostly part-time opportunities, but I-9 and AAU might be a place to gain experience in sports officiating or programming even as a college student. Additionally, the I-9 website offered franchising opportunities. (See http://www.i9sports.com/.) Ever heard of wallyball? Check out the American Wallyball Association at http://www.wallyball.com. Still not satisfied that employment may be just around the corner? Google "amateur adult sports" and "amateur youth sports."

Another example of sport programming involves a unique opportunity for soccer enthusiasts through United Soccer Leagues (USL). Headquartered in Tampa, Florida, USL sponsors leagues from the youth to professional levels. Their website indicates available positions in such areas as ticket sales, marketing, game/event operations, public relations, and camp operations. Visit http://www.uslsoccer.com/.

Sport for youth today does not include just the typical team sports. First Tee is a non-profit organization that partners with golf courses and provides youth with a chance to learn the game of golf. Private martial arts businesses offer a variety of opportunities to learn and compete. The Gatorade Free Flow Tour is the minor leagues, so-to-speak, of the Dew Tour for amateur extreme sports. Internship opportunities may be available or could be pursued in any one of these amateur sport organizations.

THE FINAL BUZZER

The intent of this chapter was to introduce the sport management student to career possibilities in Olympic and amateur sport. While many are somewhat familiar with college and high school sports, key information was relayed to broaden an individual's understanding of where internship opportunities might exist with national governing bodies, governmental and private organizations, and possible youth and adult amateur sport opportunities. Career opportunities are truly unlimited in these areas. Speaking with a faculty advisor or major professor to initiate contact with one of these agencies is a good place to start a career with an Olympic or amateur sport organization.

Classroom Experiential Learning Exercise

TOURNAMENT SCHEDULING

As the sports coordinator for the city recreation department, you have 107 entries in your wallyball tournament. You have ten leagues of eight teams and three leagues of nine teams. You have courts reserved for five weeks and will be able to play Monday through Thursday. In order to finish this tournament in the allotted time, how many games must be played per day? Utilize your tournament scheduling formulas to show your work.

Submitted by Dr. John Dollar, Department Head & Associate Professor
Northwestern State University, Natchitoches, Louisiana

Program Experiential Learning Example

BUILDING PROGRAM REPUTATION

Students at Georgia State University in Atlanta learn about research in sport in what is called a "living classroom." Their "living classroom" is the massive Georgia Dome sports arena as well as other sports in metro Atlanta. Students have conducted research related to SuperCross, United States Tennis Association events, Final Four basketball tournaments, professional bull riding, and have studied the effect of Super Bowl commercials. The students, with the guidance of the professor, then work with management who use the information in a number of ways. Students learn valuable research tools that will be utilized in future sport management professional positions and can place research skills on their résumé for increased marketability.

Submitted by Dr. Brenda Pitts, Professor

5

Sport Business Industry Overview: Support and Entrepreneurial Careers

---

"An entrepreneur must be persistent, patient, confident, self-motivated, and focused. Stay sharp and innovative and keep the ball rolling on new opportunities. Be well prepared for both the exhilarating highs and the disheartening lows."

— Brian Hoek
President, Pinstripes Media, LLC

THE WARM UP

Positions not tied to a particular team or league often are not seasonal. These organizations operate on a twelve month cycle just as any other non-sport related business. Thus, there is no hiring season. This is true of marketing and event management firms and many sport facilities that host events throughout the year. Geography may also play a role. It only makes sense that an event management firm in Florida may need interns/employees throughout the year while the same type of organization in a colder climate may hire the bulk of their interns for the summer.

SUPPORT AREAS AND ENTREPRENEURIAL CAREERS EXPLAINED AND EXPLORED

Event Management

Event management is popular among students and positions exist in all employment fields. College athletic departments may employ an event manager to handle the logistics of half-time shows, meetings, recruit visits, camps, and more. Even though an individual's actual title may not be that of an event manager, a closer look at job responsibilities of some positions may reveal the handling of the logistics of an event. Sport facilities, professional sport teams, recreation departments, sports commissions, halls of fame, and even sport marketing firms have individuals who setup and run events. All of them might not include a sporting event, but careful planning, establishment of a time line, other event logistics, and more can be the responsibilities of an event manager.

◆ ◆ TIME OUT INTERVIEW ◆ ◆

— Event Management —
LISA MCGREGOR

Position	Event Manager
Employer	Stan Smith Events, Roswell, GA
Position	President
Business Name	McGregor Events Company, Roswell, GA
B.S. Degree	Business, Bemidji State University, Minnesota

Career Path	• Hyatt Hotels—Ten years—Hawaii and Minnesota
	  • Waitress, Eight months
	  • Management trainee, Six months
	• Food and beverage/restaurant manager—18 months
	• Sales manager—Seven years
	• SportsMark—San Francisco, CA
	  • Account manager, Four years
	  • Senior Account Manager, Four years
	  • Senior Account Director, Four years

Employment Recommendation	"Be prepared to work hard and very long hours; develop relationships in the field."

Event managers must work very closely with facility managers and the information in the next section can also apply to event management. Every sporting event must have a facility. The facility for a road race can be a street and an event manager must take into account the logistics that come into play (e.g., police, road condition and closures, etc.).

Facility Management

Like event management, facility managers are needed in many of the industry segments. While most turf management positions require specialized certifications to take care of well-manicured golf courses and most professional and collegiate playing fields, there are many other positions in this area. Getting experience in facility management is easier at a larger school where you might have numerous sports and larger facilities as well as professionals who hold membership in the International Association of Assembly Managers (IAAM). There are also many well-qualified NIRSA members

◆◆ TIME OUT INTERVIEW ◆◆

⌐ Facility Management ⌐
JOHN LEE

Current Position	Associate Director—Facilities
Employer	Wichita State University
B.A. Degree	Economics, Creighton University
M.Ed.	Sports Administration, Wichita State University
Career Path	• Graduate Assistant, Two years • Facility Coordinator, Three years • Assistant Intramural Director, Five years • Associate Director, Programming, Five years, (All the above were at Wichita State University)
Employment Recommendation	"Join a professional association related to facility management. By doing so, you can develop contacts and network with other professionals in the field which could be beneficial when you apply for your first facility management position. "A degree in sport management or a related field is important, but it is just as important to work in facility management during your time in school."

(see Chapter 3) that specialize in facility management employed on college campuses. Working with these professionals will assist you in gaining some very good experience. For those attending smaller schools, seeking out apprenticeships or other experiential learning opportunities with similarly qualified individuals at any arena, stadium, convention center, or facility that hosts sporting events will assist you in gaining much needed hands-on experience.

Salary levels in this area can be determined by the type of facility and whether or not it is in the private or public sector. Privately owned facilities tend to pay higher salaries, but geography can also play a role. An average entry level salary at a publicly owned facility is between $25,000 and $35,000, and possibly has stayed the same or even slightly declined due to the number of individuals striving to enter the industry (Rick Nafe, Personal communication, November 4, 2009; John Lee, Personal communication, February 2, 2010).

The size of the facility affects the number of full-time positions available, but often some roles are contracted to outside firms. This is especially true for the areas of security, concessions, lighting, and HVAC control and maintenance. However, any local sport facility can be a very good place to gain part-time experience in facility management as an usher, security officer/

Event management is a popular career segment for many students majoring in sport management. (Courtesy of Saint Leo University)

supervisor, or concessions worker. Between October 2008 and February 2009, the Tampa Bay area hosted the American League Divisional Playoffs, the American League playoffs, the World Series, and the Super Bowl. For the Super Bowl alone, 1,500 security personnel were needed. Selection and training began in August of 2008. Good thing, because when the Tampa Bay Rays surprised everyone and made it to the playoffs, additional security was already available and the same security company, Sentry Event Services, was the outside contractor for all events. Students and faculty from Saint Leo University's sport business program and several athletic team members were role players for all of these events.

Sport Marketing

Many sport organizations have a self-contained marketing department. In Chapter 3, we touched on marketing in professional sport. College athletic departments may also have sport marketing personnel under the athletic department umbrella where promotion of events, sponsorship procurement, and ticket and advertising sales are the most prominent functions. This seg-

◆ ◆ TIME OUT INTERVIEW ◆ ◆

⌐ Sport Marketing ¬
JESSICA MUDRY

Current Position:	Senior Director of Development and Production
Employer	Van Wagner Sports and Entertainment, LLC
B.A. Degree	Journalism, Lehigh University
Career Path	• Intern, Philadelphia Eagles, Three months • Intern, Sports Information, Yale University, One year • Sponsorship Coordinator, New Haven Beast (AHL), Two years • Marketing Manager, HoopsTV.com, Two years
Employment Recommendation	"Get an internship and network with all the people you meet. Take on projects that allow you to meet more people and work in different areas of sport. 'Sports' is perceived to be a fun industry, but it is competitive. So, you need to know your business and be prepared to understand your client's needs."

ment of sport marketing will focus on this function as a support role looking at private sport marketing firms.

The role of a private firm can vary. Sport marketing firms solicit the business of teams, events, or other sport related businesses. Their functions may
include the design and implementation of a media or advertising campaign,
the design or development of organizational brochures, the development
and writing of a marketing or business plan for a client, and much more.
Sport marketing functions can also be distinguished by the marketing of
sport or marketing through sport. The marketing of sport typically involves
the promotion of a team or event or that of a sport-related product. An organization that has nothing at all to do with sport may hire a sport marketing firm if they desire to promote an aspect of their company through sport.
One very good example where this is practiced on a regular basis is that the
Susan G. Komen Breast Cancer Foundation often uses road races to raise
money for research. This foundation may hire a sport marketing firm to design all race related events, brochures, and media campaigns. Their motto,
"Race for the Cure," certainly uses sport to raise awareness of the main purpose for their existence. According to Burden and Li (2009), outsourcing is
a relatively recent phenomenon within the sport industry. In fact, Burden
and Li claim outsourcing is a main reason for the loss of marketing positions within sport organizations. As a result, the entrepreneurial sport marketing firm becomes a prime source for career location.

Public Relations/Sports Media

In Chapter 3, we briefly discussed the placement of media within a professional sport organizational structure. In Chapter 4, we discussed the role of
the media in college athletics and provided an interview sidebar for a sports
information director. In this section, we will cover other positions one could
obtain in this area.

The role of the sport media personnel working for independent television and radio stations and for the various print media outlets can be rewarding and exhausting. Travel can be a major responsibility of these individuals, especially for those who work for major media outlets and must
travel large distances to cover major sporting events. Writing and broadcasting skills are both extremely important. Often, the role of photographer
must also be assumed. The sport business major may have an inside track to
some of these positions because of knowledge of a variety of sports. However,

if the courses required for the major do not include courses in broadcasting or other desired media skills, it would behoove one to take additional electives, obtain a minor in journalism, and/or attend a sports broadcasting camp. (See http://www.playbyplaycamps.com, http://www.sportsbroadcast ingcamp.com, http://www.sportscastercamp.com, and http://www.rebecca haarlow.com.) Understanding and knowing how to record statistics for a variety of sports can qualify one to obtain entry level positions in this area.

In order to obtain an understanding of this industry segment, one can gain extraordinary experience before graduating by working or volunteering in their college athletic department's sports information office or in an on-campus radio or television station. This is a particularly difficult segment of the industry to enter and honing a complete set of skills is crucial. It is also recommended that students purchase a student membership in the College Sport Information Directors of America (CoSIDA) and attend their professional conferences.

Sports Commissions/Authorities

A sport commission or authority is usually a governing body made up of influential people nominated or selected by government officials. The purposes of such a governing body can be many, but, in most cases, these bodies are created for countries, states, counties, or local municipalities to foster the development of sport programs and facilities and increase tourism. While the building of facilities to house sporting events can be a tax burden on the local residents, bringing in or creating large events for the purpose of establishing income for local hotels, restaurants, and other businesses is the primary purpose of their existence. Promoting the image of a geographical region to what is now being coined "major league" or "big league" is another primary purpose. The term is generally used to classify large cities that have been able to attract and retain major sport franchises. A sports commission can play an immense role in attracting events and teams if the facilities exist to host large events. One of the mid-western cities recently reaching "major league" status was Oklahoma City after the Seattle Supersonics were purchased and subsequently moved in 2008, thus becoming the Oklahoma City Thunder. They built the Ford Center to house this NBA team and, according to Mayor Mick Cornett, the facility changed everything; attracting an NBA team had a profound impact on the quality of life, pride, and employment (Luschen, 2009).

◆◇◆ TIME OUT INTERVIEW ◆◇◆

‾ Sports Commissions ‾
BETH HEQUET

Current Position	Director of Meetings and Events
Employer	National Association of Sports Commissions
B.S. Degree	Kinesiology (Business), University of Kentucky
M.S. Degree	Sports Management, University of Kentucky
Other Certification	Certified Meeting Professional
Career Path	• Graduate Assistant, Univ. of Kentucky, Men's Basketball Office, Two years • Intern, Lexington Area Sports Authority, Six months • Events and Operations Intern, Indiana Sports Corporation, Nine months • Group Ticket Sales Representative, Cincinnati Cyclones, Six months • Sports Manager, Amateur Athletic Union, One year
Employment Recommendation	"Don't expect that you are owed anything; you have to work for everything! I found out about the Lexington Area Sports Authority and their work within the sports event industry while an undergraduate student. As a graduate student, I interned with them and then completed another internship with the Indiana Sports Corporation. Both of these internships showed me the world of sports commissions. These experiences eventually led to my position with the Amateur Athletic Union; this organization works with sports commissions to host their events."

Every course in sport governance should include content on sport commissions or sport authorities. Through the study of these commissions and authorities, one can learn a great deal about government, public and private organizations, and politics. Yes, politics! An examination of a variety of news articles covering sports commissions or authorities elicited a great deal of information about their political makeup and issues with which these boards have dealt. Topics revealed in the articles examined included governmental appointments (Brennan, 2004; Smith, 2006; Snel, 2005; Williams, 2005), financing/development of services, events, or facilities (Brennan, 2005a; Duffy, 2009; Grevas, 2009; Kaske, 2007; Kaske, 2008; Snel, 2005; Stark, 2007; Watts, 2005), development, dissolution, investigation, or reform of these governmental bodies (Byrd, 2004; Ellen, 2005; Meltzer, 2008; Murphy, 2005; Phillips, 2006; Wick News Service, 2008), and cutting deals to teams (Alan, 2004; Brennan, 2005b; Conte, 2007; Silva, 2010).

But sports commissions can provide tremendous opportunities for volunteer, part-time, and full-time positions when they bring major events to a municipality. Thus, future sport managers should consider these positions as major opportunities to work in event management when they provide the local citizenry with sport programming and facilities or attract major events such as the Super Bowl, college bowl games, NCAA events of all kinds, and other professional and amateur sport national championship or annual events.

Sporting Goods/Apparel

A career within the sporting goods or sports apparel industry can be widely varied. One can work within the retail industry where stores are often found in malls or shopping centers. This can be a great part-time job while in high school or college, though work hours are often unpredictable and can be quite long during holiday seasons. A manager must often fill in for other less responsible employees who do not show up. However, the rise to the position of store manager can be quick (generally from 18 months to two years) and financially rewarding if this type of environment is suitable to the individual's interest in a career. The manager must be very astute to the problems surely to be encountered revolving around human resource management and shoplifting. If working with a large sporting goods chain, a promotion to regional sales manager where you may supervise other store managers is often the next step up the corporate ladder. Extensive travel can be involved.

If the retail store is not your choice for a career work environment, working as either a manufacturer's representative or an independent sales representative can be quite lucrative. Many individuals prefer this environment if they like sales because the work schedule is typically flexible. However, to be successful here, one needs to be a very good time manager and a self-starter with a great deal of motivation for success.

◆◆ TIME OUT INTERVIEW ◆◆

⌐ Sporting Goods ⌐
PHIL LOFTIS

Current Position	Independent Sales Representative
Employer	Self-employed, Represents New Balance Athletic Shoe, Inc.
B.S. Degree	Sport Management, Flagler College
Career Path	• Retail Sales Associate, New Balance, Charlotte, NC, Seven months • Sales Representative Internship, Proball USA, Six months • Independent Sales Rep, Proball USA, Two years • Field Merchandising Rep, New Balance, Two years
Employment Recommendation	"Get retail sales experience, especially in footwear and the performance apparel industry. I learned a lot about sales techniques working with customers on a daily basis. I learned about customer service, gained product knowledge, and learned how managers, buyers, and owners operate."

A manufacturer's representative represents a single company or several companies. Most often, an individual in this type of position is self-employed and may be an independent contractor for large companies. When an individual represents a single company, generally an assignment is given to a specific territory. Phil Loftis, an independent sales rep, is self-employed and represents New Balance. He sells footwear, apparel, and accessories to 38 running specialty retailers and 12 New Balance stores in one state. His responsibilities include educating retailers about the company's footwear and apparel, executing marketing campaigns and promotions, and maintaining the currency of all accounts (Personal communication, October 19, 2009).

Different companies operate differently, but a career involving this industry can be quite lucrative for the individual who is an effective self-starter. It is recommended to start with retail sales and learn as much as possible about individual products, because product knowledge is extremely important to developing a life-long career in this segment of the industry. The positions mentioned above are not the only ones that exist in this industry, but it is a typical snapshot of what one may experience in getting started.

Entrepreneurial Ventures

Many individuals look to start their own business related to sport. A sport business can be tied to anything and, often, consulting represents some aspect of the business. Many small sport businesses are tied to event management, sport marketing, athlete representation, and consulting. Taking a class in entrepreneurship or one that assists you in walking through the step-by-step process for starting a new business is especially helpful. Some institutions offer a minor in entrepreneurial management.

Before starting a business, get experience by working with one or more sport organizations. Learning how others handle the day-to-day operations of different types of business or responsibilities can be very insightful. You can hone your skills and obtain a network of individuals that can attest to your business acumen and abilities. An entrepreneur generally develops expertise in one or more areas before beginning their own business venture. It is not

◆◆ TIME OUT INTERVIEW ◆◆

~ Entrepreneurship ~
GREG CERO

Current Position	Owner
Business Name	Mound Time, L.L.C.
B.A. Degree	Sport Management, Flagler College
Career Path	• Intern, World Golf Hall of Fame, One year • Front Desk, Nike World Campus Headquarters, One year • Manager, LA Fitness, Two years
Employment Recommendation	"It takes time to grow a business and networking is extremely important. There will be adversity and the ability to handle the hurdles that come with being an entrepreneur is key. Be prepared to work long hours with very few days off."

uncommon to work ten or more years to develop the necessary skills and business knowledge before venturing into the world of business ownership.

Greg Cero initially started his own business by helping two youths improve their pitching skills. Officially now called Mound Time, LLC, in Portland, Oregon, the business began after completing a major in sport management, playing professional baseball, and serving apprenticeships and internships. The business focuses on baseball instruction utilizing Greg's extensive background and people skills, which he said is crucial to starting a business. After four years in business, Greg had ten individuals employed within the company. After five years in business, Mound Time was considered the largest baseball development company in Oregon. Still, Greg personally fills all types of roles including typical entry level responsibilities. However, the bulk of his work is in instruction, scheduling, and marketing (Personal communication, September 9, 2009, and February 4, 2010).

Other skills a business owner should possess would be acute attention to detail, organizational skills, knowledge of business plans, and the ability to obtain business financing. Understanding accounting procedures would also be extremely important unless you can afford to hire a personal accountant. It is also recommended that an attorney be hired to make sure business paperwork is in order and to establish contracts, including waivers and other legal paperwork that will be needed in the business. Of course, attorneys are not a required hire, but one skilled in business law can assist the new business owner in making sure everything necessary is covered.

When starting a business, a full stable of employees is not always needed. Immediate staffing will depend upon the business type and its initial size, personal organizational skills, and more. Brian Hoek, President of Pinstripes Media, LLC, headquartered in Broomfield, Colorado, runs his advertising business by himself, but outsources certain tasks depending upon the current project. His recommendation when running a business on one's own is to not take on too many projects simultaneously so you do not become overwhelmed. In other words, when running a one-person business, the size and length of a project will dictate how many projects can be concurrently handled. Finding reliable companies and individuals to hire as independent contractors, when a particular project dictates assistance will be necessary, is extremely important and can lead to additional income.

Marketing personal skills and knowledge and the pricing of those skills and talents can be a tricky task, especially at the outset of a new venture.

Learning about facility management and design is important background knowledge for an individual contemplating a career in sport management. (Courtesy of Susan Foster)

Trial and error, as well as market demands for your services, will be prime factors in establishing a pricing structure. Entrepreneurs charge either on an hourly or per project basis. Obviously, pricing a project on an hourly rate will require more documentation and personal time than establishing a project fee.

Marketing your services can be accomplished through advertising or networking. Once again, the size of your business, as well as the existence of competing companies offering the same or similar product, will be relevant determining factors for the amount or type of marketing a business will need to maintain sustainable growth and a comfortable level of financial income. Word-of-mouth and networking can be great marketing and advertising methodologies at very little cost to the business. A one-person business that relies on networking and a satisfied clientele will take a business in sometimes unfamiliar or unexpected directions, leading to beneficial learning, partnerships, and relationships. Every person met can have a potential impact on your professional future. They can become trusted friends or partners that assist in those larger projects (B. Hoek, Personal communication, December 19, 2009).

THE FINAL BUZZER

The intent of this chapter was to assist students in their exploration of some non-traditional careers many may not have considered. While many only think of major teams or individual sports for employment, this chapter adds to the initial premise introduced in Chapter 1—i.e., the size of the sport industry is unfathomable to most people. This chapter supports many categories displayed in the Sport Employment Model displayed in Figure 1.1. From a sport marketing business to the entrepreneurial spirit displayed in the founding of Mound Time, LLC, opportunities available in this industry are created one business at a time. Fortunately for many aspiring interns, sport related business are created everyday.

Classroom Experiential Learning Exercise

EXPANDING STUDENT KNOWLEDGE AND SKILLS THROUGH THE INTERNET

While working in pairs, conduct an Internet scavenger hunt to learn about media and broadcasting and simulate how the working media would research a story. Different sections of the assignment are timed to test your Internet browsing skills as well as to evaluate the format and ease of navigating the webpages.

1. Identify and briefly explain the following terms: RSNs or RCNs, CPM, CPP, make-goods, and ADI.
2. What is the difference between a rating and a share?
3. From the list below, rank these sporting events in terms of their 2010 TV rating: The Daytona 500, the BCS National Championship Game, The Master's, the NCAA Men's Basketball Championship Game, and the Super Bowl.
4. How many major English-language networks are there in the U.S. and what are they?

The above entries are just a sample of questions from the assignment. There are a total of 17 questions in Part 1 and students have 30 minutes to find the answers to all 17 questions. There are two other sections for the assignment—an information efficiency search (25 minutes) and an exercise where students must evaluate several websites using class information and a provided rubric (20 minutes).

Submitted by Dr. Dianna Gray, Associate Professor
University of Northern Colorado, Greeley, Colorado

Program Experiential Learning Example
FACILITY FIELD TRIPS
The Sport Management Student Association at Mesa State College in Grand Junction, Colorado, sponsors field trips to the Pepsi Center (Kroenke Sports) in Denver each fall semester. Students are given a tour and half day workshop on facility and risk management issues. A spring break trip to Tucson, Arizona, includes tours and lectures at the spring training facilities for the Rockies and the Diamondbacks where the students are exposed to scheduling, media, marketing, and sponsorship issues. Internships have resulted from these trips!
Submitted by Dr. Richard Bell Director of Sport Management

6

Preparing for
the Internship

"The role of a quality internship is twofold: first, it provides a student with a laboratory to test and apply what they have learned to a real life setting; secondly, it gives the student a glimpse of what that particular work environment is all about and whether or not it fits their expectations or aspirations."

— Dr. Bill Sutton
Principal, Bill Sutton & Associates
Associate Director and Professor
DeVos Sport Business Management Program
University of Central Florida

THE WARM UP

Preparing to find a career position with any organization can be a full-time job. It is no different than any internship. Organization, planning, preparation, and more can make the difference between being a top candidate and securing the position or just being another résumé in the stack.

This chapter builds on the previous ones by assisting you in planning for the internship search; the information learned can be applied to any job search. Attitude and approach can make the difference, as well. However, it is recommended that any internship—paid or unpaid, for academic credit or no credit—be approached with a positive attitude and a desire to treat each opportunity as a true learning experience regardless of the responsibilities assigned. Bandy (2009) states that self-knowledge and choosing the "right" career path based on personal skills and abilities is crucial to finding a work environment that best suits an individual.

Von Mizener and Williams (2009) state that "students are more on task when permitted to make choices about academic work" (p. 110). By using the Foster Five-Step Model explained in Chapter 1 and applying the six Ps in this chapter, a student can devise an outstanding personal strategic plan for finding a quality internship and gaining employment in the sport business industry. The personal strategic plan can parallel institutional requirements for experiential learning.

MORE THAN THE 4 Ps

In 1990, four sport management students preparing for their own careers co-authored an article titled "Marketing Yourself for the Profession: More Than Just the Four Ps" (Rose, Denny, Burleson, & Clark, 1990). The article utilized the traditional four Ps of marketing—product, price, place, and promotion—as a foundation, but actually presented six Ps, as described below, to form a strategic approach to any job search. The six Ps explain an in-depth comprehensive approach that takes careful planning and attention to detail. They are presented in the order the textbook authors believe makes the most sense for those beginning the journey to securing a top culminating academic internship and a first full-time position in the industry.

Product: You, the candidate for a position, are the product. An application for any position is actually an attempt to sell yourself and your skills to an organization. Hence, developing a strategic plan and the self-confidence to get you there is of utmost importance. Knowledge and experience raises self-confidence. Thus, coursework, volunteering, and other early experiential learning opportunities will help narrow your focus to a specific industry segment. The earlier the process is begun, the earlier a prospective intern is able to answer career questions on their own. While professors and others can discuss particular careers, the student has to pave the road. Everyone's background is different and that background forms a personal paradigm upon which only you can build. Nobody knows your background or life experiences better than you. Sell it! Sell yourself! The next three Ps focus on an examination of conscience and where you really want to go in your career.

Planning: The first step in establishing a strategic plan for finding a true career path requires setting personal goals and objectives. The literature has established that setting goals and writing them down allows one to be more focused and more likely to reach those goals (Farrell, 1997; McIntosh, 2008; Pieper, 2004; Tracy, 2008; Zonar, 2007.) and according to Goldsmith (2003), that likelihood can rise by as much as 300 percent! Set personal goals high enough so that you have to reach beyond your comfort zone. Goals should be measurable so you have a benchmark for reaching the goal. Setting a goal and taking steps to reach that goal can be viewed as a series of steps on a ladder. View the sample personal strategic plan below and envision your career goal at the top of the ladder. Objective 1, then, is at the base of the ladder.

Goal:—To have a full-time position in professional sport on graduation day.

Objective 1. Get involved with the Sport Business Association (or the respective major's association) in my freshman year and participate in a minimum of two volunteer opportunities each semester made available.

Objective 2. Find a summer position as early in my academic career as possible working as an usher, ticket-taker, or concession stand employee, and use it as a required apprenticeship or summer job.

Objective 3. Nominate myself, or accept a nomination from another individual, to serve as an officer in the Sport Business Association. Follow through to establish myself as a trusted leader and a proactive Association member.

Objective 4. Explore available internship opportunities found on at least ten different sport-related websites in one or more employment areas within professional sport (ticket sales, event management, public relations, etc.). Analyze position requirements.

Objective 5. After analyzing internship opportunities, obtain additional skills that might be needed in the area of employment I have chosen by searching for additional volunteer opportunities, on-campus positions, or summer jobs.

Objective 6. During my last academic year, apply for at least five internship positions in professional sport for which I have obtained some skills and background knowledge.

Objective 7. Accept a full-time culminating internship in professional sport.

The above step-by-step plan is just one example of a personal strategic plan, but it illustrates well that a goal is obtainable through a series of measurable steps. We have heard many students incorrectly state their belief that they have to work several jobs in other industry segments in order to obtain their first job in professional sport. This is an unfounded belief! Please understand there is no guarantee you will be offered a full-time position on or before graduation day. The economy and your geographic location certainly can impact the availability of positions. Paying careful attention to goal setting and focusing on reaching those goals has proven to be a successful formula, though, for becoming the individual that does have full-time employment upon graduation.

Preparation: Preparation is where you begin to implement your personal strategic plan. According to Rose et al. (1990), most processes are made up of certain steps that facilitate a finished product, but the successful path involves a great deal of preparation. In preparing for your career in sport, preparation can begin by paying close attention in classes and doing your best work throughout your degree program. Gaining skills and knowledge about specific employment roles, attending conferences and guest speaker lectures (even if outside course requirements), and joining professional organizations and student associations are all ways for you to prepare to be the number one candidate for any internship you desire. Of course, the volunteer positions pursued in order to learn about sport and event and facility management will be of utmost importance. Caution is warranted, however. Some individuals will latch onto one organization and want to stay with the organization in the same position for the duration of their education. Although this shows loyalty, if this position is not tied to career aspirations or if the organization does not allow continuous growth by permitting constant exposure to new tasks and responsibilities, then other opportunities should be explored. While attending classes, learn as much as possible about the different industry segments and positions. This is a very important step in order to thoroughly discover all that the sport industry has to offer. The authors constantly direct their students to this approach; it is amazing how even the most dedicated student who has worked with only one organization can find there is much more to be learned by experiencing how other organizations are structured and carry out business.

Networking is also extremely important in this phase. Chapter 1 informally introduced the concept of networking when discussing the concept of who knows you. Chapter 8 explores this topic in great depth. Please read these two chapters, learn about the art of networking, and practice it often.

Price: Price focuses on what an individual can afford in terms of compensation? Can you accept an unpaid internship? Can you afford to accept a small stipend or just be reimbursed for expenses? If some organizations do not offer any compensation up front when the internship paperwork is signed, some will reward an intern for outstanding performance and decide to begin paying some form of compensation during the internship or upon completion. Finally, if the reality of the financial situation dictates that a paid internship is the only option a student can afford, there are a lot of paid opportunities. Some students take a semester off to work any available full-time position and save the income in order to pursue a desirable unpaid internship. Understanding your particular "price"-fit early, will assist you in defining other parameters of your search. Chapter 7 delves into the cost of an internship in more depth.

Place: Do you need to move away from family? Do you need to forego a summer job in the family business in order to take a position related to your future goals? Where are you willing to go? Based on the internship goals you have set for yourself, "place" can be the desire to go beyond your current geographic location in order to target a specific organization or a related organization in a specific industry segment. This is more fully discussed in Chapter 7.

Promotion: Promotion is one of the more important of the six Ps. Under promotion, you will find positioning and networking. As we mentioned earlier, several times throughout this book, promoting your skills to a potential organization or recruiter might be one's toughest sales job. On many occasions, positioning yourself to be in the right place at the right time is where prior preparation will prove to be extremely beneficial. If done correctly, previous networking, as recommended by many of your mentors, will also prove itself very useful in reaping the fruits of your labor. Continuous networking and self-promotion during this phase is important and will be discussed in great detail in Chapter 8.

SEASONAL AVAILABLITY

We discussed the seasonal nature of the sport business industry at the beginning of Chapter 3. However, a few additional comments are warranted when preparing for the internship. Seasonal availability of an internship can be problematic. Careful planning of a student's progress toward an internship

Internships are available at golf courses in the winter in some geographical locations. (Courtesy of Susan Foster)

and graduation should begin no later than the sophomore year for an undergraduate and at the very beginning of a graduate student's program. For example, if a student truly wants to work in baseball, a spring or summer semester internship is paramount and a January start date is when many teams want an intern to begin. A different example of seasonality would involve an internship with the United States Olympic Committee (USOC). The USOC has internships throughout the year. However, if an individual wanted to work in the year of the Olympic Games, the spring or summer semesters would provide that experience, but would occur only once every two years. Needless to say, most individuals would not delay their graduation to wait on an Olympic Games internship. Plus, competition for these internships is fierce and it is not recommended that a student hold out for this type of experience. Nevertheless, if an individual knows the Olympics will fall during their chosen internship semester, we encourage applications to be submitted, especially if one desires to work in event or facility management or within a specific sport. However, if one obtains an internship during the Olympic Games, there is no guarantee that the intern will get to work *at* the Games. The Games usually last two to three weeks and an intern may be asked to stay at the home office and take care of necessary business while full-time employees are working the Games. This also might be required because applications for credentials to work a major sporting event must clear security months before the actual event. An intern beginning the second week of January may not be able to obtain the necessary credentials or clear background checks in time for a February Winter Olympic start date.

UNDERGRADUATE VERSUS GRADUATE INTERNSHIPS

Some disagreement among both practitioners and professors has been observed over the years regarding undergraduate and graduate interns. Certainly, some positions in the field might be more capably filled by a graduate or law student specifically trained in sport marketing, sport law, or another specialized field. However, there are plenty of positions where undergraduate interns can perform as capably as a graduate student. In fact, many organizations prefer a student, undergraduate or graduate, who commits themselves full-time to an entire semester, season, or academic year rather than one who only wishes to work on a part-time basis. Full-time versus part-time internships are discussed in greater depth in the next section.

FULL-TIME VERSUS PART-TIME EXPERIENCES

Dedication and loyalty from an intern can leave a great impression on an organization. Beginning an internship by telling a site supervisor when you can and cannot work does not sit well with some organizations. Many organizations tell you they will work around exams or class schedules and some do this extremely well. However, when working as a part-time intern, it is very difficult to out-perform a full-time intern that is doing an exceptional job if you come in to work only when your schedule permits. Monica Rusch, Human Resources Director for the Houston Astros (Roemmisch, 2004), commented that when a student comes in for an interview and states, "Well, I can't work this weekend or that weekend, then you find another applicant who can make the commitment (p. 5)." Make every effort to select a full-time internship where you have no outside interruptions. At the very least, work your personal schedule around that of the organization. Accommodating your supervisor's schedule is just as important.

It is recommended by many organizations, practitioners, and professors that you complete a full-time internship. In fact, the first academic standards for undergraduates in sport management programs defined an internship as a 40-hour per week, 10-week experience (Sport Management Program Review Council, 2000). Ten weeks is still a short time because you are just starting to get to know the organization and the people in this brief time period. Many organizations, especially college athletic departments and professional sport teams, ask an intern to commit to a seasonal internship as previously described. This is a great way for the student to demonstrate commitment to an organization and to exhibit a desire to enter the industry; you can experience and observe the inner workings of that organization and better understand the industry segment. This is also the best way for a student to determine if the organization is a good employment fit. One full-time intern who committed to a minor league baseball team for an entire season (January through September) concluded he could not work in baseball in a position where he could not see the game. Thus, he set his goals and embarked on a career in broadcasting. His internship encompassed sales, clubhouse operations, and a little bit of media work. As an intern, had he selected a short-term assignment in just one of these areas, he may not have stumbled on his love for broadcasting. A season-long commitment often allows an intern a much broader perspective of the organization, especially if working in the minor leagues where all staff often pitch in to help each other during the course of a day's work.

SAVING MONEY FOR AN INTERNSHIP

It is very difficult to save money when pursuing an academic degree. Students often live from pay check to pay check or that monthly bank deposit from the parents. From the moment a student begins work on the academic degree, consider putting away ten dollars a week and do not touch it—*ever*. In four years, one would have $2,080 plus interest accrued. In two years, $1,040. While it does not sound like a lot of money, any amount saved can prevent one from limiting their decision and finding the best possible internship. The $2,000+ can help pay for many of the costs listed in Chapter 7.

While we do not endorse any particular savings plan in this book, we suggest looking into savings ideas such as UPromise. UPromise is a plan endorsed and supported by businesses nationwide, but requires one to open a **529 account** (an educational savings plan). All states have these savings plans available. Businesses that support UPromise donate a percentage of every transaction you or a family member makes via registered credit cards. Thus, any family member can register their credit card with your 529 plan. It does not cost anything. Every time they shop or eat at a restaurant that supports UPromise, money goes into this account. Leave the money in and when your internship semester begins, the money can be withdrawn for costs you incur. Four years of a family's contributions, even if pennies at a time, will cover some costs of the internship. It is worth investigating. See http://www.upromise.com.

If time has not been spent to investigate scholarships and there are still a few semesters before the internship, now might be the time. Scholarships today do not always have the meaning they had many years ago when one had to be at the top of the class to qualify. Many private organizations have scholarships tied to ethnicity, religious preference, geographical location, parental employment, and more. Some have very few applicants because they are not widely advertised. Googling the word "scholarships" tied to some of the categories previously mentioned may reveal available financial sources if one just applies.

The Florida State League (minor league baseball) has scholarships available. Each team in the league can recommend one intern a year for the scholarship. An individual can qualify as an undergraduate or graduate student. If you are one of those who has accepted an internship as a summer job to gain experience before the culminating senior internship or if you are considering graduate school, these scholarships can be applied to next year's tuition! Other programs like this may also exist. Check with financial aid or scholarship offices on your campus.

Yes, an internship can be costly. Planning for those expenses in advance is important. Regardless, the overall amount of money the student will spend during the internship, above tuition and semester fees, should and will be far outweighed by the value of the experience if properly selected. The student is betting on the return value expected from future employment and a rewarding career in the industry of sport. Research has shown that students who have interned have a better chance of landing a full-time job over those who have not (Gault, Redington, & Schlager, 2000).

JOB VERSUS CAREER

Job versus career is an important concept to understand. Certainly, any paid position can be considered a job. However, from a professional standpoint, there is a critical difference. Approaching these two terms from this perspective, a **job** can be defined as an hourly paid position, with or without company benefits, where one simply fulfills the requirements assigned that day and takes no work home with them related to that position. Flipping hamburgers at a restaurant could be considered a job. A **career** can be defined as a life calling whereby a series of paid positions are related to the same industry and where each new position builds in advancement and responsibility. Webster's (1997) distinguishes between the two by calling a job "a post of employment" (p. 441) and a career as "an occupation or profession followed as one's lifework" (p. 122). One could further distinguish the two by having a need for the "job" and a passion for a "career."

Gone are the days when most working adults were hired by one company and stayed with that company until retirement. Careers in sport, today, are no different. This is especially true when teams change ownership, new head coaches are hired, and loyalties change. Heritage (2001) defines a career as an "evolving sequence of a person's work experience over time" (p. 16). Heritage also explains that a career can now take on different appearances. Traditionally, one could climb the ladder and stay with one organization. However, the employment landscape of today's sport organizations embraces consultants, individuals taking on several different part-time positions linked to one industry, independent contractors, the self-employed (labeled as a portfolio career by Heritage), and multiple lateral or vertical moves with several different organizations in order to rise to top levels of management.

Russ Simons, a Senior Principal with Populous, a firm specializing in sport facility design, event planning, and facility operations, rose through the ranks in facility management after starting as an intern. He once explained his definition of career versus job in a presentation at the Georgia Southern Sport Management conference in 1995 using the following statements:

- Don't send me a résumé if you are looking for a job. I hire for jobs locally. I look far and wide for people who want a career. I look for content of character and a commitment necessary to join a winning team.
- Someone in a career focuses on something a little bigger than the job description.

Are you ready for a career in the sport business industry?

TIME MANAGEMENT

Time management skills are crucial. Can you meet deadlines? Can you get work done early in order to handle any unexpected circumstances, or are you a procrastinator waiting until the last minute to finish a project? Pro-

Maintaining a weekly, monthly, and annual calendar is an important short- and long-term time management practice. (Courtesy of Dreamstime)

crastination can kill a career or a chance for a promotion without even a re-alization of its impact. Individuals are not always aware of the perceptions of others regarding work habits within the company.

Entire books have been written on time management. We will not go into this subject in too great a depth. However, we do offer some critical in-formation on time management as it applies to the internship or job search.

Time, once lost, can never be regained. Missed deadlines or rushing at the last minute to meet a deadline are examples of poor time management skills. Is there a deadline for finding an internship within your academic program? Are you applying for several different internships? In order to prevent last minute problems such as spelling errors in cover letters or incomplete appli-cations, start as early as possible and follow these simple recommendations.

- Develop a notebook with dividers for the internship search process.
- Organize the dividers of the notebook in a manner that makes sense to you (i.e., pro sport organizations in alphabetical order, etc.).
- Make a copy of any internship or job announcements and place them in the notebook.
- Write down answers to common questions and keep a copy in the notebook. Often, an organizational employee will call without notice, and ask some questions. However informal the situation, this is an in-terview! If you are not prepared mentally for the phone call or the

questions, having this information in front of you will assist you in answering the questions with confidence and ease. We will discuss the elevator pitch later in Chapter 8 and, having a copy of this in front of you, will be of great value.

- If you call an organization, try to get the name of the individual to whom you spoke and write down the date.
- Highlight any information on closing deadlines.
- Print out a calendar that has room on which to write, and place all information on the calendar regarding closing dates for position applications.
- Apply for positions BEFORE the closing deadline; do not wait until the last minute. Sometimes interviewers will receive great résumés early in the selection process at a time when they are not yet receiving application materials from others, and they will have more time to read information submitted. Thus, your particular skills might stand out in the mind of the interviewer. If really good, your skills might be used to judge other applicant qualifications.
- Re-read position announcements on occasion. When applying for numerous positions, it is difficult to remember precise information about the responsibilities of a specific internship.
- Keep the notebook in a handy location where it can be easily accessed if an organization calls. If you receive a phone call, pull out the notebook and have the position description in front of you.
- Every Sunday night, review your calendar; make a mental note of upcoming deadlines for that week. Perhaps re-read a position announcement from a company whose deadline is approaching to refresh your memory in the event a company official calls. (This is a great time management skill for any individual and a great way of keeping track of important deadlines).
- If contacted by the company, make a note of the date and who contacted you.
- If offered an interview, write down the accurate date, time, and location on your calendar.
- Once you interview, find out before leaving when the organization hopes to make a final decision. Write this information on your calendar and on the position description.

Having all of this information in one place creates incredible organization, cuts down the time spent on the internship search, and prevents scrambling for information when a company calls. The whole process constitutes a great time management practice in which certain aspects can be transferred to other projects. Yes, all of the above information could be kept on a computer or other electronic device. If one does not keep the computer turned on at all times and others possibly share the computer, your access may be limited. Smaller electronic devices can be lost or misplaced and information can be hard to find. What you do not want is a computer error or inaccessibility to the information when that all important phone call happens!

CLASSROOM EXPERIENCES—NOT JUST HOMEWORK!

In Chapters 3 through 5 and 9 and 10, the Time Out Interviews presented contain a great deal of information from industry professionals. A continuing recommendation from these individuals is to take advantage of time in school. Most everybody working in the sport business industry has at least one college degree. In other words, we have all been there. We understand fraternities and sororities, intramural sports, and the need to have time to just relax. However, if your résumé does not reflect good use of your time to volunteer, to hold leadership positions, and a solid grade point average (GPA), some internship and entry level positions will be out of reach; getting your foot in the door may take much longer. Many individuals believe that a GPA has little or nothing to do with job success. While some industry professionals will tell you stories about their early years as a college student that may not all be flattering, at some point they woke up and realized that spending more time studying than partying was, most definitely, the best path to pursue. Starting off with a low GPA and trying to bring it up in the immediate semesters prior to graduation is a very difficult task.

GPA is important for all of the following reasons:

1. Some sport management programs require a minimum GPA in order to be eligible to intern. If the minimum GPA is not met, a student may be required to take additional courses in place of the internship. Some students believe this is an easy substitute in place of the tedious process of finding, applying, interviewing, and securing the internship. But, you want to intern! It is your ticket inside this fabulous industry! Taking courses as a substitute does nothing to increase your professional network unless your classmates are already working in the sport industry. Although very beneficial, the classroom is not the actual operation of a sport organization; it does little to increase the ex-

perience section of a résumé, nor does it establish a list of individuals willing to serve as references. You have worked too hard in your academic program to take the easy way out and elect not to intern, if opting out is an option within your program.

2. Some sport organizations seriously consider the GPA as a measure of persistence, intelligence, leadership, and excellence in work and, thus, require a minimum GPA to be eligible to apply for any posted positions. An overall GPA of 2.8 or higher is not uncommon for many prestigious internships.

3. Many graduate schools request a minimum of a 3.0 to be considered for admission. Even if an individual believes they will never go to graduate school, time and circumstances can alter future plans. A future employer may even require a master's degree for advancement within their organization.

Some individuals also believe their general education, usually the first two years of coursework in a four-year undergraduate degree program, has little to do with a career in sport. Nothing could be further from the truth. A course in psychology, for example, can expose a student to a better understanding of the behavior and actions of individuals. This is a critical business skill! A course in philosophy can establish critical thinking skills and strongly supports those planning on attending graduate or law school. Even if you find these types of courses tough, seeking them out may pay long-term dividends when dealing with the largest component of the sport business industry—people. Math, as well, plays a critical role in future business decision making. While not critical for every position in sport, the ability to understand critical business components involving math and the ability to display higher order math skills may get you a critical promotion. If there is a course at your institution that may help in a future career but is not required for your degree program, take it. A minor or an Associate of Arts (AA) degree in another field may also be beneficial. Investigate these opportunities early.

We will not prolong the discussion in this area. Other chapters have and will refer to your college education. The main point the authors wish to make is that any project and any class can impact your background conceptual knowledge and experience. The Foster Five-Step Model, explained in Chapter 1, includes classroom learning and projects as a separate step in experiential learning. It is advised that one not underestimate the importance of ANY homework assignment and give a 100 percent effort. Furthermore, keep an electronic copy of all written projects on a compact disc (CD) or flash drive and keep back-up copies as well. One never knows when one of these projects will come in handy for an interview or an assigned task at work. During the interview, those wishing to enter a position within the media are often asked for an example of a press release they have written. A facility design project may be a great one to brush up and present in a portfolio during an interview for a facility management position. This is especially important if the projects were awarded a high grade.

ESTABLISHING AN INTERNSHIP TIMELINE

This is another section where we do not intend to use a lot of print space. However, it is important to reemphasize that one should start early—as early as possible in high school or as an undergraduate or graduate student—on thinking about the culminating internship and by establishing a personal timeline with the setting of goals. Utilizing the six Ps presented earlier in this chapter is a great way to organize one's time in school, using every experiential learning opportunity afforded, and securing the internship. Not just any internship, but the right one for you that has the best opportunity to provide you a great learning experience with the right mentor. Finding an experiential learning position with an organization where you will have a great chance of being offered full-time employment upon graduation is icing on the cake. A student can never predict if this will be the final outcome, but spending quality time on this component and focusing early on the right industry segment can result in long-term dividends.

SUMMER JOBS

We mentioned in Chapter 1 that finding a summer job in sport and using it as an apprenticeship within the experiential learning model is a great idea. Why not do this each summer while pursuing an academic degree? A student could actually have three summers of different experiences with different organizations or progressive experience with the same organization. This is often just what employers want to see.

Sometimes, students indicate that they cannot afford to take an hourly job in the sport industry while foregoing a higher paying job with the family business or with a home town organization. Reality often dictates that summer jobs are a way of paying for part of next year's tuition and other bills. Nonetheless, if one truly wants to get into the industry, taking a summer position unrelated to your career goals is not the best decision. Actively searching in the sport industry for a job that will pay some of the bills is a proactive way to approach this important step toward the future. Looking early, before others across the country begin their search, is a good strategy. Late searches may not produce as many available opportunities because positions have already been filled.

If one is from a small town without any large sport organizations, it still may be possible to find a position during the summer that will help build background skills. Any small facility may have scheduled events where one could learn the beginning steps of event management. If this type of position is available but will not pay enough, then taking that family job *and* volunteering to work events may be another course to pursue. Constantly building the résumé and learning more about a specific industry segment are ultimate goals.

VOLUNTEERING

Volunteer, volunteer, volunteer! This is Step 1 of the Five-Step Model. Take advantage of every possible opportunity to learn about your career early and often. For example, if event management is where you think your future lies, find local events. If you are fortunate enough to live close to an area where a professional golf tournament is hosted, volunteer every year in a different role. Bring your significant other to volunteer as well. With major golf tournaments, there are many roles such as marshals, walking scorekeepers, security, social hosts, roles affiliated with transportation, standard bearers, maintenance crews, driving range or parking attendants, media support, and more. It is one of the best sport opportunities to learn a great deal about how a tournament or other large special event is organized and operated. Find out who the volunteer coordinator is and ask if you can help in the months leading up to a tournament. Most professional golf tournaments are not organized by the PGA, LPGA, or other professional tour staff, although these associations will send individuals in advance to a tournament. Instead, they will have a small staff of local organizers that prepare nearly year round. Volunteering often so the staff gets to know you might land you an internship or professional position.

Volunteering for a variety of positions, events, and organizations is the best way to discover one's true calling and to narrow down the industry segments prior to a culminating internship. Less time may be spent down the road jumping from organization to organization in search of your passion. This jumping around once you have graduated from college is often viewed as an inability to stay employed and can raise a red flag for individuals reading your credentials. Once you enter the professional world, you want to show persistence and continuance with an organization for at least a few years. So volunteering early often helps one become secure later on in knowing that they have found their true employment path.

THE FINAL BUZZER

This chapter focused on preparation and planning for achieving the best internship and entry level position offers. Getting hired in sport for many is a career goal. Taking the time to carefully plan early, once started in a degree program, can assist you to realize your dream and forego spending months or years in search of a life goal. The six Ps, in addition to the Five-Step Model from Chapter 1, laid the groundwork for the preparation and planning. In the next chapter, much more will be discussed for the actual application process. Coursework alone, regardless of the degree program, will not gain most individuals a position within the sport business industry. If the hints, ideas, and assignments provided in this book thus far are combined with the next chapter, obtaining quality position offerings should not be a problem.

Classroom Experiential Learning Exercise
INTERNSHIP GOAL SETTING
For the internship, all students must complete a learning contract to assist all parties involved in understanding the goals of the placement. Work on developing a set of at least five goals. Make sure the goal is measurable. For example, upon completing my internship, I would like to have completed one sponsorship proposal for selling an outfield sign, scoreboard space, or program advertisement. Just using words such as "more," "understand," and "learn" do not necessarily provide measurement to indicate the goal was accomplished.
Submitted by Dr. Martin Brett, Assistant Professor & Program Director DeSales University, Center Valley, Pennsylvania

Program Experiential Learning Example

SPORTS BUSINESS FORUM

The Center for Sport Management Research and Education at Texas A&M University hosts the Sports Business Forum annually as a means of providing students with opportunities to hear from leaders in the sport industry. This one-day forum is focused on providing students with key principles on obtaining internships and jobs and how those jobs actually function. The forum consists of two panels and one keynote. The two panel sessions include a group of young professionals and a human resources panel. The young professionals group is made up of both former students and others who are under 30 and have been successful in the sports industry. Presenters provide a real and unbiased assessment of what it is like to work in the sport business trenches.

The human resources panel consists of directors of human resources from prominent teams, leagues, or firms that provide internships and hire A&M students. The keynote chosen is usually from a facet of the industry students may not have thought about as an option for employment.

Submitted by Gregg Bennett
Associate Professor & Center Director

7

Selecting the
Appropriate Internship

"The process of selecting an internship should focus on an opportunity which will give one the most diverse experience possible. Yes, ultimately, everyone will gravitate toward a particular niche. Initially gaining exposure to a broad range of responsibilities will make one more well-rounded and marketable when pursuing job opportunities."

— Gregory Burke
Athletic Director
Northwestern State University of Louisiana

THE WARM UP

Internships have become quite an essential component of educational preparation in a variety of academic curricula, especially in sport management programs (Cuneen & Sidwell, 1994; Seagle & Smith, 2002; Verner, 2004). The selection process of your internship may well be one of the most important parts of your curriculum. Through a careful and well-planned process, the student intern can select the most appropriate organization with which to intern, and when combined with a determined and enthusiastic effort, the specific experiential learning process may lead to employment with the same organization (Figler,1999; Schambach & Dirks, 2002). The respective curriculum program should have prepared the student intern in a variety of academic areas, any one of which may serve as the basis for an internship experience. As indicated earlier in this book, the global sport markets of today are unlimited in career opportunities, and the proper internship can prepare sport management students for a very exciting and rewarding career in many corners of the world (Krannich & Krannich, 2002; Krannich & Krannich, 2001).

The wide world of sport that we have come to know today may appear to run the gamut from glamorous and glitzy (celebrity-hosted events such as golf and boxing), to treacherous and daring (the Eco-Challenge cross-country races and motor-crosses), to adventurous and exhilarating (America's Cup and balloon racing). As explained in Chapter 1, the *SportsBusiness Journal* (2008) has estimated the size of the sport industry at more than $225 billion, approximately seven times that of the movie industry. Traditionally, we have flocked to facilities or seen on television the intercollegiate and professional sport arenas from which our favorite athletes perform. In order for these sport segments to be so economically successful, each has to provide effective and enthusiastic employees willing to serve the customer base. As sport business is becoming more sophisticated and competitive, young, highly-skilled, and educated entry-level employees are needed to ensure forward growth and success. It all begins with an internship! The desires and dreams of student-interns should be just as unlimited as the expected financial return from sporting events such as professional wrestling and NASCAR. If a student wants to work in a specific field of the sport industry, a successful internship can launch a career.

THE INTERNSHIP SELECTION PROCESS

In earlier chapters of this book, the Foster Five-Step Model and the six Ps for planning and preparation were presented. Thus, you already have learned that the planning process for a successful internship begins as early as possible in the academic program of study. When starting a major in sport management, most individuals do not know exactly what industry segment or entry level niche to pursue, although many believe they do. Others will have a strong sense of direction. This is true for both the graduate and undergraduate student. Several important things have to occur for such an outcome, though. Students should first be introduced to all of the industry segments as we presented in Chapters 3 through 5. This introduction usually occurs through a foundations course in sport management offered through an approved curriculum.

Looking for an internship or a full-time position is a full-time job itself. So, do not expect to start looking a week before your internship selection deadline occurs. Once again, we are building upon the theme of starting as early as possible, but certainly by the very beginning of your capstone pre-internship course or the semester prior to your internship semester.

FINDING YOUR NICHE

Hopefully, you have already started your experiential learning by using Step 1 in the Five-Step Model, volunteering. You also did not wait around for formal experiential opportunities and created volunteer experiences for yourself. You have progressed through Step 3 or 4 and have already served an apprenticeship, perhaps, to gain experience through office observation or at an event. The point being made here is that there are a wide variety of athletic venues that exist in collegiate sport programs and many events desperately need volunteers, certainly from within the university and sometimes from the local community. A prime place for the athletic department to recruit is from the sport management program at the institution. The previous chapters discussed planning and preparation in-depth, including summer jobs; therefore, we will not belabor the discussion here. The point we are making is that by now, you have experience on your résumé and you are ready to begin the internship search process. At this point, the level of

While there is some glitz and glamour when working with large team sport organizations or college athletic departments, assisting students in finding the right fit for them is a common goal for sport management academic advisors. (Courtesy of Susan Foster)

observation, background research, and the number of experiential learning opportunities completed by the student will now determine the qualifications for an internship. The process you implemented assisted you in eliminating areas in which you have no desire to work. It is just as important to know and understand the career you do not want as much as the career you do want (Kelley, 2004; Verner, 2004).

CAPSTONE COURSES

After a student has progressed through the first four steps of the Five-Step Learning Model, it is time for the student to formally apply for the culminating internship at a professional agency and begin the selection process. Some post-secondary institutions will have what is often called a capstone course or pre-internship class. In many instances, this capstone course is organized to assist students in the internship selection process, to prepare them for all facets of the internship, and to finalize the selection and any paperwork required. Even though most students will already have prepared a résumé, especially if they followed the Five-Step Learning Model, a main topic in this type of course will be résumé writing or perfecting the résumé format (Pontow, 1999). Other topics covered include how to write proper business correspondence that include cover letters, professionalism, the importance of punctuality, management and leadership styles, and how to effectively deal with each type, as well as topics such as sexual harassment, gender bias, and the avoidance of "office politics." The interview process is usually a main topic as well, complete with a list of possible questions and "most appropriate" responses (Yates, 2000; Porot & Haynes, 1999). Analyzing job descriptions to determine whether one is qualified is also a popular topic. Some capstone courses actually use this as an in-depth management course where students create strategic plans, participate in role playing exercises, study human relations management and leadership, and more in order to immerse the student in a complete understanding of the organizational environment. The student is then required to apply this knowledge in the actual internship through a formally written analysis of their internship organization (Young & Baker, 2004). When there is a culminating internship, we recommend a capstone course approach.

Often guest speakers are invited to speak to students in the capstone course. This is a great advantage if the individuals are actually looking for interns. But not all capstone courses include the guest speaker facet because many programs invite speakers to every course within the sport management curriculum. Some believe the students should already have selected a specific industry segment to pursue when the student is nearing the end of academic coursework. On the other hand, a few students may not have found an area for which they have a passion, particularly if the student did not select sport management as their major until their junior year or transferred from another institution. If you are one of those who are unsure, we recommend two approaches. First, participate in some intense self-analysis quickly that will include how you feel your skills may fit within a specific industry segment. Engage the assistance of a career counselor at your institution. Sometimes personality tests can help identify particular strengths or weaknesses or skills. Second, begin to interview people. These can be classmates who have identified their career focus, sport management faculty who generally have intense background knowledge, other students who are currently participating in an internship, alumni, or actual practitioners in the field. If time is not on your side, you can still select and apply for any internship position that interests you. During the internship, you can then identify or eliminate a particular segment or position that is not a good fit for you. We do not recommend this approach because it could lead to the acceptance of numerous internships after graduation, just to find what does interest the student. We often call this process post-graduation meandering. The goal is to avoid this meandering, because we have found that students lose interest, need financial support, and end up looking for just any job, and thus may never become employed in the industry for which they spent two or more years preparing. Hopefully, by the time you get to this point, you are already focused and the internship you accept will lead to a confirmation of your choice and a full-time position. For more information, read Tooley (1997).

RESEARCHING SPORT ORGANIZATIONS

Employment Websites

We are going to assume an industry niche has been identified if you have progressed to the culminating internship. Begin by looking for organizations and announced positions tied to this selected industry segment.

As the saying goes in sports, "the best defense is a good offense." Being proactive in the search for the best internship is a lot like having the best offense. The internship fairy will not drop by in your sleep and place an internship under your pillow. Many of the best internships are the ones a student recruited or pursued relentlessly for themselves. In other words, the student should recruit the internship, rather than the internship recruiting the student. In the case of the former, the student intern and the pursued agency have a win-win situation, because the student may be genuinely interested in the agency and the respective role it has in the industry. In the case of the latter, the internship sites may accept anybody, because just anybody will suffice.

Applying for positions today is much easier than it was prior to 2000. With computers and technology, one can apply within minutes via the internet because, any position an organization wishes to publicize for outsiders to apply can be posted on their web-site and perhaps on several others. To find positions within an organization, most websites will have a button or a link to current job opportunities on their homepage. Sometimes, one has to search for the link and often it is in small print at the bottom. But this is the first place to look if you wish to work for a specific organization.

When looking for internships or jobs anywhere in the industry, the next place to look is on the websites that allow one to search for openings and post a résumé without paying a fee. A great place to start is http://www .teamworkonline.com, especially if a position within professional sport or facility management and operations is the goal. Teams often pay for the opportunity to post their positions, or web-advertising may underwrite the cost for this type of web-site offering. But this website certainly is not the only place to find positions. Several others exist. As mentioned previously in Chapter 4, the NCAA's website (http://www.ncaa.org) has an employment section, called "The Market," and this is an excellent place to look for graduate assistantships and other positions within college athletics. Appendix A displays a long list of websites that can link to sport business industry openings.

Print Media

Print media provides another possible location for position announcements although it is not used as widely as it once was. *The Chronicle of Higher Education* provides an outlook for locating positions on college campuses including those in athletic training, college athletic administration and coaching, and teaching positions in sport management. *The Sports Business*

Table 7.1. Internship/Entry Level Position Documentation Spreadsheet								
Site Name	Contact Person	Phone Number	Email Address	Cover Letter	Résumé	Response Y or N	Accept Or Reject	Comments
1								
2								
3								
4								

Journal occasionally has a few position announcements placed by sport organizations. Your local newspaper may also announce positions particularly if you live in an area with professional sport teams or postsecondary institutions. Small or unknown sport marketing firms or other sport organizations may also advertise in this manner. Once again, this outlet is not used widely, but if the organization is looking to hire quickly or hopes to find local applicants, it is very likely they will utilize this media outlet. Finally, do not forget to look in membership newsletters published by sport related professional associations. While many of these no longer occur in print, they may appear in an online format.

Your sport management program or library may have directories that list a multitude of sport organizations and their contact information. Conducting an Internet search for sport organizations and their contact information and then saving this information in a spreadsheet is a great way to maintain your own informational listing. Table 7.1 provides a sample spreadsheet one could easily construct to list websites and sport organization information where possible internships or entry level positions for which you intend to apply could be listed. (Constructing the spreadsheet in a landscape format provides the best space allowance).

Finding Non-advertised Positions or Creating an Internship Position

Some sport career specialists indicate that sport organizations do not need to advertise position openings. While this can be true, most advertise some openings, especially internships and entry level positions. Another strategy for learning about non-advertised positions might be to find out who receives applications for internships or positions openings. Some organizations do not have formal internship programs or, believe it or not, have never considered hiring an intern. An assertive individual might be able to create an internship position for themselves by finding the right person to contact and then sending a cover letter and résumé to that person. Caution is warranted, though. It is not recommended to apply to every organization in this manner. It can be an incredible waste of time. Be selective when using this strategy. Smaller organizations and ones not known very well are more likely to accept and read materials received in this manner.

Preferred Agency Listing

Some academic programs maintain a list of preferred internship sites. Certainly, this can make the internship search much easier for the student. Through this contact list, the university program can allow the student to choose or can assign a student to an approved internship site. Such a listing can be of benefit in some instances and extremely restrictive to the student intern in others. Of benefit, the school program may control the experience, provide guarded accessibility for the student, or have an established reciprocal agreement with another school program for shared supervision.

But through the use of a preferred agency listing, the student may be missing out on a crucial learning process by not being allowed to practice the actual job application process. Additionally, they may be missing out on the selection of an internship site that best fits their desired employment niche. Furthermore, the institution may be restricting the ability of the student intern to earn a position through hard work. If a university sends students to the same sites every term, the agency is less likely to hire students into full-time positions because of the revolving door of interns. The student may also be denied the best opportunity to meet individual wants and needs when restricted to an approved list of internship placement sites. When institutions place student interns in certain designated areas of these programs, this may be a good practice if the internship provides an outstanding experience and the site supervisor is a dynamic leader. But it is not a good situation if the organization never hires an intern into a full-time position, as mentioned earlier, or if the student has already volunteered or worked in the position in an earlier experience and relatively few new skills are learned.

Students should be encouraged to expand their network and experience the job selection process when looking for an internship and many students do seek a dynamic and challenging experience away from the four-year program that each may be close to completing. This is especially important, in our opinion, when dealing with college athletic departments. When a student remains on campus, often they are still perceived as a student and not as a working professional. They may not be invited to full-time staff meetings or other professional events due to their student status. When a student is removed from a "student" environment and the intern is treated as a professional, the student often experiences a tremendously different environment. As a maturing adult about to enter the professional world, do you want to stay home and fly kites or would you rather take off in a hot air balloon and be set free?

ANALYZING POSITION ANNOUNCEMENTS FOR INFORMATION AND QUALIFICATIONS

Chelladurai (1999) presented information on analyzing job announcements in his book, *Human Resource Management in Sport and Recreation*. He states "the purpose of job analysis is to gather the information on the job, the operations, the duties and responsibilities involved, the working conditions, and other critical elements" (p. 137). This gives the applicant clues about the organization and minimum job skills required and what it may be like working in that organization. One very frustrating element of recruiting is receiving application materials from an individual who does not even meet the basic minimum requirements of a particular position. It truly is a waste of the applicant's and organization's time. By law, an organization must hire an individual meeting the stated minimum requirements. However, if the organization uses the terminology "preferred requirements," studying the organization and the announcement a little more is critical; there is a chance you might qualify.

MARKETING YOURSELF: THE PROFESSIONAL LOOK

Promotion as one of the six Ps was presented in Chapter 6, but this section will spend a little time on how to professionally promote, present, and position yourself for hiring. Networking can be done incorrectly as discussed in Chapter 8; so, too, can self-promotion.

Professional Dress: This is a key area in which to begin. Different individuals possess different perceptions on what constitutes professional
dress. Let's begin with the basics. At the very least, when attending most
conferences, meetings, or becoming involved in any opportunity where
you might meet individuals that can assist in your career search, the
clothes to be worn should be neatly pressed. What you wear should be
dictated by the situation. A career fair or professional conference (especially the first day) most often demands a shirt and tie, dress slacks, and
sport coat, at the very minimum, for males. A suit is appropriate for
many positions dependent upon the job description. If in doubt, wear
the suit. If you plan on interviewing or introducing yourself to a speaker,
wear the suit. Some pre-internship seminars will address this issue with a
guest speaker from a local haberdashery and may demonstrate proper
dress with the use of mannequins.

For women, a professional suit should be part of your wardrobe. It can
include a skirt or dress slacks. Navy, black, gray, brown, or tan is your
best color choice. Never wear red! In all situations, never wear anything
provocative such as low cut or very tight blouses. Tight slacks or very
short skirts or dresses are out as well. It is tough to wear your best high
heels and then take a tour of a stadium walking up and down stairs and
on the playing turf during an interview. Wear comfortable shoes that still
fit with the style of dress you choose. Some individuals recommend one
should never wear open toed shoes in a professional situation. Closed
toed shoes are considered professional. Again, geographic location will
often dictate the wardrobe including the shoes to be worn.

When interviewing at the organization's offices, the situation may dictate appropriate dress other than described above. However, do not assume anything and do not ask what to wear. The interviewer may assume
that you are looking for an opportunity not to wear your business best.
As with other situations, err on the side of caution. There is rarely a
situation where you can be overdressed. Nonetheless, here is an example.

Interviewing with a recreation department or a professional baseball
team can be tricky. In either situation, often the staff wears dress or khaki-
style slacks and a professional looking golf shirt. In the professional baseball offices during the off-season, an individual may never leave their office because they are working on sales calls or marketing projects. In a
recreation department, the staff may be constantly running out of the

building to check on an event at a facility or may be checking on a youth sport league tournament in progress. In these situations, a business suit may be deemed inappropriate. Geographic location may also dictate dress as those working in warmer climates may never wear a suit while those working in an office during the blistery cold days of winter may always wear a suit for warmth. Never wear a hat indoors or at any time during an interview!

In any situation, do not be afraid to be over-dressed. It is possible that the interviewer may give a male interviewee permission to remove a coat and tie for comfort. We recommend you do not get too laid back. The staff working for a minor league organization *might* wear more comfortable dress than their major league counterparts. Again, pay attention to the environment and use your best judgment. There is a lot of truth to the saying, "Dress for success!"

One would think hygiene would not be a topic we would need to cover. But a few comments are warranted. In our experience, the most violated rule here is the failure to clean under the finger nails, and this is especially true for males. Interviewers are going to notice. A private organization can ask males not to wear earrings and can request that you not have facial hair. For an interview or any time one is meeting with an industry professional, it is better to err on the side of caution and leave the earrings at home. A good haircut and a clean shaven look is our best recommendation. While the law may not be able to prohibit a public organization from enforcing a dress code, the interviewer may have a personal bias.

The Position Application: Portraying yourself as a professional can also be demonstrated when you submit an organization's job application which is often required in addition to a résumé or cover letter. Most organizations will send an online application via e-mail. Hopefully, it will be sent in a word processing format so you can type information directly on the application. Some will ask you to print the application and sign it before sending it in the mail. Type it before printing it, even if the formatting makes it difficult to do so. Sometimes, an application will be sent in a PDF format that does not allow the applicant to type the necessary information. In today's society, some individuals have never used a typewriter and few organizations or households possess one. However, if you receive a printed application in the mail from an organization, do everything possible to type it. If all else fails, print the information in a very neat format so it can be easily read. You would not want illegible information to keep you from being considered for a position. This is another example of paying attention to detail.

Cover Letters, Résumés, and Mailings: Cover letters and résumés are definitely the professional presentation of oneself. While we discuss their content later in this chapter, presenting them to an employer in an appropriate manner is of utmost importance. It is often the first opportunity to introduce yourself and your skills. It is the most important time to pay attention to detail. No spelling errors! Proper punctuation and grammar should be exercised. Spelling the name of the individual to whom the materials are sent correctly and ensuring their proper title is used are key.

When mailing documents, the envelope is the first element observed. A sloppily addressed envelope is not a good professional presentation of the application documents. A typed mailing label with a typed return address label must be used. We no longer recommend folding the résumé; instead, mail your documents flat in a large brown or white envelope. In this case, it is okay when the résumé paper does not match the envelope. However, if you choose to fold and mail it, make sure the envelope matches the paper.

Phone and E-mail Addresses: After you have begun sending application materials, consider changing any answering machine or cell phone messages to reflect a very professional message. Eliminate music or any other material that may not be received in a positive manner by an organizational employee attempting to call to set up an interview. Notify family members or roommates of your position applications and request they answer the phone in a very positive and polite manner. The same is true for e-mail addresses. Make sure addresses do not include questionable identifiers such as "lazy eddy" or "bourbon betty."

Social Media Sites: If you intend to use social media spaces created for the purpose of marketing your professional skills, these also need to present *only* professional information. LinkedIn is a popular social media site that is used by professionals a great deal for networking and to connect with individuals in organizations. Some personal information can be viewed by everyone, but an individual determines what information can be seen. Thus, if being used to assist in a position search, most would allow access to all information. Twitter and Facebook are also popular sites to market skills. Use them wisely.

DEVELOPING A QUALITY COVER LETTER AND RÉSUMÉ

When applying for positions, never proceed without a polished cover letter and résumé. Yes, some online application processes do not ask for a cover letter. If e-mailing your application materials, the cover letter can constitute the body of the message for the e-mail or can be attached to the e-mail. When mailing your résumé, ALWAYS submit a cover letter, as well, even if one is not requested.

The Cover Letter

Learning to write a great cover letter is a key skill. Each time you apply for a position, the cover letter should be changed to fit the position description and to address how your individual skills fit that particular position. It is a crucial error to write a generic cover letter and just change the name and address at the top for each position. This practice does not position your skills in the best possible way. See Figure 7.1 for a sample cover letter. Please note in paragraph one of that document that the applicant makes very clear the position for which she is applying. Sometimes, an organization will have several positions available at the same time. Ashley also indicates where she found the announcement. This simply provides advertising info the employer likes to see. In paragraph two, Ashley brings attention to several skills she possesses and her perceived strengths. These were prerequisite skills mentioned in the position announcement.

Finally, in paragraph three, she brings attention to her résumé and is creating a networking opportunity by indicating that she will contact the organization. She also has a professional profile on the popular LinkedIn networking website and has invited the interviewer to take a look. These two items may urge the interviewer to read her materials, but there is no guarantee. She also has not limited her availability for contact which sends a message of flexibility in scheduling. One final note: if you indicate that you will be contacting the organization, make sure you do it within the time frame promised. This confirms reliability and supports the applicant's claim about paying attention to detail. If the position announcement specifically indicates no phone calls, do not call!

Ashley Q. Student
1234 Central Drive
Wichita, KS 67208

February 15, 2010

Ms. Faith M. Files, Director
Event Operations
SBC Golf Tournament
3456 Corporate Way
Land O'Lakes, FL 12345

Dear Ms. Files:

This is a letter of application for your available position as the Assistant Event Director for the SBC Golf Tournament. I found this position on womenssportsjobs.com.

My passion is using my creativity and great planning skills in Sport Event Management. My satisfaction is seeing the fruits of my labors when an event is completed with very few problems encountered. This is how I believe my skills can assist your company if I am chosen for this position. I am a team player and pay extreme attention to detail!

My résumé is attached. I also have a LinkedIn profile (ashleyqstudent@linkedin) and three individuals have posted recommendations for me. I can be reached via e-mail or my cell phone at any time. Please do not hesitate to contact me. I will call you within two weeks to see if my application materials were received. I look forward to meeting you and having the chance to interview for this position.

Sincerely,

Ashley Student

Figure 7.1. Sample cover letter.

The Résumé: Putting forth a complete and accurate portrayal of individual successes and achievements continues with the résumé. Your written presentation of personal credentials must be well ordered and concise, but also attractive enough to the reviewer's eye to pique interest and command the all-important interview. Information in the résumé should be organized under section headings preceded by the interviewee's name and complete contact information. Suggested headings can include:

- *Education Information.* This should include degrees held or pursuing, graduation dates, name and location of the degree granting institution.
- *Sport Management Experience.* Collectively placing all experience gained from the sport business industry on the front page highlights one's skills tied to sport.
- *Other Work Experience.* Exhibiting additional positions and skills outside the industry displays responsibilities that may apply to any position and demonstrates the ability to hold a job.
- *Honors and Awards.* It is not the time to be shy! Displaying accolades bestowed in jobs or in education sends a strong message to any interviewer that you take pride in your work.
- *Volunteer Work and Extracurricular Activities.* Activities outside work and education exhibits the propensity to be a well-rounded individual. These activities may also be a common interest of one of the interviewers—an immediate conversation starter. Organizations also like to see displayed interest in the local community.
- *References.* This is a must and is discussed in the question and answer section that follows.

Every job seeker has questions about format and content. Information is presented below in a most frequently asked questions and answers format.

How long should the résumé be and how should my information be presented? This is a very difficult question to answer. In our experience, some organizations want no more than one page and often believe an undergraduate has not done enough to warrant more than one page. Others want to see all experience and often it will not fit onto one page. The best answer is to find out the type of résumé the interviewer prefers. Sometimes, this can be done through a secretary or receptionist at the organization or network contacts. However, this information is often quite difficult to obtain. Consequently, the best answer is to formulate a résumé that best presents you and your skills. You want to tailor the résumé to each and every different position to which you apply. Often a functional résumé is the best way to do this. A **functional** résumé highlights skill sets and does not list experience in chronological order. This type of résumé is often better for those who have been in the industry a while who want to encapsulate their skill sets. This format can also be beneficial to entry level applicants that have built their résumé through many experiential learning opportunities but have not had a full-time position. A great deal of experience in specific areas can be sold under one large section such as "Event Management Experience" instead of displaying a series of one-week events, one day volunteer opportunities, or a series of internships.

A **chronological** format is the most common type of résumé used, especially by entry level applicants and interns. As its title indicates, sections showing education and experience are listed by dates in reverse chronological order. Employers generally want to see the most recent information first. Sample résumés have been provided in Appendix B.

Should I list high school information? The best answer to this is no. But consider the specific situations listed below that may warrant the inclusion of high school information.

- High school location can often be a conversation starter in an interview or can create an immediate tie to an individual if you know the interviewer attended the same school.
- If you were a play-by-play announcer for your high school athletic department, had the opportunity to participate in internet broadcasting, or wrote for the school newspaper, and are applying for a job in a media sector, this information may be extremely relevant.
- If you must submit a résumé when applying for an apprenticeship or summer position and you are only a freshman or sophomore, yes, some high school information may be very valuable. This is particularly important if you have not yet gained new experiences in college.
- If a coaching position is the intended employment target, but you did not play college sports or gain any collegiate related experience, summarizing any sports played and awards won may be helpful.

However, if you are nearing the end of a college degree and have actively applied the Foster Five-Step Model, you have a great deal of experience to include. Beyond the examples mentioned above, omitting high school information and allowing additional space for more recent skills and positions held is our best recommendation.

What color and type of paper should I use? The safest answer for color and type is white and a minimum of 28 pounds (the weight of the paper). Copy paper should never be used when submitting a résumé. It is generally okay to use an off-white or light colored paper (cream, light gray, or light blue), but some people will recommend white. A colleague who was in charge of screening résumés for an athletic director's position once told us four of the top five candidates submitted a résumé on non-white paper. While these are not the results of a well-designed research study, it is food for thought! Color of paper will not matter if your skills are top notch. Conversely, never use dark colored paper; it does not copy well. Résumés are often photocopied so that all members of a search committee can have a copy.

Should I present my employment information in paragraph format or use bullet points? Always use bullet points. It is much easier and faster to read phrases presented in a bulleted format. Most interviewers are too busy to read a narrative and simply want to scan information. Bullets often save space as well.

Should I use a résumé template? Personally, we do not like them. The main reason is because your résumé then looks like many of the other ones submitted, especially when using a template from a common word processing program. Templates are often difficult to use if you wish to format your information with a certain look. What you want to do is develop a résumé that is unique in appearance but easy to photocopy. Conversely, a template often provides information on categories or where to place dates and it is a good starting point to use as a guide if you have never developed a résumé.

Should I include references? This is one of the most common questions. Many campus career advisors or business personnel will tell you to simply place a statement such as "References Available Upon Request." Our recommendation is this: when applying for an internship or employment position within a sport organization, ALWAYS include references. There are two main reasons.

- Sport organizations, especially those that are well known, advertising a position on a popular employment website will often receive hundreds of résumés for one position. Think about the time involvement of going through all of the submitted documents. One way your materials may stand out is if they recognize the name or personally know one or more of your references. Do not be surprised if this happens to you even if you live in a remote section of the country. Remember, individuals in sport network very well and are very connected. This is even truer in today's market with all of the opportunities to connect through online social media opportunities. As we mentioned earlier, LinkedIn is a popular networking sight for professionals. There are no less than twenty sub-groups of networking individuals interested in sport, and this does not count the private ones that universities have started for their alumni to stay connected. On this site, individuals can post recommendations attesting to skills and work ethic. Make sure your posted information is done in an extremely professional manner. You never know who might be looking for someone with your skills.

- Because of the volume of résumés received, the person or persons charged with sorting through each one often look for ways to cut their time committed to this project. If you have already submitted reference names and contact information, this is one less step for them. They do not have to find you to first find your references. If references are not listed, it is very likely you may lose out simply because six other individuals with very similar skills to yours supplied their references in advance.

Creative Online Résumés. A final closing comment about résumés is warranted. Technology has changed the job application process. Individuals are now posting very creative résumé formats on the internet. From pages that turn to video insertions, the ability to link a creative webpage to a social media site or an online application could result in immense dividends. An online résumé developed with these bells and whistles can make a plain paper résumé seem pale in comparison. Please remember, though, some résumé information should be treated as private information and handled accordingly.

APPLYING FOR POSITIONS

We hope by now, especially after reading Chapters 3–5, that it is clear that a plethora of career opportunities are available to the sport management student in the United States and abroad. One of the most difficult decisions to be made is narrowing down the fields of opportunity if the entire realm of employment possibilities has been thoroughly examined. These factors are discussed below.

Geography

Geography impacts many decisions. In previous chapters, we briefly mentioned some considerations relating to the location of an academic program or internship. When planning the internship, proximity of the internship to the program of origin may be one factor. Potential internships located within the city where the curriculum program is offered may be conducive to travel and accessibility, as well as the personal dynamics of living arrangements and finance. Internship sites where the climate is important to the performance of the activity, but may be remote from the curriculum program need careful consideration. For instance, if the student wants to intern at a ski resort, then travel and relocation logistics play an important role in leaving major urban areas in the south for the internship. With the unique access and implementation of the worldwide web and the internet, many academic institutions can manage the progress of the internship through email and electronically-submitted correspondence (e.g., Blackboard, Web-CT, or e-College). Other transportation considerations are discussed in the section "Economics of the Decision" later in this chapter.

For the culminating internship, we strongly recommend the student not limit themselves to a specific geographical location—to only positions that would allow them to live at home or to remain with an organization where they already know everyone, the organization, and their procedures. All of these situations prevent the intern from expanding their network, learning how other organizations work, and allowing them to enter a truly professional situation away from parents or a residence hall and the typical life of an on-campus student. Change your geography, especially if you have never lived away from home or in another state! Learn how others live and work! Of course, one positive contradiction to this would be if a full-time position has already been promised in a current location.

Economics of the Decision

In Chapter 6, we briefly introduced you to paid versus unpaid internships and some financial considerations to examine when preparing for an experiential learning opportunity early in your academic career. In the present chapter, we are providing additional information to consider regarding other economic decisions that must be explored. A major consideration for the prospective intern is the cost of doing the internship.

Can you afford the actual costs of participating in an internship? "Of course!" you say. So, how does one prepare for the cost of the internship? What values does one weigh and/or sacrifice for the sake of a good internship experience?

The actual cost of an internship experience may be difficult to determine. Many items must be weighed when selecting an internship. These items are explored below. A good faculty mentor should be able to direct the student intern to resources and information necessary to answer most of these inquiries.

Tuition Costs. The student intern must pay the tuition and fees associated with the credit hours to the respective institution for academic credit applied to the internship. Some institutions require students to pay added fees (e.g., $250–$400) during the semester of the internship to help the university defray the costs of faculty to travel and visit internship sites during the semester. Some programs require at least two visits from the university supervisor and the added fees help programs afford these visits. Many students are shocked when they learn of this added cost, since most often, they will not be living on campus. Faculty members are supervising the internship, sometimes traveling to the internship site, spending time discussing an intern's progress with the site supervisor, and grading papers and projects. Internship assignments many not be considered as part of a faculty members regular teaching load and supervision may create an overload. This is particularly true during the summer term. Thus, the faculty member must be compensated for their time and travel expenses.

College costs are an ever-looming burden to most students. The internship cost depends on the number of credit hours associated with the particular internship. A graduate internship is usually three to six hours. The undergraduate intern will usually pay for six to twelve credit hours. Graduate and undergraduate programs have a minimum hourly requirement to be considered full-time students. Maintaining full-time status is important in order to qualify for scholarship monies or federal financial aid. Some graduate programs offer assistantships (see Chapters 1 and 10) to students that may cover the cost of tuition and additional incurred fees while interning. Some institutions will require a student to be full-time if living in university housing. An additional consideration is that governmental financial aid requires full-time student status and is not generally available during the summer. While the chosen industry segment and completion of courses should determine the semester of the internship, if a student's chosen industry segment does not dictate a seasonality consideration, investigating and comparing the cost of an internship during the fall and spring versus the summer is warranted. Some institutions lower tuition costs during the summer to attract students to enroll in a summer term. Even if any form of financial aid is not available, the cost of tuition during a fall or spring term may be more than in the summer. This decision will depend upon the availability of any savings the intern may have accumulated (see Chapter 6), a low cost bank loan for the summer, personal savings, or family contributions versus college tuition loans funneled through the schools.

Transportation Costs. The intern must consider the cost of travel and room and board for the duration of the internship. When the internship is in close proximity to the host institution or the student's home, an internship site will appear more conducive to the economic need, rather than recognizing the benefit of a new and different learning opportunity for the student. In either case, the cost of transportation must be included in any internship selection consideration.

In cases where the internship site must be visited by a supervising faculty member or designated program official and school budgets have been restricted, the intern may have to sacrifice a distant preference for a more local or travel-friendly site. This is becoming less of a factor, as more and more internships can be effectively monitored with internet connections, online learning platforms, and email.

We realize that often a student's family simply cannot provide the financial support for a separate automobile for a student nor the expenses involved in providing insurance and upkeep. If a student knows this early-on, a quality internship in a location with mass transportation that will still provide a great opportunity should be researched well in advance. Cities such as Atlanta, Chicago, and Washington, DC have subways and trains, but these are just a few examples. Smaller cities with less notable names where minor league teams or great sport marketing agencies are located may have great bus transportation systems or other means for local transport. The important thing, if at all possible, is to select an internship for the quality of the experience and not to limit yourself to a specific geographic area simply because you don't have a car. But, again, caution is warranted. Safety is an important consideration for anyone who would have to walk to and from a transportation stop to get to the internship site, especially when working a game that may not be completed until early the next morning.

It is not recommended a student attempt to live on campus or at home, and commute an hour or more for an internship. Since the work schedule of an intern can be unpredictable, late hours on competition dates are a common occurrence. The position may require the intern to be back at the office by 9:00 a.m. or earlier and the cost savings is often not worth the gasoline, wear and tear on a vehicle, tolls, and insurance. Insurance companies charge more when commuting long distances to and from work. Plus, the lack of sleep is not conducive to a healthy lifestyle when working a full-time position.

During the course of some internships, a student may be required to use their personal vehicle. Inquire about this in advance. Travel costs incurred while performing business on behalf of the internship agency are usually covered or reimbursed by the agency. The student intern should confirm this, have it written into the internship agreement, and have it signed by the appropriate parties. Otherwise, these transportation costs must be included in the financial summation of internship expenses.

Housing. Some internship sites may provide housing to the student intern. This is the case of internships with the USOC because on-site housing has been provided in the past. This is a huge benefit and, sometimes, is better than receiving minimum wage or a monthly stipend. Do the math! Explore the costs of local housing if one needs to rent an apartment as compared to the selection of an internship where housing is provided. Four- to six-month leases may be difficult to obtain; the cost of utility connections and moving must also be considered. As mentioned in the previous section, long commuting times nor the acceptance of a less-than-preferred internship is not how an internship selection decision should be made, even if you have a rent-free place to stay during the internship opportunity. Perhaps, another student is interning in the same area; sharing an apartment may be a good alternative.

Dress. As mentioned in an earlier chapter, most internship sites will have an office dress code in place for student interns. The student intern should inquire about any dress code that might be in effect, so as not to be in violation of that code on the first day. Remember what they say about first impressions; you only get one chance. The intern might have to incur a cost for purchasing business clothing where weekly dry cleaning or laundry maintenance costs ($50–$200 range) would need to be added to the budget.

Mailings/Correspondence. An additional cost may be incurred through mailings and email correspondence with the sponsoring institution. Students should expect to pay for their own postage and mailing assignments to the supervising faculty member. Sometimes, assignments can be mailed electronically which defrays this cost. However, some program policies call for hard copies of important documentation to be placed in a student's file. Assignments such as preparation and presentation of a portfolio and major projects may require a large amount of postage, and the student intern should expect to incur such costs personally. These are not considered agency products or part of the internship organization's daily business. Unless the student is issued a company cell phone, any cost the student may incur through use of personal electronic equipment to serve the agency (cell phone or personal computer) may or may not be reimbursable to the intern.

Do not be surprised if all internships assignments are to be mailed through the postal service. Often deadlines for submitting paperwork are steadfast as a means for measuring time management skills. Problems can be encountered when the clock on an organizational fax machine does not work and the time on the faxed documentation does not meet the required deadline. Another reason for not allowing e-mailed documents may be due to the fact that some assignments may require actual supervisor signatures, and some organizations have not created this capability through electronic communication. Be prepared to cover the cost of mailing a hard-copy of all internship assignments.

Certifications and Insurance. Of benefit to some interns is the availability of personal certifications and in-service training that may be offered through or by the internship agency. Some agencies will require the prospective interns to be CPR (cardiopulmonary resuscitation) or First Aid certified. Some training may be for security sensitive information and documentation by the human resources (HR) department, while others may require in-house training to obtain keys and building access. In cases where the intern is dealing with equipment and player locker room/facilities, Occupational and Health Safety Administration (OSHA) guidelines and certifications may be required, to which the agency may be willing to reimburse or pay for in advance. For international internships or international travel, the intern will be required to bring shot charts and booster inoculations up to date. Incurring the personal cost for such items must be calculated and included in the overall cost of the internship. Some internships, such as fitness or event management or college coaching, may require an intern to purchase liability insurance. This is often available through the academic institution at a nominal cost and may also be available through a parent's insurance policy. Student teachers often have to purchase a similar insurance package, effective for the semester of the internship or student teaching experience. Even if not required by the organization or your institution, it is worth investigating. A $3 million liability policy can often be purchased by a student for less than $20 and provide coverage for 12 months. It is better to be covered with a policy and not need it, than to need the insurance and not be covered.

Job Search Costs. While searching for a full-time job should not really be considered as a cost for completing an internship, one can often tell early in an internship if the sponsoring organization may not be hiring for full-time positions once the internship is complete. Thus, including the cost of a job search during the internship is not a bad idea.

If a student maximizes their efforts in seeking an appropriate internship, costs will be incurred during this search process. It is no different when searching for a full-time position. One will need to set aside some money for this process. While some organizations allow an individual to apply online, thus reducing mailing costs, not all individuals are hired in this manner. As recommended earlier for the internship search, purchasing memberships to websites that require a fee is a great idea. Often, competition for the job is lessened because not everyone is willing or cannot afford to purchase a membership. But if fewer people are applying to positions found on these websites, it is well worth the cost. Most often you can purchase a two to three week membership, three months, or more. We recommend nothing less than a three-month membership because this is generally a better value. Annual memberships are also available, but, hopefully, one will find a full-time position in less than three months. Be aware! A downturn in the economy can make the job search much longer.

Table 7.2. Internship Budget Worksheet				
Fixed Costs		**Variable Costs**		
Rent/Insurance	Amount	Water/Electric/Other Utilities	Amount	
Car Payment		TV/Cable/Internet		
Phone Service		Entertainment		
Liability Insurance (If required)		1. Foods		
Credit Card Payments		2. Other (Movie, Club, etc)		
1.		Dry Cleaning		
2.		Non-Auto Travel		
Student Loans (If not deferred)		Clothing/Uniforms		
Laundry		Gifts (Xmas, B-days, weddings)		
Savings (min. $25/month)		Gasoline/Tolls		
Other		Groceries		
		Miscellaneous		
		1.		
		2.		
TOTAL F		TOTAL V		
* Total F + Total V = Ts	Ts x 12 months=	Amount you will spend in 1 year		
**To spend $2500 a month	For 12 months	One needs to earn an absolute minimum of	$35,000 /year	
**The 2009 federal income tax was between 10 and 15% for individuals earning what could be considered a student income. Tax bracket varies based on income, marital, and filing status.				

One very good way the student intern can hedge on the cost of a job search, during the internship experience, is to make your talents become very valuable to the agency. Many individuals interviewed for this book have mentioned this: a strong work ethic and the personal determination to do a good job on any assignment the agency requests may lead to a full-time position. If the intern spent a great deal of time in choosing the right internship and maximized the opportunities to impress the staff at the agency, then, hopefully, the agency will not let the competition hire the graduating intern. Many first jobs have been earned through a well-performed student internship.

This section has focused on the costs involved in the completion of an internship. Some internship programs provide the student intern with a budget worksheet to help in the planning of the financial arrangements for the duration of the internship. If the student intern already has established a personal budget, subsequent estimated projections will allow for a much easier comprehension of the cost to live while interning. An example of a personal budget worksheet is provided in Table 7.2. One can insert or eliminate items; obviously, fixed and variable costs will fluctuate depending on one's individual situation. Amounts will vary based upon geographic location of the internship site.

Use of the worksheet will assist in making financial decisions about the internship. If a student has financially planned for the internship from the beginning, the opportunity to select the best possible placement, regardless of location, will maximize this career-making experiential learning opportunity.

Applying Over the Internet

Applying for jobs over the internet can be convenient, but tricky. We all take the time to format our résumé perfectly, but not all word documents transfer easily into online résumé submission programs. The Ontario Council of Agencies Serving Immigrants has placed some very good information on their website at http://www.settlement.org/sys/faqs_detail.asp?faq_id=4000254. Three job search experts recommend you learn how to create your résumé in plain text, e-mail, and scannable formats in addition to the word processed format (Dikel, Ireland, & Joyce 2009). There are also links to the *Riley Guide: Résumés & Cover Letters* (Dikel, 2009b), *How to Job Search* (Dikel, 2009a), and other great information for applying online.

Contacting the Organizations after Applying

Two common questions heard from students are: "If I have not heard from an organization, how long do I wait before contacting them?" and "How often and how should I contact them?" First of all, review the position announcement. Make sure calls are accepted about the position. Calling individuals or organizations when there are specific directions not to call can be disastrous. We mentioned earlier that paying attention to detail is important and this is one situation where making an error can take you out of the running for a position. Make sure you read job announcements and follow the information in them explicitly.

In Figure 7.1, paragraph three indicated the applicant would contact the organization within two weeks. This is a good length of time to first contact an organization after applying. This inquiry is primarily to ensure your materials were received, but it may not hurt to ask when top candidates may be contacted or when interviews may be conducted.

INTERVIEWING

Advance Planning

Interviewing for any job can be a nerve racking experience. Advance planning, though, can decrease or even eliminate the feelings of anxiety. The key to creating a successful experience that allows the interviewee to control a great deal of the environment is preparation. You have already done some of the work by developing a notebook with all of the position announcements as recommended earlier in this chapter. Now you have been contacted for an interview.

Do your homework! Your first step is to review the position announcement and refresh your memory. Second, go to the organization's website and study it intensely. Learn as much as you can about the organization. Of particular importance is studying the organizational chart if one is available. At the very least, find a staff directory and try to learn as many names and position titles as possible. Definitely, concentrate on finding the individual(s) who might be meeting you at the airport, with whom you may be sharing a meal, and any individuals who you will most likely meet during the interview process.

Another place to find information about the organization would be within the pages of the *Sports Business Journal, Athletic Business*, the *NCAA*

News, or any other trade journal linked to the particular position for which you are interviewing. Besides journals, many professional associations have newsletters that highlight news, awards, and other information about organizations and individuals. If these newsletters are online and do not require a membership, information about an individual might be found by conducting a name search. Googling an individual also may raise information about personal news items or accolades. Perhaps they have their own website. Try to find about impending facility projects, spectator attendance, an organization's bottom line, and more. Regardless, your goal is to find as much information about the organization and its employees as possible and arm yourself with critical information that may be asked in an interview.

The Interview Week Has Arrived

What you do during the week, and especially the two to three days before the interview, can also make or break your chances of being hired. We already discussed some elements of professional dress and hygiene earlier in the chapter. Now is the time to make sure your clothes are neatly pressed and you have everything you need. Depending on the position for which you are interviewing, you may want to have a portfolio neatly prepared with work you have completed. These can be sample press releases, that risk management project you completed, or at least portions thereof, and anything else that represents the type of work of which you are capable.

Mock Interviews. If you have not already participated in a mock interview, now would be a great time to initiate a practice interview with family members or professionals on campus. A campus career office can probably assist. Individuals who have been employed and have experience in interviewing can provide you with a realistic situation and professional feedback on your performance. Supply anyone assisting you with a copy of the job description and your résumé in advance. Websites exist that present a set of commonly asked questions in a job interview. Type "mock interview questions" into an internet search to find some sites. Most provide you with solid answers for specific questions, but some of these internet sites, have questions related to a sport business. Appendix C presents extensive lists of interview questions categorized by industry segment to assist in interview preparation.

Preparing Questions for the Interview. Prepare intelligent questions to ask during the interview. Most interviewers will make sure the interviewee has time to ask questions. Some interviewers do this on purpose to see what type of planning the applicant has done in advance. The quality of the question is extremely important. This is a tough situation because it is possible the interviewers will have answered every question one prepared during the interview. Questions that deal with the organization's strategic plan including mission, vision, and goals are often very good topical areas particularly if these have not been addressed in the interview. Top level managers love discussing their organization's mission and vision. Just make sure your questions are honest and sincere and that you can intelligently respond if they follow up with questions for you. Appendix C also has a set of questions to ask interviewers or to prompt one's thinking when developing questions more applicable to the specific organization with which you will interview.

Some questions you may not want to ask. Information about company benefits may be readily available on a company website. Asking questions about a topic that can be found on their website may send a message one is not adequately prepared. A question about benefits is best addressed when you have been offered the position. Asking about vacation time and sick days does not display an approach that focuses on work ethic but rather how much time off you get from the organization.

Another approach to developing solid questions is to exhibit that you did your homework. For example:

> "I noticed on your website that your organization recently secured a sponsorship with NIKE. The marketing project I completed for my degree focused on NIKE. Will the person being hired for this position have a chance to work with and learn from the individual responsible for monitoring the satisfaction levels of the client?"

Besides showing preparation for the interview and knowledge about the organization, it also shows that you are anxious to work with, assist, and learn from individuals tied to this project. It does not show arrogance that you will want to come in and take over the project. Obviously, here, the position for which the applicant applied would be tied to marketing or sponsorship sales.

There are two more points we need to convey that are applicable to the sport industry, whether writing a cover letter or résumé or during an interview. First, never tell an organization you are a fan of their team. This is a turnoff for many managers because, when working for an organization, you may have very little time to actually watch an event. This raises a red flag and may eliminate you from consideration. Reconciling tickets, taking care of facility problems, or handling other situations not near the actual event, are typical responsibilities.

Second, be careful of how much you praise the organization in an interview or a cover letter. Some refer to this as fluff. Praising a particular aspect of the organization in an interview on one occasion, depending on the topic, is usually appropriate. Continuous accolades might be considered overkill and may be received as insincere in hopes of simply getting the job.

The Interview Location. Make sure you know the exact date, time, and location down to the room number if interviewing in a large building home to many businesses. If the interview is local and you have never been to the facility, take the time the day before the interview to scope out traffic and directions, find the building and locate the room or general area without being too conspicuous. This preparation will prevent you from having to concentrate on one more thing or risk being late when you should be thinking about the interview itself. On the day of the interview, plan to arrive at least ten to fifteen minutes early to the parking lot and arrive at least five minutes early to the actual interview location at the reception desk or designated interview area.

If the interview is not local and you will be renting a car, arrive the day before in plenty of time to prepare as recommended in the previous paragraph. It is even more crucial if you have never been to the city. Having maps and directions or a portable global positioning system (GPS) will ease this task, but do not rely on these tools being absolutely correct. Still arrive in plenty of time the day of the interview in order to find the interview site.

Always carry with you the phone number or numbers of individuals who you will be meeting. Just in case something unexpected happens over which you had no control, you will be able to call the individual and alert them to the situation. Make sure it was something under which you had no control. Just being late because traffic was too thick or you got lost are not acceptable excuses in this situation. You want to send a mes-

When traveling for an interview, arriving early and finding the interview loca-tion in advance are extremely important, especially when the interview will be conducted in a place such as Disney's Magic Kingdom, where the magni-tude of the grounds could make locating the interview area more difficult.

sage to the interviewers that you are calm and well prepared. On time ar-rival sends this type of message. Remember, on time means at least five minutes early!

One of the toughest questions for a prospective intern or entry level applicant to ask when the interview offer is extended is whether the host organization will reimburse the applicant for interview expenses, espe-cially if a plane fare and hotel expenses are involved. It is definitely okay to ask the question if presented in a very tactful manner. For example: "Will I be reimbursed for my expenses?" Dependent upon the answer, the interviewee can accept or decline the interview, but if this is a posi-tion you really want, we recommend finding a way to finance the trip if the organization does not plan on paying expenses.

Listening and Answering Questions. During the actual interview, lis-ten very well to the interview question being asked. Let the interviewer finish the question before you start your answer. It is okay to pause a few seconds and gather your thoughts to completely and confidently answer the question. If you do not understand a question, ask the interviewer to rephrase or explain some aspect of the question. However, you do not want to do this for numerous questions. With advance preparation, most questions can be answered with ease, but do not monopolize the inter-viewer's time by doing most of the talking.

The Phone Interview. Some organizations offer phone interviews, especially for interns who have little money to pay for expensive travel. One should prepare in the same manner as they would for an on-site experience. It is even recommended to dress up for this experience to understand the interview is as important as one taking place face-to-face. Many will not go to this length. The key thing to remember is your approach and preparation for this type of interview is no less critical.

Voice intonations are also important. Record yourself to see how you sound over the phone. If you come across as monotone or have very little change in the sound of your voice, you may not be portraying your personality to the interviewer, something you can do more easily in a face-to-face interview. Since the interviewer cannot see facial expressions, it is important to display an upbeat and positive approach through voice tone and even humor when and if appropriate.

THE FINAL BUZZER

Serious consideration must be given to the selection of an appropriate internship experience. In this chapter, we have attempted to provide the student with enough resources and information to present oneself in the utmost professional manner and to assist in making the absolute best decisions for a successful internship experience. The student must pursue the internship with diligence and knowledge and have reasonable expectations for the final outcome. Application for several internships may be necessary due to the competition among the agencies to recruit the very best personnel and the number of individuals pursuing sport business industry internships. The student that has prepared themselves throughout their educational career should have little trouble securing a quality internship provided they adhere to the start early mentality, utilize the six Ps from Chapter 6, and apply the information presented in this chapter.

The internship is likened to a "golden egg" and, when properly nurtured and hatched, it can grow into the most beautiful and rewarding learning experience leading to a lifetime of career successes. Truly, a dream come true—a career in the management and business of sport!

Classroom Experiential Learning Exercise

UNDERSTANDING THE WORK ENVIRONMENT

Senior Seminar (Company in Practice) is designed to present an environment that provides a transition from the classroom to the boardroom. Each class will be run as a staff meeting where students will represent the following departments: Management, Human Resources, Marketing, Sport (amateur, professional, international), Media, and Finance. You are required to read the *Sports Business Journal, In Search of Ethics* (required texts), and other media resources regularly as a preparatory requirement for "staff" meetings and are expected to display professional behavior. This includes arriving to work on time prepared for the "meetings" and to offer insights and thoughts drawing from your four years of undergraduate learning. Staff projects will be assigned and special projects may arise. We will investigate the total industry using current events and issues and apply theoretic solutions. Staff meetings will include strategic planning and problem solving.

Submitted by Sandra Slabik, Professor & Program Director
Neumann University, Aston, Pennsylvania

Program Experiential Learning Example

STUDENT MENTORING

The University of San Francisco holds a class internship meeting where older students meet with younger students. The older students give a short presentation on how they have worked their way into the sport business industry. Successes, failures, pitfalls, and more are presented to provide ideas, connections, work expectations, and to establish an aura of self-confidence when pursuing their first experiential learning arrangement.

Submitted by Dr. Daniel A. Rascher
Director of Academic Programs & Professor

8

Networking: Establishing Internship Relationships

"Networking is critical to one's success within the realm of sports business. Possessing excellent skills in this area can lead to opportunities seen and unseen. The value of establishing and cultivating networking relationships cannot be overstated."

—Cameron O'Connell
Marketing Services Coordinator
Ironman World Headquarters

THE WARM UP

In several earlier chapters, we introduced the concept of networking. In this chapter, we will delve deeper into networking as a professional art form. It is crucial in this industry. New employees are hired based on a colleague's recommendation. People know people; they may call colleagues working in another organization or country. It is extremely important students thoroughly understand networking and not simply rely on the contacts of a faculty member.

NETWORKING DEFINED

Networking is a professional skill utilized to meet industry professionals for a variety of reasons. It is a way to meet individuals with whom you want to do business, but it also provides an avenue for meeting individuals who might be hiring or who work for a particular organization. This is a skill that should be learned early and learned well. While some individuals will make mistakes in their attempts to network with busy professionals, some networking skills take practice. In the following sections, the authors provide valuable networking information and common pitfalls to avoid.

Networking can take several forms. Telephone, e-mail, blogging, socials, social media sites, planned meetings, mentor relationships, attendance at conferences, and chance meetings all provide networking opportunities. Used appropriately, networking can mean an immediate job offer or it can lay the groundwork for future possibilities. Even so, it must be done properly or it can actually turn individuals away.

STUDENT ROLE

Just as a student is responsible for beginning their volunteer experiences as soon as they step foot on their college campus, so, too, are they responsible for beginning the development of their network. We realize some students are more outgoing than others. Perfecting one's networking skills decreases the time others must spend assisting with an experiential learning placement opportunity and increases employment possibilities. Though some institutions will provide volunteer opportunities and insist on placing students in apprenticeships or practica, often a student's contacts can be just as valuable in fulfilling their experiential learning needs.

A faculty member cannot find placements for every single student from a practical standpoint. Students have unique career goals, varied skills, and differing personalities. One organization might be a perfect fit for one student but may not be even a close fit for another. Even faculty members with an extensive network of professionals working in sport business may not know of a placement within a specific industry segment every single academic term. Thus, it is imperative for students to begin early in establishing a network and continue to build it throughout their academic careers. As discussed in earlier chapters, this can be done in a variety of ways found throughout the Foster Five-Step Experiential Learning Model. For a review of this model, please revisit Chapter 1.

From a legal perspective, liability is often transferred to a student when an institutional policy prohibits a faculty member from placing or requiring a student to work with a specific organization. In this situation, the student assumes the risk for accepting a placement with a particular industry. One example of this is *Nova Southeastern University, Inc. vs. Gross* (2000); (Foster & Moorman, 2001). Nova Southeastern, a private university was named in a lawsuit for the placement of an intern in what was determined to be an unsafe area of town. Where a policy exists that prohibits institutional control over placement, a faculty member can still provide information about available experiential learning opportunities. It is up to the student to take action and contact the appropriate individuals or apply to intern with the organization through the appropriate channels.

FACULTY ROLE

In sport business, a faculty member has many opportunities through conferences, meetings, field trips, and invited guest speakers to expose and introduce students to industry professionals. Every academic year brings new opportunities to search for individuals in different industry segments and involve them in the academic setting or program. Faculty members can also volunteer to work events to further extend professional networks.

A wide network still does not guarantee an internship placement for any student. Organizations go through periods where no interns are needed or may have accepted an intern from another institution. Seasonality, as previously discussed, may vary internship needs at different times of the year.

Students benefit from a faculty members' network early in an academic career. This is especially true when finding volunteer opportunities for freshman or recommending an organization to a student for a summer position or apprenticeship. When students work on developing their own networks, the pressure is removed from the faculty member to provide a perfect fit for student placements and students begin to establish professional independence.

TAKING ADVANTAGE OF OPPORTUNITY

Cities, counties, and university campuses always have opportunities for a sport business student to build a professional résumé and expand a network. Campus sport management programs and student associations often search for special events where a student can play a role and gain valuable experience. One can never know who they may meet or what type of responsibility they may be given simply by working a sporting event, regardless of its size or impact. Even if you have built a solid résumé, the very next person one greets at the next event may be the all-important owner or business person who will offer that chance of a lifetime!

Volunteering to work any sporting event, small or large, is a recommended opportunity for anyone preparing for a career in the sport business industry. (Courtesy of Susan Foster)

Sometimes a particular reporting time such as 6 a.m. may deter a student from accepting an early morning responsibility. A Super Bowl work day can begin as early as 4:00 in the morning. The Super Bowl, a divisional playoff, and a professional golf tournament are examples of events that happen once a year and, sometimes, once in a lifetime. Foregoing this fantastic opportunity to gain experience and meet the professionals working the events or organizations may be a colossal missed opportunity; the sad closure to this example is that the individual who chose the preferred social event will never realize the professional opportunities that may have been missed.

Many experiential learning opportunities turn into a full-time internship or entry level employment. It is not uncommon. However, it often happens to very-involved individuals especially if extra effort was expended. For example, one student served an apprenticeship with a minor league team during the summer between the sophomore and junior year. The apprenticeship required him to work alongside the Director of Concessions. When it came to serve his senior culminating internship, the student was offered the position as Director of Concessions and, upon graduation, was employed full-time by the same organization. The student never planned on entering the food services arm of minor league baseball, but the opportunity offered him entry into the sport business industry. Ultimately, he moved into sports media. Yes, an unlikely path, but nevertheless, full-time employment within the industry of his choice. This is confirmation of Bernie Mullins' identification of career paths as a unique parameter of the sport business industry discussed earlier in the book.

THE ART OF NETWORKING

We have addressed networking in several different ways in this book. However, we have not provided a step-by-step strategic plan for assisting the novice. Examples below will cultivate ideas and, hopefully, motivate even the most timid individual in starting a professional network.

Getting Started

Networking can be affirmed as an art for meeting people. We mentioned earlier that networking is difficult for some individuals. As with many things, one gets better with practice. We recommend a variety of pathways to establishing one's own professional network.

Observing how others network is a great place to start. Once different outward methods of networking have been scrutinized, it is time to embark on the development of a personal networking style. If meeting people for the first time is uncomfortable, begin by writing an introductory letter to a particular professional in the industry. This person might be someone who spoke in a sport foundations course and invited students to contact them. This letter can simply be an opportunity to introduce yourself and your desire to tour the organization's facility or to conduct an informational interview, as discussed later in this section. The worst that can happen is that you do not hear back, a sad display of professionalism especially since the individual invited students to contact them. However, you are more likely than not to get a positive response.

Perhaps you have a course assignment where you have to research career paths as we have done in several chapters in this book. Construct a very professional letter free of all writing errors and select a certain niche area within the industry, for example, event managers. Address a letter to each event manager in a particular league, conference, or state, personalize the letter for each person using their actual name and specific title, explain your assignment, and craft a set of questions that will satisfy your assignment's directions. Anyone can go online and find out what others say about certain positions in sport. However, there is no better research method for discovering the necessary information about a certain position than asking those who hold that position. Many professionals will respond to this type of inquiry much faster than to a newspaper interview or a researcher's survey. This is primarily because many individuals working in sport had the same dream you do, completed similar assignments, and performed an internship. Because they are living their dream of working in the sport industry, of waking up every day loving their work, they have a strong desire to help students in the same pursuit.

After the letters are sent, sit down and create additional questions you would like to ask if this individual calls you. Craft answers to questions the individual might ask you. Preparing in advance will allow you to talk to this individual in a professional manner should they pick up the phone and desire to initiate a conversation with you. Most will not have the time, but being prepared will work in your favor should the unexpected happen. Above all, write a personal thank you note to anyone who responds. Do not send a text message or an e-mail. Take the time to write a personal note free of all writing errors, and mail it in the conventional manner. As we mentioned in Chapter 6, very few people take the time to complete this step and, most often, it will leave a very favorable impression on the individual to whom it was sent. It might even change someone's mind about using your services. Maybe the very next week a position does open and it is offered to you just because you took the time to send a personal thank you.

If you feel completely comfortable in talking with these professionals, request the opportunity to schedule an informational interview, a facility tour, or perhaps a chance to shadow an individual and assist with the set-up or take-down of an event. Someone you contact will grant these types of requests. It happens more likely with those in the minor leagues or less popular sports, but do not be surprised if an extremely busy individual in a high profile position takes the time to assist in your pursuit of gaining knowledge of and experience in this industry. This was the case of the example involving Pat Summitt we used in Chapter 1.

An informational interview is not considered an interview for a job but is a great networking tool. It is a professional situation one arranges to learn more about an organization or an individual's job while exploring different career options. Working professionals are busy. Offer to take someone to lunch as, even on the busiest of days, individuals must eat. Be prepared to initiate the discussion with well-thought out questions. Most individuals will go with the flow in this type of casual atmosphere and the conversation should proceed with ease. Do not ask for a job in an informational interview; however, do bring an updated résumé just in case one is requested. Bring a nice portfolio with paper to take notes and store the résumé where it will not get bent or wrinkled. After the meeting, follow immediately with a thank you note in the mail. Individuals will appreciate the time taken to express your gratitude.

If a chance meeting results in an invitation to stay in touch, do so, but do not hound the individual. The same recommendation applies. Follow up with a letter that mentions the meeting and thank them for their time. Why a letter? Busy individuals get a bunch of e-mails. They may not recognize your name or it might get sent to their junk mail. There is a better chance they will remember you and the conversation if you remind them in a letter sent directly to them at their work location. Yes, they might get a lot of mail as well, but a personal letter might have a better chance of reaching them and getting read than an e-mail sitting in their junk box.

Demonstrate creativity! Even a student can develop a business card and use it in networking. Microsoft Word and Publisher are easy programs to use and business card paper can be purchased at office supply stores. Develop a sharp looking card with correct contact information. Be careful about using logos that may be copyrighted. When in doubt, develop your own logo or do not use one. Invest in a portable business card holder so the cards do not get creased or dirty and keep them with you at all times. When meeting individuals, some will be impressed that a student had a card. It is easier for people to maintain a card than holding onto a full résumé. A card may also help them remember you more readily. An exchange of business cards should become a standard part of your professional greetings.

Networking is not without its pitfalls. Errors can be made in networking. Listed below are a few situations to consider.

- *Do not consistently call individuals or e-mail them when given permission to do so.* Most often, many individuals in the sport industry are extremely busy and may receive hundreds of résumés in a given week or month. Respect their time. Yes, it is okay to call to follow up on a conversation, to find out if your application materials have been received or to find out the status of a job search if you have not heard from an organization within a predetermined amount of time—generally about two weeks. However, we suggest you do not pester anyone at the organization with continuous e-mails or phone calls. Some will reward

FLORIDA STATE UNIVERSITY
SPORT
MANAGEMENT

Some sport management programs sponsor conferences for students and invite a variety of speakers for student networking. (Courtesy of Susan Foster)

those who conduct simple follow-ups and perceive these contact attempts as a measure of assertiveness, a trait organizations want in a candidate.

• While we mentioned attendance at conferences as a preparation tool in a previous chapter, attending conferences or job fairs, for the main purpose of meeting individuals, is one of the best ways to position oneself to promote your background, professional goals, and skills. Some individuals actually go too far and "stalk" a certain individual in hopes of getting a personal interview. Chance meetings can happen in an elevator or at a drinking establishment; be prepared for those types of situations with what some call a 30-second "elevator pitch," but do not monopolize an individual's time or conversation by prolonging the chance meeting. One can usually tell if that individual wants to prolong the meeting by asking additional questions and showing a true interest.

• Job fairs and conferences afford job seekers an opportunity to mingle with industry professionals at a social or in a bar. Regardless of the site, these events are not the time to drink a lot of alcohol. Yes, if one is of legal drinking age, it is okay to have one or two drinks dependent upon the situation. Erring on the side of caution and not drinking at all is the best recommendation if one is unsure.

- If you make any promises during a networking experience, follow through. If a promise to send an e-mail or to make a certain phone call is given, do it by the day or time promised. The individual may be testing you!

Improving Your Networking Skills

You are pursuing Step 2 of the Five-Step Experiential Learning Model, the apprenticeship. You *can* take the broad approach explained in the previous section where you wrote letters to a variety of individuals hoping one or more will respond, but it is time to practice a more direct approach. Do not wait until one or two weeks before your institutional assigned deadline to approach a specific individual and confirm an apprenticeship offer. Select an organization and an individual in a position for whom you wish to work. Draft an introductory comment before you dial the phone just in case you are able to talk with them on your first call. Know what you want to say and how you want to say it, but do not read it off a sheet of paper. Many can tell when you are doing this. Get a faculty member to help you draft some questions or advise you as to how best to introduce yourself. Make the call. Many times you will be asked to leave a message. It is our recommendation, if this happens, to follow-up your phone call with an e-mail that is very clear regarding the purpose of your call. It is also suggested you not use a cell phone when making these important calls. You may believe your cell has great coverage and messages you leave are not garbled, but one can never be sure. Land lines are the best option to ensure your message is clear and that all information is received.

By starting your pursuit early to fulfill Step 2, in all probability, you will be able to find an apprenticeship or summer paid position to satisfy your academic requirement and more than satisfy your need for professional growth. When starting late in the process, often a student has to accept just anything that becomes available when, in reality, they know the opportunity offered to them would not have been their first choice. Even if you must accept a less than ideal choice for you, you never know how that decision can change your life and your path for entering the industry. Make sure you make the most of any opportunity afforded you. Approach it with a positive outlook and an open mind that you will learn everything possible and be the best apprentice the organization has ever had. Even if you do not end up liking the position or the responsibilities, your co-workers will not be able to tell and you will come away with great recommendations to utilize for your future internship search. Oh, and did we mention, after you leave, follow it up with a personal thank you letter to your site supervisor, boss, or anyone with whom you worked, even those who may not have been 100% in your corner?

Do not be disheartened if the first individual contacted does not respond. Move on to the second person on a list you have created of potential worksites and professionals to contact. Not getting a response most likely has nothing to do with you. Perhaps that individual has moved to another organization or is going to be moving on and cannot yet announce the move. Yes, they might just be displaying poor ethics or professionalism by not responding even if only to tell you they cannot accept your services at this time. Maintain your positive outlook and the confidence you now have in your abilities to network.

One never reaches ultimate perfection in networking. Yes, some individuals are very good at it, but even the most accomplished networker will tell you they can always find a better approach or a more creative way to ask a question. Many will tell you there was that thank you letter they never wrote. With social media outlets increasing and the opportunity it affords individuals to meet or stay in touch with colleagues they knew ten or more years ago, this is another avenue where even the most accomplished networker can learn and hone this important skill. Oh, and did we mention to take the time to say thank you to individuals who offer comments or words of encouragement on these social networking sites? This time, it is OK to e-mail them because, chances are, you do not have their mailing address or would not be able to find it without asking them directly.

THE FINAL BUZZER

Hopefully, this chapter will assist anyone, even the most apprehensive individual, in improving their networking skills. We challenge you to come up with a networking exercise or event not presented anywhere in this book and introduce it at one of your on campus sport management association or other group meetings you attend. You will not only be able to get feedback on your networking skills, but you can assist fellow students in honing their networking abilities. Remember that every one of your fellow classmates represents a network connection, as each of you are pursuing your individual paths in the same industry.

We have constantly reinforced the practice of saying thank you in this chapter. We cannot emphasize enough the importance of this simple practice, a networking exercise in and of itself, and the effect it can have on the individual at the receiving end. Though this practice is, in actuality, an act of paying back the good deeds of another, it can truly end up being a practice of paying it forward, just as in the practices established by the young boy in the movie *Pay it Forward* (McLaglen, Treisman, & Leder, 2000). However, no expectations should accompany the thank you. Send a thank you today to someone that has assisted you! Surprise a current faculty member, a mentor, a family member, a high school teacher, or coach!

The intent of this chapter, to discuss networking in depth, was presented to emphasize the importance of learning the art of networking early so the pursuit of finding the culminating internship, Step 5 in the Experiential Learning Model, results in a less complicated endeavor. Remember, your ultimate goal, presented earlier in this book, is to have a full-time job in the industry on graduation day! Icing on the cake is having the offer extended as a result of the internship, thus eliminating the job search process.

Classroom Experiential Learning Exercise

COMBINING CLASS PROJECTS WITH NETWORKING

You are assigned to submit a bid to host the International Special Olympics using the bid format provided by Special Olympics International. After developing the bid proposal, your group will have 30 minutes to present followed by a ten-minute question and answer period. All presentations must include a webpage or PowerPoint and audio. Video and charts/graphs are encouraged, but not required. Your goal is to be awarded the bid and each presentation will be judged on the professionalism of the group and the ability to convince the judges that their city will be the best host for the event. Sell your city's strengths and address any weaknesses during the presentation. You may use the following site http://www.games bids.com/english/bids/2014.shtml and pay particular attention to Candidate Procedure, Part 2 IOC Questionnaire on page 66.

After the assignment is completed, individuals from the Greater Cleveland Sports Commission will visit the class and compare their actual bid to yours. This will give you a chance to meet, network, and discuss the bid process with sport managers.

Submitted by Dr. James Thoma, Director of Sport Business & Associate Dean
Mount Union College, Alliance, Ohio

Program Experiential Learning Example

PROGRAM NETWORKING

Georgia Southern University hosts a well-attended sport management conference every year during the spring semester. In planning for that event, their sport management club leadership attends some planning meetings. The club also provides one student host for each speaker. The student hosts spend two days networking one-on-one with their assigned speaker. They transport the speaker to and from the hotel and to the different conference rooms where the speaker is scheduled to appear. The club also works many events throughout the year. These events have included the Orange Bowl, the Super Bowl, golf tournaments, NASCAR events, and Jacksonville Jaguar games. Thus, the students have many opportunities to engage in networking.

Submitted by Dr. Willie Burden, Associate Professor
Statesboro, Georgia

9

Ending an Internship and Starting a New Position

"As the intern enters the work force, it is essential to develop and nurture the skill sets that are in alignment with the prospective position. Furthermore, the intern must be cognizant of the competitive nature of those entering the work force and demonstrate the skill sets and the people skills that will set them aside from other applicants."

Barry Mestel
President, Winning Ways Sport Management, Inc.
Winning Ways Pro International, Inc.

THE WARM UP

Congratulations! Successfully completing an internship and graduating with any academic degree is an outstanding milestone. How you finish an internship and start a new position is vitally important. Both of these situations lend themselves to important ways for handling both. The sections below will explain in more detail.

REQUESTING ADDITIONAL RESPONSIBILITY

If you have not already done so, during the last weeks of an internship, ask for additional responsibility. You understand your capabilities; you are comfortable with the work environment, and you want to learn and do more.

One of the most prolific efforts put forth by a student intern to enhance the quality of the internship, is that of seeking additional responsibilities. Interns have plenty to do some of the time; conversely, there can be down time between projects or assignments. Interns also become very familiar with their work environment and have a keener awareness of where their skills complement an unmet need within the organization. In these situations, ask for additional assignments, propose a plan to fill the unmet need, or go above and beyond on even the smallest of tasks. Perhaps you will be running an errand or delivering a finished product and will be able to further coordinate the movement of the product beyond what is expected. The little bit of extra effort expended to get the item one step above your destination, to upper level management, can make a difference in just being an intern or being an exceptional intern. The following story will illustrate this point.

An undergraduate student was serving an internship with a major league baseball team in one of the southern states. The student intern was working on a group project in early spring, and the agency had not completed its hiring for the upcoming season. The project was a major marketing effort requiring coordination between three in-house departments of the agency. The organization had one coordinator on staff, but hiring efforts had not yet filled two additional coordinator positions for the project. The student intern was very proficient and detail-oriented in her work efforts. Before long, she was moving the information and project items between the three separate departments working on the project. The coordinator and the intern were able to get the marketing project completed ahead of time, and it was a huge success for the team. The internship supervisor for the agency called the sponsoring university program coordinator and requested the student intern be hired before the completion of her internship, all based upon her work efforts and commitment to the organization. Yes, the project required overtime on the part of the intern (four separate 70+ hour weeks), as well as functioning with three supervisors instead of one, but consider the payoff. She started at the agency with a $32,000 salary in a job she basically designed for herself! Needless to say, the agency did not bother to re-hire for the two open coordinator positions. True story!

Similar opportunities may not always be available in an internship. In this setting, it was the young lady's diligence and willingness to go the extra mile that made a difference. She did not act out of self interest; on the contrary, her actions were to make the workload easier for the organization. She simply assumed additional responsibility to make a situation better for all of the workers involved. This was simply maximizing the purpose of the internship experience and providing a win-win result for all involved parties.

COMPLETING AN INTERNSHIP

One of the biggest mistakes we have seen students make is leaving an internship relationship inappropriately or without any intent to continue networking with individuals within an organization. Just because one is not hired full-time does not mean your contributions were not valued and the colleagues do not want to maintain contact. Hopefully, full-time employees extend to you the appropriate gratitude and well-wishes for success and a desire to maintain communication. However, this does not always happen.

We will assume you did a great job in the internship and, if so, several individuals will be willing to write a letter of recommendation and allow you to retain them as a reference on your résumé. Accept these offers graciously. In return, never list an individual as a reference for a position unless you send them a copy of any positions to which you apply along with an updated résumé. If significant time has passed, before you list them as reference, contact them and ask their permission. It can be very frustrating for an individual serving as a reference to get an e-mail or phone call out of the

Graduation is a grand milestone, but only the beginning of an exciting career in sport business. (Courtesy of Saint Leo University)

blue indicating a particular person has listed them as a reference, while not having all of the necessary information in advance. Additionally, it does not allow a reference to give you the best possible recommendation because they are unfamiliar with recent responsibilities. They are unaware of the requirements of the position for which you are applying and cannot attest, in the best possible way, to how your skills meet those requirements. An individual serving as a reference is devoting time from their own very busy work schedule when a letter of recommendation is required; respond with gratitude and provide as much information as possible before they are contacted by the organization. After you leave your institution or an organization, maintain contact with former professors and coworkers. You never know what can become of this continuous networking opportunity.

If, by chance, your internship presented a rocky road or you are not leaving on the best of terms with some of your coworkers, in your last weeks of the internship, do anything possible to show the organization your best work. Make every attempt to smooth any bumps that may remain. It is immensely important to leave on a positive note. Perhaps you made some mistakes in how you communicated or worked with one particular person. Take time and make the effort before you leave to apologize and show gratitude for their assistance helping you to grow as a professional. Any extensions of appreciation will be observed positively and that is the impression you want to leave with the organization. Ignore the often heard saying, "Apologizing is a sign of weakness." This is not true, especially in networking and creating relationships.

The same is true when you are applying for internships or graduating and leaving your university. Depart on great terms with all of your professors and individuals for whom you may have worked. Professors are the first individuals an organization might contact for a recommendation, especially if they are well-known by one or more employees within that organization. Also, not listing a professor from an institution that is well known may work against an applicant, particularly if the professor has a good track record of recommending outstanding interns and employees.

SALARIES TO EXPECT

Your work as an intern may be limited to an uncompensated internship. Paid internships can certainly be found and those who receive any form of compensation during the internship are very fortunate. Upon completion of the internship, one should graduate to an entry-level working position. In times of a tough economy when organizations may not be hiring full-time employees, accepting another internship might be necessary. However, we would not recommend consenting to another unpaid position. Although this can vary, repayment of student loans generally start within six months after a degree is completed and some income will be important. Likewise, we do not advocate leaving the industry to take a full-time paying position if a career in the industry is truly the goal. When you have lost daily contact with a network of sport professionals, it is much tougher to get back into the industry. If you have no full-time career offers and are in a paid internship, strongly consider staying in that position after you graduate if the opportunity is extended.

Should you remain at the internship site and your position is converted into a paying job, you may have the opportunity to negotiate your initial salary. Some agencies may not have an open position available immediately and will offer to pay an hourly wage to keep you on board. The individual would have to make that decision at the appropriate time and should weigh such factors as the actual wage amount, any benefits associated with employment, and the expected length of time until a salaried opportunity becomes available. Basically, if you optimized your required internship time at the site (usually 400–500 hours per semester for the undergraduate intern) and maximized your experiential learning opportunities within the organization, you may be qualified to be hired at the entry level. After all, you now have several months of on-the-job training with the organization. If the agency has no positions available for you, there are other organizations that would be interested in offering you a career position. Some agencies will not train and teach you their respective "secrets" and then turn you away to work for the competition. This is the beauty of the internship process; if done well, you can, more than likely, expect an offer for employment if any positions are available.

So how much is one to expect in the form of salary and compensation? Entry level positions are on the low rung of the pay scale ladder. With your degree in hand, you can expect to start in the sport industry anywhere from $23,000–$35,000 a year, plus benefits. Even when entering the field with a master's degree, the salary can be the same. These entry level rates are especially true in professional team sport organizations. Because there are so many individuals hoping to enter sport business through professional sport, the law of supply and demand is quite applicable. Teams can offer low salaries and be assured they will find a qualified applicant who will jump at the chance. Salaries for sales jobs may even be lower, but many offer a commission based on individual sales. Additionally, basic perks are often given to all employees regardless of position title. Tickets for your family and friends and logo clothing are common.

Salaries in other industry segments will vary based on several factors. We mentioned some of these factors in earlier chapters. Private and public sector salaries may differ. Any entrepreneurial business that requires you to earn income for the organization may offer higher income with the expectation that the employee will recoup that income through their position. An example would be in sport marketing where the procurement of corporate sponsors is part of the job description. Of course, the higher salary may also come in the form of a commission based on the size of the contract. Five percent on a $1 million dollar sponsorship deal is a hefty payday! Starting salaries in recreational sport management and athletic administration often pay more than an entry level position in professional sport, however, a master's degree is often a prerequisite for entry. In 2009, the average salary for an intramural sport employee with less than five years of experience was $37,413 (NIRSA, 2009).

After you have proven yourself, promotions would gradually increase your salary. Looking for positions with other organizations is a common way to gain promotions and achieve salary increases. Other organizations will have openings. Perhaps your organization is top-heavy where individuals with families feel very comfortable and choose not to move a family or seek out a move up the corporate ladder.

As you climb the corporate ladder in sport business, additional perks may accompany upward mobility in most sport organizations and agencies. Upper management positions may include company phones, a company car, an expense account, and a travel budget. Because you are working with a sport organization, a variety of sport-related perks may be offered. Access to the owner's suite, additional tickets, and signature memorabilia and equipment are common. Trips to championship or special events that may include family are also considerations.

Usually the pay scale is directly proportionate to the length of employment time and the quality of job performance and few positions, if any, in the sport industry will pay an employee for little or no work. Accepting the realization early that to be successful in the sport industry, or in any industry, and remain employed, long hours and producing a profit or added value to the agency is a necessity. It will help immensely if you have a passion for this type of work!

YOUR NEW POSITION IN SPORT BUSINESS

Congratulations! Your hard work has paid off and you have taken the first step into what can be a long and very satisfactory journey—your career in the sport business industry! Welcome to an industry where individuals wake up each day loving their work and are enthused about tackling a new sponsorship proposal or the opportunity to initiate the registration process for a new youth league. A career in sport business, in many instances, is different each day; the uncertainty of the outcome of a game or event where new challenges and rewarding outcomes result are often the ingredients for an exciting career. Carpé diem! Seize the day!

We could have ended the book before this chapter, but we would have been remiss in leading you to believe your work is done. A career in sport now becomes a series of experiential learning opportunities that can lead you to promotions, new directions, and new geographical regions of the United States, as well as internationally. Sport is ever expanding and the globalization of sport will continue to reach even the most remote areas of the world. What you do in your first full-time position can define your career. Aiding you in the realization that seizing every opportunity to make those experiences the most rewarding possible is the intent of this chapter.

Your First Week

A great way to approach one's first position in this industry is to perceive it as a training ground for your next promotion. During your first week, in most instances, you will be meeting many people. As everyone knows, first impressions are important. Take interest in those introductions and the work of your colleagues. Show an enthusiastic interest in their work responsibilities and learn how your tasks will serve or impact their work as you become an integral part of the organization's team environment.

The faster you learn everyone's first name and their role, the more impressed your colleagues will become. It will also aid you in communicating with colleagues and enhance your productivity and, perhaps, that of your coworkers.

Establishing Positive Work Habits

During the first few months in a new position, the importance of establishing positive work habits cannot be overemphasized. However, nothing we recommend should come across as a surprise as these work habits should already be part of the positive work ethic shown throughout the internship.

Arriving at least five to ten minutes before the organization's start time is recommended. This means arriving early enough so you are at your work station and beginning work at the designated time. If a meeting is scheduled, you are at the meeting with necessary writing materials and your full attention given to the meeting manager. There is nothing more frustrating to a supervisor than to have a meeting scheduled for an allotted time in the day and then have key individuals arrive late and unprepared. The meeting then becomes abbreviated and rushed, in order to maintain the remaining daily agendas. As a result, the productivity of colleagues and the group as a whole is diminished. In fact, late arrival by some often dictates the need for additional meetings—something nobody likes.

As in the internship, you are also not darting out the door at the designated end of the work day. Yes, there will be times where family or outside event interests will determine a need to depart quickly on occasion, but professionals ensure that a project the boss needs at the very start of the next work day is completed and ready for delivery before they leave the office. In fact, it is a very good practice to get projects completed and submitted in advance. If by chance, your supervisor wants to change a component or requests additional material, you then will still have plenty of time to complete the additional requests long before the original deadline. Quality work is best completed well in advance, allowing time to proofread, to review the requirements requested, and to add the finishing touches to enhance the project. The finished product will produce evidence of the quality time and effort taken to complete the work, and your supervisor will notice even if nothing is communicated.

Yes, additional work is often assigned to an individual who completes projects in a timely manner with exceptional quality. Sometimes, within your particular work environment, it might appear that more work is coming your way as compared to the amount being sent to your colleagues. While this can be true, it can also mean your supervisor respects your work and, when it comes to that important promotion you are pursuing, it is quite possible you will be at the top of the considered list. If your organization is looking to release workers because of low ticket sales, tough economic times, or a redirection of the organization's mission and vision, a supervisor would be remiss if they dismissed you even if you were the most recent hire. Obviously, there are no guarantees and the seniority of other workers may work against you. Even if you are released for one of the reasons above, your supervisor should be more than willing to provide an outstanding reference for another organization.

Office Etiquette and Rules

Arriving for the work day and meetings on time, as previously mentioned, is just one element of proper office etiquette. This practice also shows respect for all others in your work environment. However, there are often more rules, manners, and protocol for proper office etiquette.

It is not appropriate to utilize office supplies, letterhead, or company postage for personal uses. Nor is it appropriate to surf the internet, send personal e-mails, or make personal phone calls, especially long distance ones, on company time. All of this can allow a supervisor to charge an individual with inappropriate use of company resources which can be grounds for dismissal. If you ask permission from your supervisor and it is granted, then it is probably okay, but having it in writing via an e-mail, memorandum, or in some other format is recommended. Save this correspondence. Nevertheless, the best recommendation is to not use any organizational resources for personal needs.

Participating in office gossip is, first and foremost, a practice in which one should never participate. It is of particular importance for a new hire to refrain from this practice. You are attempting to establish your professionalism and your importance to the organization. Nothing will ruin another's perception of you faster than this type of discussion at the water cooler, over lunch, or in any other environment. Sometimes, you cannot prevent someone from pulling you aside or an inappropriate topic being raised in a lunch time conversation. The best recommendation, if you cannot excuse yourself from the situation, is to simply listen and forget. At no time, should you share what you heard with anyone else. Additionally, any information you learn should not cloud your perception of a working relationship with the colleague who was the target of the possible misinformation.

Purchasing proper attire for the interview or when starting a new position is a necessary expense. (Courtesy of Dreamstime)

Professional Dress and Appearance

We spent quite a bit of time on professional dress in Chapter 7, so we will not belabor the point here. We do want to emphasize the point that private organizations can dictate office dress, facial hair policies, or any other facet applicable to appearance. It is up to you to accept those policies as a new hire. Any policy can change down the road with new management or with a relaxation of current policies.

A public organization has to pay more attention to the rights afforded individuals in state or federal constitutions. Hopefully, this was learned in a legal issues class. For example, an athletic director at a public institution, by law, should not be allowed to dictate hair length simply because of personal taste. However, such rules can be tied to a strong rationale for the establishment of such a rule. An employee can choose to comply or address the situation in another way. If no rationale for the rule can be established, the rule might be a violation of the First Amendment of the United States Constitution, specifically freedom of expression.

However, it is not our recommendation as a new employee and, perhaps, even at any other time, to challenge such rules. While it would be difficult for an employee to be dismissed based on such a rule, a supervisor can find other reasons to release an individual with no claim or a perception presented that it was tied to the employee's questioning of the rule. Plus, the rule's rationale, even if it would not be accepted by a court, is often to establish a team environment, a sense of camaraderie. When an individual attempts to go against the desires of the majority of individuals in order to promote their own self interest, the situation rarely has a positive outcome.

Listening and Observing

As a new hire, listen to others and observe as much as you can. Listening is a skill that will serve you extremely well. You are in a new setting where others probably have more experience, have worked more events, and perhaps have designed a policy or procedure that has been revamped many times over to derive certain results. While you may have worked a few events or experienced similar office or work procedures at another location, it is not in your best interest to come into a new work environment and promote another organization's process just because it worked well elsewhere. Yes, maybe your ideas might be better and may result in better productivity or a simpler process, but it is best to wait and observe until an opportunity arises where you can, very tactfully, present an alternate solution or process. Many individuals are resistant to change, especially those who have been with an organization for a long time and have tried many different ways of accomplishing a task or running an event. Respect their experience. If the solution you present is not accepted, then at least you tried.

Observing how others perform can increase the speed of your learning curve. Learn through these observances. If you show respect for the skills and abilities of coworkers through attentive listening and careful observations, eventually the same respect will be given to your performance. This is especially true when others utilize your recommendations. Coworkers will pick up on how your work, and possibly theirs, is enhanced or streamlined, resulting in a more timely result.

Being a manager may be part of a new role. Entire textbooks and majors cover human resource (HR) management; this is not the purpose of this section, but a few comments are warranted. The content of the previous paragraph is just as important if you are hired into a supervisory role. Asking, learning, and listening is an exceptional method to being accepted quickly as a new supervisor. Learn about the organization before proposing or making sweeping changes. Make a point to meet with any individuals who will be reporting to you; get to know them and their strengths. Exhibit an honest interest in each employee and trust everyone, unless someone gives you a reason to question their actions. Managing employees can be extremely rewarding, but it can also be very frustrating and time consuming if everyone is not on the same page. Trying to foster a team-oriented environment is a good approach. After all, you are working for a sport organization.

Establish an environment where each individual's background and skills are valued. Asking for input before making important decisions always invokes a sign of respect. An environment where everyone does their part to establish collegiality is important. It starts with leadership and setting an example.

Communicating With Clients: Manners and More

While many are very polite and were taught by parents at an early age all about manners, a few tips on communicating with clients are still important. Many entry level employees deal directly with clients. People expect quality customer service and poor service over the phone is one setting that can lead to contentious situations. Hopefully, your organization continually conducts training sessions with individuals who will be dealing with customers, such as would be encountered in a ticket sales position. This is not the time to be rude or return an acrimonious comment. If you are unsure of how to handle a frustrated customer, ask for assistance from your supervisor. The same is true if you are in a position where you might need to deal with parents or coaches. This is more likely to be the case if you are working in youth or high school sports. Newspapers and television have increasingly portrayed accounts of parents who address coaches and officials in an unproductive and irate manner. The National Association of Sports Officials (NASO) reportedly receives over 100 testimonies annually of incidences involving officials, coaches, players, and fans (Topp, n.d.). While most of these incidents involve violence against referees, other instances include a fourth grader filing a $10,000 lawsuit against a coach for violence during a game (Findlay, 2002), athletes versus athletes, fans versus Athletes or coaches, and parents versus coaches. Furthermore, there are probably cases of violence against league administrators or sport supervisors. The key point here is that an employee can infuse tranquility into situations involving irate individuals by calmly addressing the situation and being educated in advance on how to do so. Therefore, as a new employee of a sport organization, treat a customer, client, or coach involved in any negative or volatile situation with courtesy and respect. Curt responses to comments or conditions can result in the escalation of a situation to an unnecessary stage involving rage and anger.

Using Modern Communication with Colleagues

"Excuse me. I need to take this call." No problem, it happens all the time. Where would our society be today without the cell phone? Even when not talking on it, we juggle it, flip it, scroll it, scan it and text on it incessantly. Modern communication has come a very long way in the last twenty-five years in improving connections with the important people in our lives: family, friends, children, students, bosses, and employees. Answering emails alone consumes a large part of most people's days. We can receive emails, text messages, and videos on our phones; thus, we are available 36/8—at least it seems more than 24/7! Answering a phone or continuing to work with earphones when another individual is talking is a sign of disrespect. When a colleague is attempting to communicate, give your full attention.

Technology allows us to keep notes and running lists, schedule appointments on an interactive calendar, or command a computer from a remote location. Do we need technology to be effective in sport business? Yes, when it allows one to be more productive, decreases work hours, and increases how we effectively contend on a level playing field with the competition. When conducting business, today's technology is indispensible! However, its primary purpose must remain in focus—operating and serving a sport business agency and its clients. We discussed proper use of letterhead and office supplies in a previous section. As an intern or a new employee, the same rules apply in the use of technology. The organization may provide access to the most advanced office equipment and technology and one should follow a polite and sincere code of behavior when using that equipment and technology. The key to this code would be recognition and acknowledgement of the proper rules of use and access and restriction of usage for personal reasons, especially on company time. Many pieces of office equipment, especially in larger organizations, will have a log-on user code assigned to individuals or departments, and abuses of the equipment or sharing a personal log-on code could result in dismissal from the agency. Surfing the internet on company time for reasons unrelated to the business is discouraged. Know your parameters—maintain your boundaries and illicit use of technology in the work place can be avoided.

Respect those who despise technology; yes, some individuals would rather not use a BlackBerry® or other similar pocket size life organizer. In fact, those that feel very comfortable using the most advanced equipment on the market can be a true asset to the organization; many non-users simply may not have the time to learn. Offering to show how a computer program or a top of the line personal organizer can make one's tasks easier and faster can make you a hero! In fact, Tyrone Brooks, a Time Out interviewee in Chapter 3, indicated he was retained after the completion of an internship in baseball operations with the Braves because of his technology skills (Personal communication, February 3, 2010). Today, generations are growing up with technology usage and non-technology users will very soon be a thing of the past! But there will always be newer and more complicated equipment. As an example, we can remember teaching our professors how to use a computer! Today's generation can assist with the insertion of YouTube videos into a power point presentation. The cycle will always continue. Be patient with your colleagues who are not using the latest and greatest. One day, you may be in their shoes and will be asking for assistance from your new employees!

WHAT IF YOU ARE RELEASED BY THE ORGANIZATION?

It is recommended that a generic letter of reference not addressed to any one individual be obtained before the last day of an internship or a full-time position. It is not uncommon for a supervisor to leave the organization, as well, and sometimes it can be difficult to locate a former supervisor for a reference. Additionally, any future reference letter from that individual will not be on the respective organization's letterhead. Sometimes this is important to future employers or human resource offices.

Finally, perhaps your supervisor and you are being released. Your work habits may be the very thing the supervisor remembers when s/he moves on to another sport organization. Do not be surprised if you are contacted to come and work under that supervisor at a different organization. This is a common happening in sport business.

FINDING A MENTOR

Everyone would like an edge to help them be successful in their chosen work endeavors, especially when new to a job setting or location. You would like to find someone you can approach with questions, to help resolve a dilemma in the work setting, or from whom to occasionally seek advice when making difficult decisions. This person to whom you would go in your new work setting is known as a mentor. A **mentor** is generally an older, wiser, or more experienced individual who has worked in the industry for several years and made such an impact as to have earned an important title or name recognition. This particular person may have several additional people under his or her supervision as "under-studies," learning and experiencing training from this particular mentor. This person of high esteem usually provides important feedback for decisions, conflict resolutions, or future agency or organizational direction within the job setting. They may or may not have a legal background, but would be able to call upon vast knowledge, information, and experience in order to render a good judgment or decision. As a student, this person may have been a distinguished faculty member or major professor. In the work setting, keen observations of colleagues and the work environment will assist when choosing a mentor. Sometimes, one does not have to choose a mentor. Such a relationship can result simply from a close working relationship with a colleague or supervisor.

Mentors provide advice; weigh that advice and act appropriately in order to be effective and successful in your job. As a young employee, you want a mentor! A good mentor will ALWAYS go to bat for you whether it is in seeking a promotion, making a phone call to a colleague for an open position in another organization, or serving as a great reference. A mentor is in your corner! As you learn and grow from that mentor's example, one day, you may become a mentor for others to seek out and follow.

ORGANIZING YOUR NETWORK

Having a network of individual people upon whom you can call within the sport industry can mean the difference between the success and failure of your organization. Knowing whom to contact with an inquiry or a request for information is paramount in keeping at the forefront of competition with other similar agencies. One of the best ways to stay ahead is to organize your contacts and your method for reaching them as needed. Early in a career, practice gathering necessary information from your contacts in the industry. An imperative resource is the personal business card.

A business card is not a very expensive item if you have to purchase your own ($25–$30 per 200). It is a vital exchange item for keeping track of individuals met and introductions made within the sport industry. One could literally gather one hundred or more a year when attending seminars, symposiums, and conferences. Remember, other individuals seeking internships or employment are a valued source of networking contacts, and contact information can be hard to keep organized. One of the best methods for the necessary organization of all of the cards accumulated is to file them alphabetically by name or organization in plastic card-holder sheets with indexing tabs, generally available at a local office supply store. Based upon the number of cards, you may have a one-, two-, or three-inch ring-binder full of business cards with contact information of individuals in all sectors of the sport industry. Either alphabetized by name or agency, one can then access information needed quickly and accurately by retrieving the notebook and accessing the appropriate tab. Update the listing frequently (at least once a year), in order to maintain the most recent contact information. This prevents excessive time spent in finding information in a moment's notice for your use, a fellow student's, or another interested party's. Knowledge is power, and this technique puts the necessary knowledge at your finger-tips, literally!

Hiring a Consultant

A career coach, consultant, or a head hunter can be hired to assist in finding a job. By doing so, one may actually be extending their personal network. Career coaches or consultants may have worked with individuals within sport organizations and have a good track record of recommending quality individuals. It will cost you, but if a full-time position results, it is money well-spent. An average cost to hire a consultant can vary but most charge $125 an hour or more. Some may give package deals especially for individuals just graduating and starting in the industry. Consultants and career coaches generally do not guarantee a client a full-time position in the sport business industry. These individuals do not control the hiring practices of sport teams or organizations. Their role is to assist in preparing application documents, reviewing cover letters and résumés, making recommendations, providing interviewing tips, and perhaps assisting in locating available positions for which the client may be qualified. Most students looking for internships cannot afford to hire a consultant, but it should definitely be an option, especially in a tough job market. If a student has built a great résumé and they market themselves well, a consultant is not necessary. For those laid off from full-time positions, a career consultant may accelerate a new position search resulting in an earlier return to much needed income. Thus, the money spent may return an earlier dividend.

Head hunters or professional recruiters are usually paid by organizations to actively recruit individuals on their behalf for a position opening. Using a head hunter may cost you, especially if you contact them. However, their fees are usually paid by an organization so if a head hunter has your résumé, it might not cost you anything. Their fees will often depend on how the

◆◆ TIME OUT INTERVIEW ◆◆

― Recruiting Firms ―
MICHAEL GARNES

Current Position	President
Employer	Next Level Executive Search (Subsidary of Next Level Sports, Inc.)
B.A. Degree	Political Science, University of Maryland
M.S. Degree	Sports Management, University of New Mexico
Career Path	• 2nd Lt., Captain, & Major, U.S. Air Force and U.S. Air Force Reserves, Thirteen years • Sales & Marketing, Johnson & Johnson, Five years • NCAA Enforcement Rep, NCAA, Two years • President, Next Level Sports, Inc., Twenty-one years
Employment Recommendation	"A recruiting company is a number 1 priority for many hiring managers. Some companies are always seeking top-talent not readily available via job boards, classified ads, the internet, or unemployment."

contract is written with the employing organization. Be aware that head hunters are normally only used for top level positions. Hiring a career coach or consultant can be a desired route for an entry or mid-level employee if finding a position by oneself has not resulted in a position.

THE FINAL BUZZER

The intent of this chapter was to provide the new employee with information to effectively make the adjustment from completing an internship to starting a new position. Education, concept knowledge, and skills assist one in doing a job well. Manners, etiquette, and establishing positive professional relationships are equally important. The fortunate intern may be the one who has the internship converted into a job with the same agency. There may be advantages and disadvantages to this situation, so the intern-employee should weigh all options carefully.

Ending an internship properly can reap many benefits. Maintaining contact with agency colleagues leads to the strengthening of a professional network. Strange things can happen; an unexpected turn of events can result in immediate employment openings when just a few days before, no apparent opportunities existed. Having proven oneself in the internship, and having shown true gratitude for that internship and the learning opportunities an organization provided may lead company executives to look first to exiting interns for open positions.

When starting a new position, making the right moves at the right time are equally important. No two office environments are the same. Seniority, political positioning, egos, and pursuit of promotions have an interesting way of changing an individual's perspective and motivation. Remaining neutral on many issues, as a new employee, is a positive move. There will be plenty of time to learn how any issue, positive or negative, will impact each individual and the organization.

Individual work habits and skills can enhance opportunities with a hiring agency. Seeking a mentor can help one integrate into a new setting more gracefully and effectively. Remember that mentors provide advice and one must act upon that advice and their own convictions in order to be effective and successful in a new position.

Should you be released from the internship or the new job, exit gratefully and refrain from burning any bridges. One way or another, those who know your work ethic and assets will be looking out for you down the road. Finally, as you live and learn in this new career setting in the industry of sport, know that your own experiences from both successes and failures will contribute to the wealth of knowledge and wisdom that will one day make you a mentor for those to follow you.

Classroom Experiential Learning Exercise

WORKPLACE TRANSITIONING

At Slippery Rock University, students must take a Seminar before interning in their final year which they must pass with a "C" or better. The students are required to wear professional business attire to all classes (professional demeanor begins with professional dress). To carry out the theme of professionalism, all assignments are expected to be written in a professional manner and the course is writing intensive. Papers are returned if writing does not represent the professional level and students receive an "F." It is recommended that students rewrite each assignment five to six times before submitting the final draft for a grade by the due date. *The Sports Business Journal* and the *APA Manual* are the required textbooks. The students are also expected to demonstrate competency as a sport management researcher and must design, collect, implement, and synthesize research data. All of this exhibits the abilities of the students to transition from student to professional in their internship and in the everyday world of work.

Submitted by Rob Ammon, Professor & Department Chair
Slippery Rock, Pennsylvania

Program Experiential Learning Example

EVALUATING THE INTERN AND CONCLUDING THE INTERNSHIP

Faculty at Bowling Green State University supervise field students closely. Faculty supervisors contact all field students every seven to ten working days, and those students within a 3-hour driving radius of the main campus receive one site visit per session. Practicum students must complete a research paper on a specific sport career, then conduct a field observation of a sport professional working in that area, as well as a concluding practicum summary and self-reflection. Interns must consistently consult with their faculty and site supervisors regarding a required project designed to make a lasting contribution to the agency. Faculty also communicate with all site-supervisors at the mid-term and the conclusion of a field student's experience for the purpose of assessment. All field students must have an exit interview with the site-supervisor and receive a final assessment from the faculty supervisor.

Submitted by Dr. Jackie Cuneen, Professor
Bowling Green, Ohio

10

Just for the Graduate Student

"The life of a university professor is stimulating and varied. The opportunity to interact with students and peers in an energetic and constantly changing environment is deeply gratifying and rewarding. It is important for young graduates who aspire to work in the university environment to seek the best fit in terms of their long-term goals and interests."

— Dr. Karen Danylchuk
Associate Professor
University of Western Ontario

THE WARM UP

The workplace of today has changed quite drastically from that of 1995. At that time, a student graduating with an undergraduate degree from an accredited four-year institution was fairly assured of employment opportunities based upon completion of the "college" degree. College graduates were recruited and provided exciting career opportunities in their respective fields. A college graduate could expect to earn, on average, $43,000 a year across a 30-year career, as opposed to a high school graduate with no college experience earning $19,500 a year in the same career span (Lacey & Crosby, 2005). The United States Department of Labor (DOL) reported in 2003, workers with a college degree earned, on average, 62% more wages than workers with only a high school education. Additionally, between 2002 and 2012, 14 million plus job openings are projected to be filled by entry-level workers who have earned a college diploma. In the time span since 1995, enough students have passed through graduation doors from accredited university undergraduate programs to glut the job market. In order to create a job market edge in the competition for employment, one must now supersede the undergraduate degree; in many sport business professions, one must have a master's degree!

Thus, many employees are returning to graduate school in search of the next boost up their personal career ladder, both financially and status-wise. This movement has been accelerated by the "demand" for advanced training for promotion-worthy employees. Essentially, one must get ahead to stay ahead. The master's degree has been a very successful vehicle for the faster track. Touted as the highest applied degree, the master's degree is based upon a successful undergraduate degree from an accredited education institution, a minimum overall GPA for all undergraduate coursework, successful application to the respective graduate program, and an acceptable performance score on any one of several standardized post-graduate examinations (e.g., the Graduate Record Exam). Upon successful completion of this graduate degree, the graduate student should have a litany of new, cutting-edge academic skills to apply to the respective job setting. Thus, the career ladder continues with leadership opportunities and advanced financial status, all in response to the degree.

In the field of Sport Management, the graduate student can pursue the master's degree in Sport Management (MA or MS), choose the business route and seek the master's of business administration (MBA) degree, or seek an education related degree (MEd) if, perhaps, they wish to move into college coaching or institutional administration. All three of these graduate degrees can provide successful educational support for advanced training and career advancement in the broad scope of employment in sport and sport organizations. So, how does one go about getting into the right graduate program for their a specific career goal?

WHEN IS A MASTER'S DEGREE REQUIRED?

The three areas of sport management where one should strongly consider heading straight to graduate school after completing an undergraduate degree are college athletic administration, college coaching, and campus recreational sport. Since you would be working in a collegiate setting, often the master's degree is the minimum degree expected in order to join faculty and some staff ranks. The easiest way to enter into any one of these three industry segments is through the graduate assistantship defined in Chapter 1, briefly discussed in Chapter 4, and explored later in this chapter.

If you are aspiring to enter into professional sport management (Chapter 3) or any of the entry level positions discussed in Chapter 4 (Olympic and Amateur Sport), many industry professionals would recommend getting full-time experience before heading to graduate school. In some cases, at least two years is recommended. In fact, some organizations will pay for you to attend graduate school after you have been with the company for a predetermined length of time. The PGA TOUR is one such organization. Time to go back to school!

Graduate School: Now What?

You have decided to enter a master's degree program. Much of the information in the previous nine chapters is applicable to you. Those of you graduating with an undergraduate degree in sport management probably already have experience. However, many probably did not select sport management as an undergraduate field of study. Begin getting experience right away! Your professional network is probably weak if you have not served an internship with a sport organization. Hopefully, the graduate program selected expects or recommends everyone to get involved. With the number of online graduate programs in sport management increasing, the face-to-face contact with well-connected faculty is seriously diminished, if existent at all. If this is your situation, get to know your online professors and ask them to help you establish network contacts. If they do not have any, you will need to embark on your own network building project and make the contacts on your own. This book was designed to help you do exactly that.

Most master's degree curriculums are comprised of approximately 33–36 hours of coursework (nine to ten classes), culminating with a major research paper (three credit hours) and an internship (three or more credit hours) as capstone courses to the degree. Some programs require more than 36 hours once the capstone courses are included which are usually completed during the last semester of the graduate degree. Once finished, the graduate student should have a clear indication of the course they wish to pursue. On occasion, one may have decided to remain in school. What? Are you kidding me? Yes, the doctoral degree will be discussed later in this chapter.

In a previous chapter, we mentioned that some academic programs may have specialty areas. The following examples will help to illustrate program specialties in more depth.

The University of North Carolina offers a specialty program to graduate students with a specialization in Sport Administration. Claimed to be the "first" in the United States, this two-year curriculum focuses on preparing graduate students for professional careers in collegiate athletics administration. However, students pursuing this curriculum also obtain teaching experience in their first year which complements our discussion in Chapter 4 about the dual responsibilities of college coaches. More information can be found at the following address: www.unc.edu/depts/exercise/sport_adminis tration/program_description.htm.

Texas A&M University's Sport Management program also offers a specialty program which addresses intercollegiate athletics. The Laboratory for the Study of Intercollegiate Athletics has a primary mission to advance and enhance how intercollegiate athletics is managed through conducting scientific research. (See http://lsia.tamu.edu.)

The University of Southern Mississippi provides students with the opportunity to participate in the National Center for Spectator Sports Safety

Learning how to develop a risk management plan for facilities, events, and other programs is an important skill learned in many sport management programs. (Courtesy of Susan Foster)

and Security, promoted through their master's degree in Sport Management, with an emphasis in Sport Event Security Management. This program is the first of its kind in the United States. The design of this 36-credit hour program is to provide special event managers with specialization skills and knowledge needed to meet risk management capabilities and challenges associated with homeland defense and security in sports environments. One can find more information on this program at www.usm.edu/sporteventse curity/contact.php.

There are many other such opportunities available to the inquiring prospective student. A quick means to access those graduate programs with Sport Management curricula and, perhaps, additional specialty opportunities would be to access the North American Society for Sport Management (NASSM) website at www.nasssm.org. Choose your preferred graduate school and embark on a graduate program search. More information on master's degrees also appears in the next section.

HAVE YOU CONSIDERED TEACHING SPORT MANAGEMENT?

In consideration of career opportunities after graduate school, most sport management textbooks do not include nor discuss the position of sport management instructor/professor as a career field. While instructors and professors are not working directly with or for a sport organization, most courses in the graduate program encircle sport. Thus, the authors decided to include this very rewarding career segment in this chapter. There are many career paths that may lead to one making the decision to teach sport management where obtaining the terminal degree is the ultimate goal for many. In the ensuing paragraphs, the authors discuss several rewarding teaching paths, two of which do not include obtaining a doctorate.

Before discussing the doctoral degree, the authors feel it important to describe the pursuit of this career field in a little more depth. En route to the doctorate, some individuals pursue a master's with an emphasis in sport management while others may obtain a master's of business administration (MBA) since the majority of sport management courses include the application of business to sport. While obtaining a business related degree is not necessary, a business degree may carry more influence when pursuing a position, especially, within a college or school of business at a post secondary institution. Understandably, this depends on the particular academic insti-

◆◆ TIME OUT INTERVIEW ◆◆

— College Teaching —
TREY CUNNINGHAM

Position	Chair and Assistant Professor, Department of Sport Management
Employer	Shorter University
Position	Adjunct Faculty, M.B.A. Sport Business Specialization
Employer	Saint Leo University
B.S. & M.S. Degrees	Louisiana Tech University, Exercise Science
PhD.	Health and Human Performance (Minor in Educational Research), University of Southern Mississippi
Additional Certifications	Certified Strength and Conditioning Specialist (CSCS); Several Department of Homeland Security (DHS) Certifications
Career Path	• Graduate Teaching Assistant, Strength and Conditioning Lab; Head Powerlifting Coach, Louisiana Tech University, Two and One years, respectively • Graduate Assistant, Two years while full-time doctoral student • Operations Director, Center for Spectator Sport Security Management & Adjunct Faculty, University of Southern Mississippi, One year while full-time doctoral student • Assistant Professor, Sport Administration and Exercise Science/Graduate Faculty, Department of Health and Human Performance, Northwestern State University of Louisiana, Two years
Employment Recommendation	"In reality, the sacrifices you make during the completion of your doctorate are truly rewarding for a lifetime. The flexibility, independence, and challenging nature of a professorship will benefit all facets of your life. Guided perseverance and patience is the key to an efficient and meaningful completion of the degree. Do not leave campus until you have finished the dissertation!"

tution. The majority of professors in sport management, at this time, do not possess a business degree because the preponderance of sport management degree granting programs, at any academic level, are not housed in business departments. However, there has been an observable shift of the positioning of some programs in this direction. In order to staff the programs moving in this direction, business departments are recognizing that

◾◆◾ TIME OUT INTERVIEW ◾◆◾

— College Teaching —
GREG SULLIVAN

Position	Assistant Professor
Employer	Otterbein College, Department of Health and Sport Sciences
BA Degree	Economics, Brooklyn College of the City of New York
MBA Degree	Sport Management/Finance, Seton Hall University
PhD	Sport Management, The Ohio State University
Employment Path	• Assistant Men's Basketball Coach, Brooklyn College, Two years • Commodity Trader, Enbelhard Minerals and Chemicals, Five years • Commodity Trader, CitiBank, One year • Commodity Trader and Assistant Vice President, Deutsche Bank, Five years • First Vice President, Prudential Securities, Five years • Director, Dresdner Kleinwort Wasserstein, Two years
Employment Recommendation	"If your passion is to research, do not apply for positions at teaching colleges and vice-versa. If you choose to work at a teaching college, then you must have a love of teaching. To be a quality teacher, you must be willing to learn how to become a good teacher through continued education; you must consider yourself always to be a work-in-progress. Quality teachers are devoted to staying current in their discipline by attending conferences and reading journals."

excellent teaching professors with equally impressive research agendas can very capably fill positions within schools of business without possessing a business degree. This is primarily due to the reality that professors with a sport management background possess the qualifications to teach the application of business to sport because many have held positions within the sport industry at some point in their careers. Students respect the ability of their professors to relate real world industry experience in the classroom. In fact, this type of background makes the classroom come alive for many students. The classroom and program experiential learning examples at the end of each chapter in this textbook are strong testimonials to the business related assignments being taught in sport management programs. In fact, an examination of many sport management professor position descriptions will display the desire for applicants to have sport industry experience and may not require a business degree.

Pursuing a Doctorate in Sport Management

Some master's graduates will choose to remain in school and pursue yet another graduate degree. Known to be a **terminal** degree or the highest attainable degree in the academic field, this degree is formally called a doctorate, and those earning it are referred to as "Doctor." Many faculty teaching in colleges across the country have earned this degree and most institutions offer either a PhD or an EdD. The **PhD** degree is a Doctor of Philosophy degree, and is granted to anyone matriculating from the institution, having completed all degree requirements (approximately 72 hours above the master's degree), including a dissertation. The **dissertation** usually takes a minimum of one academic year to complete; for some, much longer, especially if the degree is being pursued on a part-time basis. Some may consider this to be a seriously *long term* paper, but it is a major research undertaking with guidance by at least three established professors. As an alternative to the PhD degree, the **EdD**, is considered to be a doctorate in education. When sport management programs are housed in an education department, this is often the degree granted. In most graduate program settings, the pursuit of either doctorate can be identical. However, at some institutions offering both degrees, sometimes the PhD. is touted as the "research doctorate," while the EdD is considered the teaching doctorate. Some universities offer specialized doctoral degrees that use different designations, but these are rare.

Teaching sport management in graduate school, or in an undergraduate program, is a career with advancing salaries. Six-figured salaries are possible; of course, one would not start at that level of pay. Different career paths are possible. Some professors desire to build their careers around a very productive research agenda, and, often, this is dictated by the type of post-secondary institution at which the professor is employed. However, there are many institutions where professors are encouraged to focus on teaching. Regardless of the path chosen, most institutions require all professors to perform in three to four core academic elements, teaching, research/professional development, service, and academic advising.

◆◆ TIME OUT INTERVIEW ◆◆

⎯ College Teaching ⎯
CHIA-CHEN YU

Position	Director, Undergraduate Sport Management and Associate Professor
Employer	University of Wisconsin—La Crosse
B.S. Degree	Physical Education, National Taiwan Normal University
M.S. & EdD. Degrees	Sport Administration, University of Northern Colorado
Employment Path	• Physical Educator & Swimming Coach, Yang Ming Junior High School, ChangHua, Taiwan, Two Years • Graduate Teaching Assistant, Sport and Exercise Science, University of Northern Colorado, Three years • Assistant Professor, Exercise and Sport Science, University of Wisconsin—La Crosse, Six years
Employment Recommendation	"It is critical to get practical experience with a sport organization before becoming a professor for three reasons. This experience will help you understand in which areas you want to specialize for teaching and research; you can illustrate examples in the classroom; any previous experience with a sport organization can assist a student's networking in their careers."

Either or both of the doctoral degrees mentioned above are attainable for any aspiring graduate student who is willing to work and study hard for the additional three to four years. Before moving forward and discussing more about teaching sport management, a clear understanding of academic tenure and the promotion process must be explained. **Tenure** is typically defined as the process by which a professor is rewarded with a place of employment for as long as they wish. However, there are caveats to this "for life" situation. Becoming involved in an illegal or inappropriate activity are scenarios that can result in termination. An example of this would be sexual harassment of a student. But dissolution of an academic program can also result in a professor's release. Institutions do everything they can to honor the tenure contract, but difficult economic times, refocusing of institutional direction, or low enrollment are other reasons a tenured faculty member could be released from employment.

Most collegiate institutions use the same titles and progression for faculty. An individual at the lecturer's or instructor's level generally has not completed a doctoral degree or may not be under a tenure track contract (under an annual contract where one can earn tenure). The title of assistant professor is usually granted to a beginning professor who has completed a doctoral program. Usually, an assistant professor must complete five years of work at the assistant rank, before applying for tenure (undergoing tenure review) during the sixth year. How well one teaches, how much research or professional development with which one becomes involved, the quality of work, and amount of service (e.g., committee involvement, special assignments) in which one becomes engaged usually determines the granting of tenure. Academic advising may be included in the teaching component or may be an entirely separate component also considered in the tenure granting process.

In many institutions, one cannot apply early for tenure, but this policy is based on institutional choice. Many institutions allow an assistant professor to apply for promotion to the next level, associate professor, at the same time as tenure review. If tenure is not granted, the individual is usually given a seventh year of employment, after which they cease employment with that institution. If tenure is granted, many institutions provide an increase in pay with the promotion, but it is less common to receive an incremental pay raise for gaining tenure. Faculty applying for tenure or promotion are initially judged by a committee of their peers based on institutional guidelines. The committee then forwards any recommendation to the appropriate administrators who then provide their recommendations. Granting tenure at a non-profit institution is usually the ultimate decision of an institution's Board of Trustees. A Board generally does not overturn any tenure or promotion decisions especially if a faculty member has received positive recommendations at all levels.

In general, there is no limit to the length of time one can stay at the level of associate professor. But if pay increments are granted, many individuals seek an eventual promotion. The requirements for a promotion to the highest rank of full professor vary greatly. However, this is a time when many professors seek the publication of a textbook or continue to develop and firmly establish a specific research agenda. A promotion to the rank of professor elicits the highest of faculty salaries, which can reach six figures and not just at the largest of institutions. Field of employment, geographic region, and presence of a faculty bargaining unit can all have an impact on salary. Those professors teaching in a medical field, business, engineering, law, or architecture often elicit the highest salaries. There are sport business professors who fall into this category.

Ironically, one does not have to have a teaching certificate/license in order to instruct at the college level, but having completed courses in education, teaching methodologies, and classroom management can certainly be beneficial. Many institutions make quality in teaching a requirement for obtaining tenure or to be offered contracts of continuation. The majority of sport management professors in the 1970s and 1980s initiated their careers in a physical education teaching program. When sport management majors began to gain popularity in the 1990s, the vast majority were still housed in physical education departments, but some programs allowed students to choose between student teaching or serving an internship centered around sport.

To be successful as a professor in the field of sport management, one must devote one's career to professional development. Continuous attendance at professional conferences is typical of the work, and, in this industry, there are plenty of them. The premier organization for most professors in sport management is the North American Society for Sport Management (NASSM). However, one's teaching specialty can determine the appropriate conferences to attend, especially if school reimbursement funds are scarce. For example, if one chooses to specialize in the teaching of facility and event

management, organizations such as the Stadium Manager's Association
(SMA), the International Association of Assembly Managers (IAAM), the
Florida Facility Manager's Association (FFMA), and the National Intramural-
Recreational Sports Association (NIRSA) all have conferences that focus all
or part of their conference agenda to the design and management of facilities and the operation of events. To become tenured, most professors must
develop and present their research projects at these professional conferences.

Service is usually the third component of the tenure-earning contract. Service can take many different forms, but usually involves committee participation and leadership at the institution. Service to the local community, as
well as active involvement within professional organizations, is also accepted.

If academic advising is considered for earning tenure, this segment is
usually based on an advising model that extends beyond assisting students
with registering for classes. A quality academic advisor treats this role just as
important as any of the others. Assisting a student in finding their career
path and being available when they seek solutions to other encountered
hurdles can be part of a professor's role in advising. At the graduate level,
guiding students through master's theses and doctoral dissertations is also a
major part of an academic advisor's role. In research institutions, it would
not be uncommon for a professor to be advising several graduate advisees at
the same time that they are pursuing their own research projects. The research professor must have a working knowledge of a variety of research
methodologies and statistical tools to manage their work and that of his/her
graduate students. This responsibility, however, is often reserved for professors that have achieved the rank of associate or full professor.

In the Time Out Interviews in this chapter, we have selected individuals
with a variety of backgrounds in order to emphasize that there is no one-
clear-path to becoming a professor. In interviewing all of these individuals,
a common recommendation was to obtain practical experience before accepting a full-time position as a professor. Ironically, all of the individuals
who have provided information for this chapter have some coaching experience, but very different backgrounds. As you read the Time Out Interviews,
compare the different degree fields of each interviewee.

Calvin Hunter, an Assistant Professor at Catawba College in Catawba,
North Carolina, has coaching experience. This experience was augmented
by the practical knowledge he gained as a YMCA youth sports director and
two event management positions, including one as an event coordinator in

equestrian and mountain biking events for the 1996 Olympics. According to Dr. Hunter, in addition to a graduate teaching assistantship, all of these experiences, "provided me a framework and a reference point for things I want my students to learn and I think they enhance my lectures" (Personal communication, January 10, 2010). Dr. Hunter's background also includes two master's degrees—one in sport management and the second was an M.B.A. with a concentration in Sport Business.

Dr. Greg Sullivan, one of our Time Out Interviewees in this chapter, began teaching before he had practical experience beyond coaching. During a **sabbatical** (paid time-off to work on professional projects), he worked as an interim high school athletic director and indicated he could not wait to get back into the classroom to share his experiences with his students. This is testimony to the powerful lessons learned in the sport business world and how important it is to bring those experiences alive for sport management students.

The Law Degree

The law degree, the Juris Doctorate (JD), is not considered a sport management degree, and some academic departments do not consider it a terminal degree. However, since most sport management curricula include one or more sport law classes, some institutions will hire an individual with a law degree to teach these and other courses. A law degree is certainly not required to teach risk management or legal issues, even though some institutions prefer an individual with this credential.

Some students graduating from undergraduate sport management programs become interested in pursuing a law degree after being exposed to one or more legal issues courses. Many law schools offer at least one course in sport law. Two law schools, in particular, have developed specialty tracks related to sport. The Marquette Law School in Madison, Wisconsin, has a Sports Law Program, and offers a wide array of sports law courses and complimenting internships with sport organizations. The Marquette website proposes that students receive a "theoretical and practical education concerning legal regulation of the amateur and professional sports industries" (Marquette University, 2010, para. 1).

A newer law school which has entered the Sport Law arena is Florida Coastal School of Law, located in Jacksonville, Florida. Students may obtain a concentration in Sport Law or enter a Sport Law Certificate Program,

― College Teaching ―
BARBARA OSBORNE

Position	Associate Professor
Employer	University of North Carolina—Chapel Hill
Position	Of Counsel
Employer	Ice Miller, LLP
BA Degree	Communications, University of Wisconsin—Parkside
MEd Degree	Human Movement, Sport Administration Concentration, Boston University, (attended part-time while working full-time)
JD	Boston College Law School. • Member of the North Carolina and Massachusetts State Bars
Career Path	• Intern, Media Relations, The Athletics Congress, Two years • Media Relations Director, Goodwill Games, Three months • Interim Sports Information Director, University of Wisconsin—Parkside, One year • Public Relations Coordinator, Bob Woolf Associates, Inc., One year • Television Analyst Freelance, Various networks including ESPN, Nine years • Assistant to the Athletic Director, Brandeis University, Two years • Newsletter Publisher, Massachusetts Race Place and Boys and Girls • Track Coach, Needham High School, Massachusetts, Two years • Associate Director of Athletics, Brandeis University, Eight years • Adjunct Professor, University of North Carolina Law School, Three years • Assistant Professor, University of North Carolina, Six years
Employment Recommendation	"Explore the reasons for wanting to earn a doctorate. If you are passionate about teaching and research, then an additional degree is warranted. I would also advise you to conduct a cost/benefit analysis. What is the cost in time and money to earn the additional degree versus what you would earn without it?"

which consists of coordinated sport law courses covering a variety of legal issues (Florida Coastal School of Law[b], 2010; Florida Coastal School of Law[a], 2010).

After graduating from law school, one does not have to pursue the life of a practicing attorney. Some individuals pursue the law degree for prestige, for the knowledge learned, and to obtain a wider array of career options. Thus, applying for sport management teaching positions after obtaining the law degree is an option.

Teaching with a Master's Degree

Individuals with a master's degree can successfully teach in undergraduate sport management programs. Competition will come from those with completed doctorates if the position is advertised nationally. However, many smaller programs only advertise locally, so contacting educational institutions in a chosen geographical area that have an established sport management program is one path to pursue. It also would not hurt to contact local institutions, including community colleges, and make an appointment with their chief academic officer. Find out if they have plans to begin a sport management program, or perhaps they plan to offer sport management classes. Some two-year colleges are transforming into four-year colleges and your timing could be perfect! Consider that some may be in the process of entering into articulation agreements with a four-year college and, thus, the addition of sport management teaching positions may be on the horizon. In this case, an **articulation agreement** would be an agreement where a two-year school may begin offering classes for their students to make transferring to a four-year school easier with less loss of credits. For example, a two-year school may partner with a four-year school locally, or somewhere else in the state, that has an established sport management program. The two-year school may develop an Introduction to Sport Management class or other classes that are generally offered by the four-year school at the freshman or sophomore level (100 or 200 level courses). Examples might be Sociology of Sport, Event Management, or Facility Management. If the students take those courses at the two-year school, the agreement stipulates that those courses will transfer equally to the four-year school. Thus, articulation agreements could create teaching opportunities. In most cases, there is a requirement to coordinate agreeable course content with the four-year school in order to satisfy transfer credits to the four year institution.

◆◆ TIME OUT INTERVIEW ◆◆

— College Teaching —
JANET COMFORT

Position	Full-time employee (Advising & Retention); Part-time Online Instructor
Employer	Missouri Baptist University
BS Degree	Business/Accounting, Liberty University
MAC Degree	Accounting, Lynchburg College
MS Degree	Sport Management, Wichita State University
Additional Certifications	CPA
Career Path	• Assistant Softball Coach, Randolph Macon Women's College, One year • Assistant Softball Coach, Lynchburg College, Two years • Accountant, Self-employed, Three years • Adjunct Instructor, Friends University, Three years • Adjunct Instructor, Andover Community College, Three years • Adjunct Instructor, Wichita State University, Three years • Accountant, McBride and Son, Three years • Owner, Radical Resale, Four years
Employment Recommendation	"I began teaching when I was asked to teach an online accounting class for M.B.A. students. I really enjoyed the student interaction, so I decided to see if any other community colleges needed adjunct instructors. My advice is to find a specific area and begin to know it."

Teaching Online

Many sport management programs, particularly at the master's level, are increasingly turning to the internet. This methodology has opened up many opportunities for online teaching. Institutions may hire part-time adjuncts to fill these positions. This offers a great deal of flexibility to the instructor because, most of the time, they do not have to relocate. It may not be the best situation for the institution from a consistency in teaching stand-point or from a face-to-face advising perspective, but many institutions have found that online programs bring in a great deal of revenue. Some professors believe degree quality is an issue in an online format especially for sport management where concurrent course discussion and group projects are often difficult to require. However, if quality instructors with sound academic and experiential backgrounds are hired, a quality online methodology for delivery is used, and a mandate for consistent content are all part of the formula, quality online classes are possible. But most professors of sport management will agree that an online format will never replace the hands-on team projects, field trips, or face-to-face discussions in the classroom environment where critical discourse can be bantered back and forth—particularly if the online courses are offered using **asynchronous delivery** methodology (students participating on their own time schedules).

Sport Education at the High School Level

Education has also changed at the high school level. Some high schools have initiated Academies, where students stipulate the desire to enter a specific course of study, pre-approved by the state government or the private school. In Florida, this option is called a Career Academy, and they are defined as "small, personalized learning communities within a high school that select a subset of students and teachers for a two-, three-, or four-year span" (Florida Department of Education, 2010, para. 1). An application, acceptance, parental knowledge and support are required in this voluntary process. A college preparatory curriculum is then developed and partnerships with local organizations and colleges are also developed. Most follow the Career Academy National Standards of Practice. For more information on these national standards, go to http://www.fldoe.org/workforce/careeracademies/ca_standards.asp#2.

In the 2008–2009 school year, 67 schools in Florida were registered as offering at least one academy (FDOE, 2010). Forty-three had academies related to business. While only two on the list indicated a link to sport management. Rockledge High School recently instituted a Sport, Entertainment, and Tourism Academy (SET). Steinbrenner High School opened in 2009, in the town of Lutz, Florida, and boasts preparation of students for a career in sport marketing through their Kinsman Academy, complete with a Sports, Recreation, and Entertainment Marketing elective listed on their 2009–2010 curriculum (2010).

But sport management courses at the high school level existed long before the rise of the Academies as noted above. Palm Bay High School in Melbourne, Florida, offered a sport management careers course in 1980. Fairfax County, Virginia, offered a sport marketing course in 1989 and, as of 2009, 24 of 25 high schools in the district offered introductory and entertainment marketing courses (Swanson, 2009). In the fall of 2010, New York City opened a Business of Sports School with a planned enrollment of 120 students (Swanson, 2009). With community colleges in New York extremely active in offering sport management curricula, no doubt more schools in the state will adopt sport business related curricula.

◻◆◻ TIME OUT INTERVIEW ◻◆◻

⁓ High School Teaching ⁓
JENNIFER PINSKY-NEWMAN

Current Position	School to Career Transition Coordinator, Dulaney High School
Employer	Baltimore County Public Schools
BA Degree	History, University of Maryland, College Park
MEd	Curriculum and Instruction, Loyola College, Maryland
Other Certifications	Advanced Professional Degrees, Work-Based Learning and Social Studies Secondary Education, Maryland State Dept. of Education
Career Path	• Resident Teacher Certification Program • General Educator, Milford Mill Academy, Baltimore County Public Schools, Five years • School to Career Transition Coordinator, Patapsco High School, BCPS, Three years
Employment Recommendation	"I feel it is most important to be a strong teacher. I do not think it is necessary to have a college degree in sport management; however, it is important to have experience in sport management in order to effectively teach the subject to high school students."

Baltimore County Public Schools, one of the largest school districts in the United States, have comprehensive high schools and special schools, some of which have programs focusing on fields related to sport management and athletic training. All of the high schools allow students to participate in internships in a variety of fields when they are seniors if they have fulfilled general graduation requirements. Jennifer Pinsky-Newman, our Time Out Interviewee for this section, is responsible for managing the students involved in work-study and internship programs as well as working with students in the classroom as they explore various career fields. She conducts site visits, is responsible for performance evaluations of the students working an internship, and recruits employers willing to serve as mentors. (Personal communication, February 2, 2010). Jennifer states, "Right now things are in a state of flux in education. We are trying to meet all of the 'No Child Left Behind' standards and the national movement to provide data-driven assessments as proof of academic achievement. As a result, sport management education at the high school level is not a primary focus as the basic core subjects are most important. At the same time, within the state of Maryland, students are no longer mandated to be in school the entire day during the senior year if they have met graduation requirements. As a result, there are more opportunities for students to participate in structured internship opportunities . . . if they so desire." Please visit http://www.bcps.org/offices/omp/high/Sports-Science-Academy.PDF for additional information on the Sport Science Academy Program for Baltimore County Public Schools.

Undoubtedly, other states have similar course and internship offerings related to management or they may be in the curriculum development stage. If the trend continues to allow schools to be flexible and allow specialized curriculum while also maintaining high standards for teaching basic educational core courses, it is probable that more teaching positions may be available in the high school setting. This is a good thing for sport management majors, particularly those who are required to take basic education courses as part of their degree program. Many sport management students desire to go back to their high school alma maters and work as a coach, but many coaching positions these days are not full-time. Possessing the credentials or background knowledge to accept a teaching position in a sport management related curriculum opens up more opportunities for individuals wishing to become high school coaches and educators.

Graduate Assistantships: Teaching, Administration, Research

In Chapter 1, we defined an assistantship as a graduate level form of experiential learning and expounded a little about assistantships in Chapter 4. Here, we will discuss the purpose of graduate assistantships (GAs) and their relationship to graduate study.

Financial aid is not prevalent (other than personal loans) in support of students pursuing an advanced degree. Thus, some institutions offer graduate assistantships. Academic departments hire graduate assistants to assist professors with regular duties and responsibilities. These graduate assistant positions often take the form of teaching, administrative, or research assistantships. In sport management, graduate professors teaching undergraduate courses may allow a graduate teaching-assistant to develop and/or deliver lectures to a class of students. This is an excellent training ground for GAs to learn the art of teaching, especially if the supervising professor is an excellent professor of instruction. While serving as a teaching assistant, the student may also provide assistance with roll call and attendance, tutoring, grading papers, and monitoring or overseeing undergraduate students taking exams. As an administrative assistant, the GA may be assigned duties and responsibilities important to the daily routine of the department. They may assist with department or school projects, grant-writing, screening of applications for student admissions in either a master's or doctoral program for an upcoming academic year, or contribute to any project in which their supervising professor or another professor in the department may be involved.

Research assistantships are mostly offered to doctoral students to provide research assistance to professors. This is an excellent training ground for students learning how to conduct literature reviews or in learning about statistical or legal research methodologies prior to embarking on their own dissertation research.

While we discussed in Chapter 1 the amount of time expected of a GA (usually 20 hours per week), we need to more fully discuss salaries and benefits. In some cases, the amount by semester may be as little as $300 per month. Some GA positions may pay as high as $12,000 or $15,000 distributed on a monthly basis for nine months. Full or partial tuition expenses and a monthly stipend are generally provided. The amount of tuition covered can depend on state laws and may stipulate whether in-state and out-

◆◆ TIME OUT INTERVIEW ◆◆

~ Graduate Assistant ~
JOE COBBS

Position	Assistant Professor, Marketing & Sports Business
Employer	Northern Kentucky University
BS Degree	Marketing, Ohio University
MA Degree	Sport Management, The Ohio State University
PhD	Management (Sport Management), University of Massachusetts—Amherst
Employment Path	• Credentials and Volunteer Management Intern, Tennis Master's Series, Cincinnati, One year • Graduate Marketing Associate, Ohio State University Athletics, One year • Strategic Corporate Sponsorship Consultant, General Sports, Detroit, MI, Two years • Director of Marketing, Miami University Athletics, Four years • Graduate Research/Teaching Assistant, University of Massachusetts, Four years
Employment Recommendation	"Proceed to a doctorate when you are confident in the area for which you have a passion for research and teaching. Pursuing a PhD. is a commitment unlike previous educational levels and the perseverance necessary for success is more easily mustered when you have a clear vision of your goal. Selection of a program that fits your own interests will best prepare you to reach your goal."

of-state tuition is waived. However, it is not uncommon for all tuition expenses to be waived for the graduate assistant. At larger schools, graduate student housing is often available. This can substantially lower living costs or can be offered as an additional benefit at no cost to the student. Some states/institutions will even provide full medical coverage as a benefit for graduate assistants. Thus, it can be financially affordable to pursue a graduate degree full-time without holding other employment.

Eligibility for graduate assistantships will vary and policies generally stipulate who can and cannot qualify for assistantship positions. Policies will also exist for keeping any assistantship position, and maintaining a minimum grade point average (3.0) is part of most policies. Deadlines for applying for graduate school and assistantships are usually early with many schools establishing a January or early February deadline for the submission of all application materials and admission test scores for a fall semester entry. Some institutions only accept new graduate students in the fall term and conduct rigorous screening of all applicants.

Graduate School Admission Test Scores

Most sport management graduate programs require prospective students to submit admissions test scores. If the program is housed in an education or sport-studies related department, the required admissions exam is usually the Graduate Record Examination (GRE). A score of 1000 out of 1600 is generally the absolute minimum a student could score to be admitted into most graduate school programs. If one is pursuing a degree housed in a School of Business, the Graduate Management Admissions Test (GMAT) is often the preferred exam. The maximum score on the GMAT is 700 and some business schools expect a score of at least 550. Others require much higher achievement. However, because some students just do not test well, some institutions will make exceptions. If a student has been identified by a professor for a graduate assistantship, admission can be granted in this instance as well. Some schools have eliminated required test scores or may grant a waiver, especially if the individual has many years of experience prior to applying to the graduate school.

INTERNING AS A DOCTORAL STUDENT

Some individuals in graduate school, or contemplating the submission of an application to graduate school, inquire about internships as a doctoral student. This opportunity really depends on the individual. Consideration of the information below is warranted.

Internships can never be wasted. Even if the experience results in a poor experience, one has learned that not all organizations have quality internship programs or well-designed internship positions. Still, information about the organization has been learned from the inside. The intern has possibly learned what not to do and how they may wish to design internships for their future employer. Most internships at the doctoral level turn out to be a positive learning experience. If a doctoral student is contemplating a career as a professor, an internship in the sport business industry provides the practical experience recommended by all of our interviewees. Assuredly, great contacts will be made and the personal experiences can be relayed to their students in the future.

Most doctoral programs in sport management do not require an internship. The graduate assistantship will often substitute for an internship. After all, being a graduate assistant for three or four years is an experiential learning opportunity unto itself! If one is pursuing a doctorate and does not have a GA position, sometimes the individual is also working a full-time job outside of sport. This can be detrimental to obtaining much needed on-campus networking and social experience. Students should participate in sport and campus opportunities afforded through athletics, recreational sports, public relations departments, and committee assignments, and these opportunities should be pursued, whenever possible, both formally and informally.

Not all doctoral students plan to teach at a university or college upon graduation. In the next section, we discuss the pursuit of a doctorate for purposes other than teaching. Internships should definitely be an integral part of the educational plan for this particular graduate student.

THE DOCTORAL DEGREE FOR OTHER AREAS OF THE SPORT INDUSTRY

Once employed in sport, some individuals contemplate the pursuit of a doctorate. The need for a doctorate is only dictated by the organization or the demands of the industry. As mentioned previously, the master's degree, the highest *applied* degree, is the main degree expected of a college athletic administrator. Some institutions offer free tuition as an employment benefit and, accordingly, some employees will pursue an advanced degree, law degrees included. Possessing a JD may open doors not available to even those with PhD or EdD degrees. Many individuals with a law degree receive strong consideration for positions as athletic directors, especially in NCAA Division I schools. More than likely, this is due to the number of contracts involved in the yearly operations of an athletic department, as well as the number of legal issues impacting such operations. Individuals with a law degree may even be considered for top positions in athletic departments without any previous sport-organizational experience. It does not regularly happen, but it is certainly possible.

Sometimes, individuals will pursue a doctorate because they hope to achieve the level of Athletic Director. Since the doctorate is the terminal degree and is associated with advanced education and learning, this degree may catapult someone to the front of the line for an Athletic Directorship. When applications are made for top level positions and individuals possess similar experiential qualifications, an earned doctorate degree may be the deciding factor.

FINDING A MENTOR

We discussed mentoring in Chapter 9 for the benefit of an intern or new employee. As a graduate assistant or a new professor, it is equally important to have a good mentor. We look to have a "go-to" person to test our ideas, to give us the "been there, done that" input, so that we, hopefully, do not repeat their mistakes. As a graduate student begins work on a degree in a sport management program, they should look for a professor who is willing to develop a rapport with students, serve as a faculty advisor for a degree curriculum, and then guide them through the academic processes of being

A faculty member actively engaged with sport organizations can create great networking contacts for a mentee. (Courtesy of Dreamstime)

a graduate student. The GA will still have to do the work and grow and develop academically until it is time for the professor to gently push them out of the graduate nest and into life. Some student-mentor relationships last a lifetime. Many GAs will pursue a particular research topic or a subject matter for the rest of their lives, because it was passed down from an outstanding mentor. Good mentors can influence and persuade performances one would never believe possible. In the exalted realms of higher education, no greater compliment can be had than that of a great and gentle mentor. If one does not have a mentor, you could possibly be missing out on great advice on issues important for maximum development of the graduate student. Seeking a mentor is a very positive move.

THE FINAL BUZZER

Teaching or conducting research in the college setting can be a very rewarding career path. Talking to current professors or graduate teaching assistants can provide a great deal of insight into this profession. However, as pointed out in the chapter, it is important to first find out where your passion lies and then embark on a search for the right graduate program that fits your needs and, perhaps, your wallet. Graduate assistantships are the best course to pursue if looking to attend graduate school on a full-time basis. Whether in pursuit of a master's or a doctoral degree, the resourceful use of the graduate assistantship can lead to rewarding and enlightened learning experiences. The dedicated GA can also find a willing mentor to provide advice and guidance along the way. Though the master's degree may only last for three or four semesters, the student-mentor relationship may well continue for a lifetime.

Some determined graduates will pursue the doctorate degree, in spite of all the advice to the contrary. Having read this chapter, it is hopeful that the aspiring graduate student will have realized that there is a tremendous amount of effort and study necessary for a doctoral program. In order to survive, indeed to thrive in such a program, a good mentor is of paramount importance. Proceeding through the curriculum and sharing teaching and learning symbiosis with a mentor, one can blossom into a well-educated and insightful assistant professor, ready for your first class and mentee. Graduate school and being a graduate assistant can be very rewarding. The whole reward for the process will not be for the pay, but for the payback to those you will teach and mentor during your career.

Classroom Experiential Learning Exercise

SECOND-YEAR SEMINAR

The University of North Carolina—Chapel Hill encourages their master's students to consider working on a doctorate through the following class assignments in a second-year seminar.

1) Thesis Oral Proposal (All first-year students and faculty are encouraged to attend the presentation).

2) Students must submit a research abstract for at least one academic conference (e.g., SRLA, NASSS, NASSM, CSRI, etc).

3) Thesis Defense (see number 1 above).

4) All students are required to convert their thesis into a manuscript suitable for submission to a peer-reviewed journal. Research-based manuscript.

5) Students organize, plan, and manage the College Sports Research Institute (CSRI) academic conference. This allows them to interact with scholars from across the country in developing the three issue symposium panels.

Our program's mission is to combine theory and practice to prepare students for leadership positions in college sport; we feel providing these learning opportunities gives students a real-world glimpse at what going on to get a PhD. might involve.

Submitted by Dr. Richard Southall, Assistant Professor & Coordinator
Graduate Sport Administration Program

Program Experiential Learning Example

ENCOURAGING DOCTORAL STUDY

If a master's student is thinking about doctoral study or is undecided, we recommend taking one of our doctoral seminars as an elective in the master's program. We also encourage them to talk with one or more of our current doctoral students. This gives the student opportunities to see what to expect in the program.

Submitted by Dr. Brian Turner, Associate Professor & Program Coordinator
The Ohio State University, Columbus, Ohio

References

About GA&M. (2010). Global Athletics Marketing, Inc. Retrieved from http://www.globalathleteics.com/about.php

Academic degrees no longer a luxury in the burgeoning business of sport. (2008, June 9–15). *SportsBusiness Journal*, p. 29.

Africa. (2010). Africa's dress rehearsal. *SportsPro, 2* (17), 34–35.

Alan, S. (2004, December 14). Sports authority approves Tampa Bay Lightning tax break. *Tampa Tribune*. Retrieved from Newspaper Source database.

Application of the Fair Labor Standards Act to Employees of State and Local Governments. (2007). 29 C.F.R. ß 553.

Apprentice. (2010). In *Merriam-Webster online dictionary*. Retrieved from http://www.merriam-webster.com/dictionary/apprentice

Balfour, F. (2007, October 23). A slam dunk for the NBA in China. *Business Week*. Retrieved from http://www.businessweek.com/globalbiz/content/oct2007/gb20071023_180498.htm

Bandy, K. (2009, March). Launch your career with self-assessment tools. *Student Lawyer, 37* (7), 16–19.

Behind the blue disk: FCS, Division II and Division III. (2008, September 26). Retrieved from http://www.ncaa.org/wps/ncaa?key=/ncaa/ncaa/media+and+events/press+room/current+issues/behind+blue+disk/behind+the+blue+disk_+football+postseason+-+fcs%2C+division+ii+and+division+iii

Bell, J., & Countiss, J. R. (1993). Professional service through sport management internships. *The Journal of Physical Education, Recreation, and Dance, 64* (3), 45–47, 52.

Belson, K. (2009, May 27). In sports business, too many hopefuls for too few positions. *The New York Times.* Retrieved from http://www.nytimes.com/2009/05/27/sports/27class.html?_r=1&scp=1&sq=In%20sports%20business,%20too%20many%20hopefuls%20for%20too%20few%20positions&st=cse

Bennett, G., Henson, R. K., & Drane, D. (2003). Student experiences with service-learning in sport management. *Journal of Experiential Education, 26* (2), 61–69.

Brennan, J. (2004, May 13). Arena backer nominated to fill sports authority seat. *The Record.* Retrieved from http://www.northjersey.com

Brennan, J. (2005a, June 28). $60M Xanadu rent check due to sports authority. *The Record.* Retrieved from http://www.northjersey.com

Brennan, J. (2005b, July 22). New Jersey sports authority cuts New York Jets' rent. *The Record.* Retrieved from http://www.northjersey.com

Bridgstock, R. (2009). The graduate attributes we've overlooked: Enhancing graduate employability through career management skills. *Higher Education Research & Development, 28* (1), 31–44.

Burden, W., & Li, M. (2009). Minor league

baseball: Exploring the growing interest in outsourced sport marketing. *Sport Marketing Quarterly*, *18* (3), 139–149.

Byrd, T. (2004, August 4). Hillsborough County, FL, leaders seek probe of Tampa Sports Authority. *Tampa Tribune*. Retrieved from http://www.tampatrib.com

Chelladurai, P. (1999). *Human resource management in sport and recreation*. Champaign, IL: Human Kinetics.

China's market for sport is growing rapidly but state controls are holding back potential. (2009, October 5). *The Wire*. Retrieved from http://www.golfbusinesswire.com/story/207176/

Commission on Sport Management Accreditation (2008). *Accreditation principles and self study preparation manual*. Retrieved from http://www.cosmaweb.org/sites/all/pdf_files/accrPrinciples.pdf

Commonwealth. (2010). Commonwealth blames. *SportsPro*, *2* (17), 36–37.

Constitution. (n.d.). North American Society for Sport Management. Retrieved from http://www.nassm.org

Conte, A. (2007, March 14). Pens, officials strike arena deal to keep team in 'Burgh. *Pittsburgh Tribune-Review*. Retrieved from http://www.pittsburghlive.com/x/pittsburghtrib/sports/penguins/s_497572.html

Cuneen, J., & Sidwell, M. J. (1994). *Sport management field experiences*. Morgantown, WV: Fitness Information Technology.

Cunningham, G. B., & Sagas, M. (2004). Work experiences, occupational commitment, and intent to enter the sport management profession. *Physical Educator*, *61* (3), 146–156.

Dewey, J. (1938). *Experience and education*. New York: Macmillian.

Dikel, M. (2009a). *The Riley Guide: How to job search*. Retrieved from http://www.rileyguide.com/execute.html

Dikel, M. (2009b). *The Riley Guide: Résumés and cover letters*. Retrieved from http://www.rileyguide.com/letters.html

Dikel, M., Ireland, S., & Joyce, S. (2009).

Prepare your résumé for email and online posting. Retrieved from http://www.rileyguide.com/eresume.html#irr

Dorschner, J. (2006, June 15). World catches NBA fever: The NBA has made basketball into a truly international sport—as 38 teams come to Miami to broadcast the finals worldwide. *Miami Herald*.

Duffy, G. (2009, May 14). Sports authority insists Marana is spring training option. *Tucson Citizen*. Retrieved from http://www.tucsoncitizen.com/ss/byauthor/116566

Ellen, G. (2005, January 20). County to study ejecting Tampa Sports Authority. *Tampa Tribune*. Retrieved from http://www.tampatrib.com

Emmett, J. (2010). Fighting its way to the mainstream. *SportsPro*, *2* (17), 87.

Employment under special certification of messengers, learners, and apprentices. (2005). 29 C.F.R. ß 250.

Extreme sport. (n.d.). Retrieved from http://en.wikipedia.org/wiki/Extreme_sport

Extreme sports. (n.d.). Retrieved from http://dictionary.reference.com/browse/extreme+sports

Facilities. (n.d.). Retrieved from http://www.recsports.osu.edu/facilities

Farrell, C. S. (1997, June 26). Black coaches convention focuses on job-hunting strategies. *Black Issues in Higher Education*, *14* (9), 25–27. Retrieved from http://findarticles.com/p/articles/mi_m0DXK/is_n9_v14/ai_20055265/?tag=content;col1

Fédération Internationale de l'Automobile. (2009). About FIA. Retrieved from http://www.fia.com/en-GB/the-fia/about-fia/Pages/AboutFIA.aspx

Fielding, L. W., Pitts, B. G., & Miller, L. K. (1991). Defining quality: Should educators in sport management programs be concerned about accreditation? *Journal of Sport Management*, *5* (1), 1–17.

Figler, H. E. (1999). *The complete job-search handbook: Everything you need to know to get the job you really want* (3rd ed). New York: H. Holt Publishers.

Findlay, H. A. (2002). Violence in sport: Policy consideration for the amateur sport organization. Presentation at the Symposium "Sports management: Cutting edge strategies for managing sports as a business." Retrieved from http://www.sportlaw.ca/articles/bullying_violenceinsport_policy.php

Fisher, E. (2005, November 7). Baseball calls up young guns. *SportsBusiness Journal*, 1. Retrieved from http://www.sportsbusinessjournal.com/index.cfm?fuseaction=article.preview&articleID=47732

Florida Coastal School of Law. (2010a). *FCSL Certificate in Sports Law*. Retrieved from http://www.fcsl.edu

Florida Coastal School of Law. (2010b). *Suggested schedules and course concentrations*. Retrieved from http://www.fcsl.edu/academics/

Florida Department of Education. (2010). *Appendix Y: 2007–2008 career and professional acadamies registered with the Florida Department of Education*. Retrieved from http://www.fldoe.org/workforce/fcpea/pdf/0708Academies.pdf

Fonda, D., & Healy, R. (2005, September 8). How reliable is Brown's résumé? *Time*. Retrieved from http://www.time.com/time/nation/article/0,8599,1103003,00.html

Foster, S. B., Gillentine, A., Pinsky-Newman, J., & Fay, T. (2003). Future directions for the NASPE-NASSM Standards: What changes are needed for 2007—Part I. Paper presented at The North American Society for Sport Management Annual Conference, May 2003, in Ithaca, NY.

Foster, S. B., & Moorman, A. J. (2001). *Gross v Family Services Agency, Inc.*: The Internship as a special relationship. *The Journal of Legal Aspects of Sport, 11*(3), 243–267.

Fraser, A. (2010). The rise of Russian sport. *SportsPro, 2* (17), 109–111.

Fudger, G. (2010). More than just a pipe dream. *SportsPro, 2* (17), 82–85.

Gault, J., Redington, J., & Schlager, T. (2000). Undergraduate business internships and career success: Are they related?

Journal of Marketing Education, 22 (1), 45–53.

Goldsmith, B. (2003, November). The outrageous power of self-evaluation. *Cost Engineering, 45* (11), 30.

Grevas, L. (2009, August 5). Sports authority discuss priorities. *Worthington Daily Globe*. Retrieved from https://secure.forumcomm.com/?publisher_ID=24&article_id=25838

Helyar, J. (2006, September 16–17). Failing effort. *Wall Street Journal*, p. R5.

Heritage, A. (2001, March). Career management: From ladders to wings. *Training Journal*, 16–20.

Higdon, L. (2004, September). Preparing students for a tough job market. Retrieved from http://www.universitybusiness.com/viewarticle.aspx?articleid=356&p=1

History of the YMCA movement. (n.d.). Retrieved from http://www.ymca.net/about_the_ymca/history_of_the_ymca.html

Holden, G. (2008). World cricket as a postcolonial international society: IR meets the history of sport. *Global Society, 22* (3), 337–369.

Jowdy, E., McDonald, M., & Spence, K. (2004). *European Sport Management Quarterly, 4* (4), 215–233.

Kaske, M. (2007, April 17). New Jersey Sports Authority to sell $21 million for practice facility for NFL's Jets. *The Bond Buyer, 360* (32609), 7.

Kaske, M. (2008, September 3). New Jersey to begin retail order period for sports authority bonds today. *The Bond Buyer, 365* (32953), 3.

Kelley, D. R. (2004). Quality control in the administration of sport management internships. *Journal of Physical Education, Recreation, and Dance, 75* (1), 28–30.

Kelley, D. R., DeSensi, J. T., Beitel, P. A., & Blanton, M. D. (1989). A research based sport management curricular model: Undergraduate and graduate programs. Retrieved from http://www.eric.ed.gov/ERICDocs/data/ericdocs2sql/content_storage_01/0000019b/80/1f/c0/27.pdf

Kelly, W. W. (2007). Is baseball a global sport? America's 'national pastime' as global field and international sport. *Global Networks, 7* (2), 187–201.

Key executives. (n.d.). Retrieved from http://www.teamusa.org/about-usoc/usoc-general-information/leadership/key-executives.html

King, B. (2008, July 14). Path to the corner office—Part 1: Landing the job. *Sports-Business Journal,* 1–10. Retrieved from http://www.sportsbusinessjournal.com/index .cfm?fuseaction=article.preview&articleID=59504

King, B. (2009). New lessons to learn. *Sports-Business Journal, 12* (17), 4A, 5A, 7A–10A.

Krannich, R. & Krannich, C. (2001). *Directory of websites for overseas job seekers: A click & easy special report.* Manassas Park, VA: Impact Publications.

Krannich, C. & Krannich, R. (2002). *The Directory of websites for international jobs.* Manassas Park, VA: Impact Publications.

Lacey, J., & Crosby, O. (2005). Job outlook for college graduates. *Occupational Outlook Quarterly, 48* (4), 15–27.

Lambrecht, K. W., & Kraft, P. M. (2009). Opportunities and challenges in offering a sport management program in the B-school. Paper presented at the North American Society for Sport Management Annual Conference, May 2009, in Columbia, SC.

Lawmakers respond to Dubai's ban on Israeli tennis player peer by proposing professional sports anti-discrimination law in New York. (2009, February 27). Retrieved from http://assembly.state.ny.us/mem/?ad=025&sh=story&story=30363

Learn and Serve America's National Service-Learning Clearinghouse (2004). What is service learning? Presentation at the National Conference on Community Volunteering and National Service, June 2004, in Kansas City, MO. Retrieved from http://www.servicelearning.org/what_is_service-learning/service-learning_is/index.php

Luer, M. (2010). Asia 2010 and beyond: The evolution of Asian sports. *SportsPro, 2* (17), 17.

Luschen, B. (2009, May 11). Oklahoma City grows into a big league city. *The Oklahoman.* Retrieved from http://www.newsok.com/article/3367811?searched=Oklahoma%20City%20grows%20into%20a%20big%20league%20city&custom_click=search

Major League Baseball Players Association (1997). *MLBPA regulations governing player agents.* Retrieved from http://www.sportsagent411.com/products/sports-agent-course/certification/index.htm

Manchester building its credentials in international sport since hosting the Commonwealth Games in 2002. (2006, February 13). *The Times,* p. 79.

Mansasso, J. (2008, March 4). Former Atlanta Spirit chief Bernie Mullin forms Aspire Group. *Atlanta Business Chronicle.* Retrieved from http://atlanta.bizjournals.com/atlanta/stories/2008/03/03/daily13.html

Marquette University. (n.d.). *Sports law program.* Retrieved from http://204.11.208.101/cgi-bin/site.pl?2130&pageID=162

Marx, A., Walker, H., & Weaver, T. (2009). An analysis of career interest and academic preparation of graduating sport management students. Paper presented at the North American Society for Sport Management, May 2009, in Columbia, SC.

McIntosh, C. R. (2008, November). Yes, you can! *Essence, 39* (7), 140–143.

McLaglen, M., & Treisman, J. (Executive Producers), & Leder, M. (Director). (2000). *Pay it forward* [Motion Picture]. United States of America: Warner Brothers and Bel Air Pictures, LLC.

Meltzer, E. (2008, March 5). County closer to forming sports authority. *Arizona Daily Star,* p. B4.

MLBPA info: Frequently asked questions. Retrieved from http://mlbplayers.mlb.com/pa/info/faq.jsp#agent

Morrison, R. (2008). *A message from the executive director.* Florida Department of Business & Professional Regulation. Retrieved from http://www.myfloridalicense.com/DBPR/os/documents/AthleteAgents_news.pdf

Mullin, B. (1980). Sport management: The nature and utility of the concept. *Arena Review, 4* (3), 1–11.

Murphy, B. (2005, April 4). Sides form over sports authority's future. *Houston Chronicle*. Retrieved from http://www.chron.com/CDA/archives/archive.mpl?id=2005_3858577

National Association for Sport and Physical Education/North American Society for Sport Management. (2000). *Sport Management Program Standards and Review Protocol*. Reston, VA: AAHPERD.

National Basketball Players Association. (1991). *NBPA regulations governing player agents*. Retrieved from http://www.nbpa.com/downloads/NBPARegulation.pdf

National Football League Players Association. (2007). *NFLPA regulations governing contract Advisor*. Retrieved from http://cms.nflplayers.com/images/pdfs/Agents/NFLPA_Regulations_Contract_Advisors.pdf

NIRSA. (2009). *2009 NIRSA salary census*. Corvallis, OR: National Intramural-Recreational Sports Association.

Nova Southeastern University, Inc. v. Gross. (2000). 758 So. 2d 86.

Octagon. (2009). Retrieved from http://www.octagon.com

Our history. (2010). *Boys and Girls Club of America*. Retrieved from http://www.bgca.org/whoweare/history.asp

Oxford Business Alumni News. (2007, Winter). *From MBA to successful sports agent*, p. 2.

Pacheco, A. C. (2007). Cooperative education as a predictor of baccalaureate degree completion. PhD dissertation. Retrieved from Proquest Dissertations and Theses: AAT 3377827.

Parks, J., Quarterman, J, & Thibault, L. (Eds.). (2007). *Contemporary sport management*. (3rd ed.).Champaign, IL: Human Kinetics.

Parrish, R. (2008). Access to major events on television under European law. *Journal of Consumer Policy, 31* (1), 79–98.

Phillips, T. (2006, September 18). N.Y. lawmaker calls for reform at Lake Placid Winter Sports Authority. *The Bond Buyer, 357* (32468), 6.

Pieper, S. K. (2004, November/December). The mentoring cycle: A six-phase process for success. *Healthcare Executive, 19* (6), 16–24.

Pontow, R. (1999). *Proven résumés: Strategies that have increased salaries and changed lives*. Berkeley, CA: Ten Speed Press.

Porot, D., & Haynes, F.B. (1999). *The 101 toughest interview auestions; And answers that win the job!* Berkeley, CA: Ten Speed Press.

Profile: Todd Crannell. From MBA to successful sports agent. (2007, Winter). *Oxford Business Alumni News, 2*. Retrieved from http://www.q2agency.com/documents/Oxford_Alumni.pdf

Riordan, J. (2002, December 16). Epstein lights up the career path. *SportsBusiness Journal, 35*. Retrieved from http://www.sportsbusinessjournal.com/index.cfm?fuseaction=article.preview&articleID=27285

Rockledge High School. (n.d.). Academy of Sports, Entertainment, and Tourism Management. Retrieved from http://www.rockledge.brevard.k12.fl.us/Academies/SET/main.htm

Roemmich, L. (2004, February). Q & A with Monica Rusch. *Insider, 2*, 5. Retrieved from http://74.125.113.132/search?q=cache:BU5N4l4atkrJ:cohesion.rice.edu/Humanities/sportmanagement/emplibrary/newsletter0402.pdf

Rose, T., Denny, D., Burleson, C., & Clark, C. (1990, Spring). Marketing oneself for the profession: More than just the four P's. *NIRSA Journal, 14* (3), 24–26, 51.

Saty, S. (2009). *Information paper*. Armed Forces Sports Program. Retrieved from http://armedforcessports.defense.gov/AFS_Info_Paper.pdf

Schambach, T. P., & Dirks, J. (2002, December). Student perceptions of internship experiences. In the *Proceedings of the International Academy for Information Management (IAIM) Annual Conference*. International Conference on Informatics Education Research (ICIER), December 2002, in Barcelona, Spain. Retrieved from ERIC database: ED481733.

Schneider, R. C., & Stier, W. F. (2006). Sport management field experiences as experiential learning: Ensuring beneficial outcomes and preventing exploitation. *The Sport Management and Related Topics Journal, 2* (2), 36–43.

Schrag, D. (2009). 'Flagging the nation' in international sport: A Chinese Olympics and a German World Cup. *The International Journal of the History of Sport, 26* (8), 1084–1104.

Scott, I. (2006). The government and statutory bodies in Hong Kong: Centralization and autonomy. *Public Organization Review, 6* (3), 185–202.

Seagle, E. E., Jr., & Smith, R. W. (2002). *Internships in recreation and leisure: A practical guide for students*. State College, PA: Venture Publishing, Inc.

Silva, C. (2010, January 13). Under new deal, Al Lang Field could be home to baseball again. *St. Petersburg Times*. Retrieved from www.tampabay.com/news/localgovernment

Simons, R. (1995). Presentation at the Georgia Southern University Sport Management Conference, February 1995, in Statesboro, Georgia.

Sinclair, D. (2005). Sports education—A priority for Caribbean sports tourism. *International Journal of Contemporary Hospitality Management, 17* (6/7), 536–548.

Skinner, J., Zakus, D. H., & Edwards, A. (2008). Coming in from the margins: Ethnicity, community support and the rebranding of Australian soccer. *Soccer and Society, 9* (3), 394–404.

Smith, D. (2006, September 13). Blunt will look at sports authority list. *The Kansas City Star*, p. B11.

Snel, A. (2005, June 3). Former official, developer named to Sports Authority. *Tampa Tribune*. Retrieved from http://www.tampatrib.com

Snel, A. (2005, September 15). Sports authority, Bucs dispute cost of NFL rule: Most teams pay for security. *Tampa Tribune*. Retrieved from http://www.tampatrib.com

Southall, R. M., Nagel, M. S., LeGrande, D., & Han, P. (2003). Sport management practica: A metadiscrete experiential learning model. *Sport Marketing Quarterly, 12* (1), 27–31, 34–36.

Spence, K. K., Hess, D. G., McDonald, M., & Sheehan, B. J. (2009). Designing experiential learning curricula to develop future sport leaders. *Sport Management Education Journal, 3* (1), 1–25.

Sport Management Program Review Council. (2000). *Sport Management Program Standards and Review Protocol*. Reston, VA: National Association for Sport and Physical Education.

Sports Agent Responsibility and Trust Act. (2004). 15 U.S.C.A. ßß 7801, 7802, 7803.

Stark, J. (2007, July 12). Pittsburg Sports Authority plans $300M for hockey arena. *The Bond Buyer, 361* (32669), 35.

Steinbrenner High School. (2010). *2009–2010 special elective programs and courses*. Retrieved from http://steinbrenner.mysdhc.org/2009-10

Stier, W. F. (2002). Sport management internships: From theory to practice. *Strategies, 15* (4), 7–9.

Stratta, T. M. P. (2004). The needs and concerns of students during the sport management internship experience. *The Journal of Physical Education, Recreation, and Dance, 75* (2), 25–29, 33.

Strong growth in UK sports industry. (2008, June 19). *USA Today*. Retreived from http://www.usatoday.com/sports/olympics/2008-06-19-3860996986_x.htm

Sutton, W. A. (1989). The role of internships in sport management curricula—A model for development. *The Journal of Physical Education, Recreation, and Dance, 60* (7), 20–24.

Swanson, E. (2009). High schools reach teens via sports business. *SportsBusiness Journal, 12* (17), 11A.

The team. (2010). Joe Gibbs Racing. Retrieved from http://www.joegibbsracing.com

Thibault, L. (2009). Globalization of sport: An inconvenient truth. *Journal of Sport Management, 23* (1), 1–20.

Thiel, G. R., & Hartley, N. T. (1997). Cooperative education: A natural synergy between business and academia. *S.A.M. Advanced Management Journal. 62* (3), 19–24.

Tooley, J. (1997, November 17). Working for credit: How to make the most out of a semester-long internship. *U.S. News & World Report*, 76–78.

Topp, B. (n.d.). Poor sporting behavior incidents reported to the National Association of Sports Officials. Retrieved from http://www.naso.org/sportsmanship/badsports.html

Tracy, B. (2008, June). Success is no accident. *T + D, 62* (6), 76.

Uniform Athlete Agents Act (UAAA) history and status. (2009). Retrieved from http://www.ncaa.org/wps/ncaa?key=/ncaa/ncaa/legislation+and+governance/eligibility+and+recruiting/agents+and+amateurism/uaaa/history.html

US Sports. (2010). US sports hit Europe hard. *SportsPro, 2* (17), 32.

USOC Affiliated Organizations. (n.d.). Retrieved from http://www.teamusa.org/resources/usocaffiliatedorganizations.html

Van Riper, T. (2008, July 29). How to get a job in pro sports. *Forbes*. Retrieved from http://www.forbes.com/2008/07/29/sports-jobs-biz-sports-cx_tvr_0729sportsjobs.html

Verner, E. M. (2004). Internship search, selection and solidification strategies. *Journal of Physical Education, Recreation and Dance, 75* (1), 25–27.

Von Mizener, B. H., & Williams, R. L. (2009). The effects of student choices on academic performance. *Journal of Positive Behavior and Interventions, 11* (2), 110–128.

Watts, J. (2005, July 18). Arizona Sports Authority plans final bonds for stadium. *The Bond Buyer, 353* (32176), 3.

Wehmeyer, M. L., Lattimore, J., Jorgensen, J. D., Palmer, S. B., Thompson, E., & Schumaker, K. M. (2003). The self-determined career development model: A pilot study. Journal of Vocational Rehabilitation, 19, 79–87.

Wick News Service. (2008, July 7). Sports authority for Pima County fails in Phoenix. Inside Tuscon Business, 18(5), 7.

Willenbacher, E. (2004). Regulating sports agents: Why current federal and state efforts do not deter the unscrupulous athlete-agent and how a national licensing system may cure the problem. 78 St. John's Law Review, 1225.

Williams, B. Y. (2005, March 22). 3 women tapped for sports authority. Kansas City Star, p. B3.

Williams, J. (2002). Sport management internship administration: Challenges and chances for collaboration. NACE Journal, 63(2), 28–32.

WNBPA. (2000). WNBPA regulations governing player agents. Retrieved from http://www.sportsagent411.com

Yang, X. S., Sparks, R., & Li, M. (2008). Sports sponsorship as a strategic investment in China: Perceived risks and benefits by corporate sponsors prior to the Beijing 2008 Olympics. International Journal of Sports Marketing & Sponsorship, 10(1), 63–78.

Yates, M. J. (2004). Knock 'em dead with great answers to tough interview questions. Holbrook, MA: Bob Adams, Inc.

Young, D. S., & Baker, R. E. (2004). Linking classroom to professional practice: The internship as a practical learning experience worthy of academic credit. The Journal of Physical Education, Recreation, & Dance, 75(1), 22–30.

Zonar, S. (2007, November). Five steps to a life that works! Coach and Athletic Director, 77(4), 70–71.

Appendix A

Internship/Employment Websites

SITES OR LINKS TO SITES FOR SPORT-RELATED CAREER OPPORTUNITIES

In today's internet society, many organizations post their employment opportunities online. However, many also utilize websites hosted by other organizations. Some of these sites charge a fee while others allow the person looking for a position to look for free. There are so many sites available that there is no way to list all of them. Teams, colleges, and other sport organizations have websites and a few have been listed. Most organizations usually have a button for "job opportunities." The websites below provide numerous opportunities to find employment positions in the sport industry. Some provide direct links; others may include career announcements somewhere on the website.

www.acm.org

www.active.com

www.adage.com

www.adidas.com

www.aema1.com

www.arenafootball.com

www.athleticlink.com

www.athleticsearch.com

www.batsbaseball.com

www.canadiansport.com/jobs

www.canyonranchjobs.com

www.careerbuilder.com

www.careerpath.com

www.cbdr.com

www.cityseach.com

www.clubjobs.net

www.cnnsi.com/jobs

www.coachhelp.com

www.coachingjobs.com

www.collegegrad.com

www.collegiatewaterpolo.org

www.cooljobs.com

www.coolworks.com

www.cubs.com

www.dice.com

www.dodgers.com

www.eosports.com

www.eventsonline.com

www.fifaworldcup.com

www.flipdog.com

www.footwearnews.com

www.gamefacesportsjobs.com

www.golfemployment.com

www.grand-rapids.mi.us

www.hcareers.com

www.helpwantedpage.com

www.hire-ed.org

www.hospitalityonline.com

www.idealist.org

www.indeed.com/q-Amf- Bowling-jobs.html

www.internabroad.com

www.internshipprograms.com

www.internweb.com

www.jobs.hospitalityonline.com

www.jobvertise.com

www.laga.org

www.laworkout.com

www.leisurejobs.com

www.lwonline.com

www.marketingjobs.com

www.minorleaguebaseball.com

www.mls.com

www.nationjobs.com

www.disneycareers.com

www.dsusa.org

espn.go.com/sitetools/help/jobs.html

www.exercisejobs.com

www.fitnessmanagement.com

www.footlocker.com

www.foxsports.com

www.golfingcareers.com

www.golfsurfin.com

www.hartfordciviccenter.com

www.helpwanted.com

www.higheredjobs.com

www.homestead.com

www.hotjobs.com

www.imgacademies.com

www.intermatwrestle.com

www.internjobs.com

www.internships-usa.com

www.jobs.com

www.jobsinsports.com

www.jupiterisland.com

www.latpro.com

www.law.vill.edu

www.lucky.com

www.malakye.com

www.milwaukeejobs.com

www.mlb.org

www.naia.org

www.nationwidearena.com

www.nba.com

www.nfl-monster.com

www.njcaa.org

www.onlinesports.com/pages/jobs.html

www.paidinternships.com

www.pbeo.com

www.pgalinks.com

www.prosports.com

www.recsport.indiana.edu

www.reebok.com

www.seanhylandmotorsport.com

www.snagajob.com

www.sportbusiness.com

www.sportscastingjobs.com

www.sportsline.com

www.sportsworkers.com

www.summerjobs.com

www.teamworkonline.com

www.thegolfclassifieds.com

www.tvjobs.com

www.universalstudios.com

www.usahockey.com

www.usoc.org

www.volleyballseek.com

www.wbca.org

www.welltech.com

www.womenssportsfoundation.org

www.workingsports.com

www.workopolis.com

www.ncaa.org

www.nikebiz.com/jobs

www.nsga.org

www.outdoornetwork.com

panthers.nhl.com/index.html

www.pepsicenter.com

www.pgatour.com

www.racecityresumes.com

www.recsports.ufl.edu/gradassist.aspx

www.rsinternships.com

www.sgma.com/jobs/index.html

www.soccerhall.org

www.sportscareerfinder.com

www.sportsemploymentinc.com

www.sportswork.com

www.stpetetimesforum.com

www.teammarketing.com

www.tennisjobs.com

www.timesonline.com

www.ujobbank.com

www.usa-gymnastics.org

www.usgolfjobs.com

www.vans.com

www.waterski.org

www.wellnessnwi.org

www.womenssportscareers.com

www.womensportsjobs.com

www.workinsports.com

www.wsnsports.com

Appendix B

Sample Chronological and Functional Résumés

SAMPLE CHRONOLOGICAL RÉSUMÉ

Susan C. Forrester
808 Larkspur Street—Titusville, FL 32780
scf@email.com
111-111-1111

SUMMARY OF QUALIFICATIONS	• Successful tournament scheduler with advanced skills in set-up and operation • Excellent time management, social media, and web design skills • Experience with a wide variety of sporting events • Effective project manager
EDUCATION SPORT	**Ohio State University—Columbus, Ohio—2008** M.S.—Sport Management 3.78 GPA —Oberteuffer Award Winner **Florida State University—Tallahassee, Florida—2004** B.S.—Sport Management Minor—Business Law 3.0 GPA
BUSINESS EXPERIENCE	EVENT AND TOURNAMENT MANAGER—FLORIDA AMERICAN UNIVERSITY—2009–PRESENT • Planned, organized, and executed tournaments and meets in eight sports • Designed, sold, and executed tournament sponsorship packages • Assisted with community outreach programs • Competition manager for U.S. Association of Blind Athletes Summer Nationals • Created and maintained day-to-day media relationships • Executed all tournament contractual elements GRADUATE ASSISTANT—OHIO STATE UNIVERSITY—CAMPUS RECREATION 2007–2008 • Undergraduate staff supervisor—Special Events • Facility management night-time supervisor • Graduate student representative—Recreation Advisory Council SPORTS OFFICIAL—NORTH BREVARD SPORTS ASSOCIATION—SUMMERS, 1998–2004 • Softball, volleyball, basketball SPORTS OFFICIAL—DEPT. OF CAMPUS RECREATION—FLORIDA STATE—2001–2004 • Softball, volleyball, basketball, swimming, and track and field VOLUNTEER • LPGA Legends Tour Championship—Player Check-In—Safety Harbor, FL—2009 • XLIII Super Bowl—Merchandising Stock Manager—Tampa, FL—2009 • American League Playoffs—Media Security Support—St. Petersburg, FL—2008 • Little Everglades Steeplechase—Parking Attendant—Dade City, FL—2007 • Chrysler Championships – Driving Range Concierge – 2004 & 2005

REFERENCES

Name, Title Company Name Address City, state, zip Approved phone # Approved e-mail	Name, Title Company Name Address City, State, Zip Approved phone # Approved e-mail	Name, Title Company Name Address City, State Zip Approved Phone # Approved e-mail

SAMPLE FUNCTIONAL RÉSUMÉ

JOHN E. DAMIAN

5151 NORTHWESTERN ST. BIRMINGHAM, AL 10001
JED@EMAIL.COM 222-222-2222

SPECIALIZED SKILLS

MARKETING & PROMOTIONS

GROUP AND SPONSORSHIP SALES

LEADER AMONG PEERS

CONFIDENT SOCIAL MEDIA COMMUNICATOR

EDUCATION

Bachelor of Science in Sport Management, Minor in Business Administration

Northwestern State University of Louisiana 3.88—Magna Cum Laude

AWARDS AND HONORS

Dean's List Student

Outstanding Sport Management Major

Track and Field Athlete

REFERENCES

Reference #1
Name, Business title
Company Name
Full mailing address
City, State, Zip
Approved phone number
Approved e-mail

Reference #2
Name, Business title
Company Name
Full mailing address
City, State, Zip
Approved phone number
Approved e-mail

Reference #3
Name, Business title
Company Name
Full mailing address
City, State, Zip
Approved phone number
Approved e-mail

PERSONAL PROFILE

- Proactive, decisive, and result-oriented leader
- Proficient in Microsoft Word, Excel, and PowerPoint
- Effective web and social media designer
- Ethical team player

AREAS OF STRENGTH

SPONSORSHIP SALES

- Proven sponsorship sales record
- Effective communicator with sponsors to maximize year-to-years sales retention
- Detailed sponsorship program designer

GROUP SALES

- Continuous leader in development of group sales packages
- Creative packaging for customer satisfaction and retention
- Developer of innovative services and service delivery
- Effective sales presenter

MARKETING/PROMOTIONS

- Experienced half-time promoter for increasing spectatorship
- Developer of marketing plans for college athletics
- Proven results for increased attendance
- Implemented program social media program for online marketing

VOLUNTEER/COMMUNITY INVOLVEMENT

- PGA Zurich Classic of New Orleans—Media Logistics—April, 2010
- New Orleans Saints NFC Playoff—Game Day Support—2010
- University of Alabama—Game Day Operations Assistant—2009
- Northwestern State University—Game Day—Ticketing & Marketing Assistant—All Sports—Four years
- YMCA of Birmingham—Developed Saturday Career Day Program for High School Students—Sport Management and marketing

PERSONAL PHILOSOPHY

Make . . . each day count
. . . each project your best, . . . each client #1,
and keep all promises!

Appendix C

Sample Interview Questions

COLLEGE ATHLETIC ADMINISTRATION/COACHING

1. What experiences, good or bad, have you had that you believe will be most helpful to you in fulfilling the responsibilities of this position in our athletic department?
2. What do you see as the biggest threat to big-time college athletics?
3. When and why did you decide to take an interest in being a _____ for an athletic department?
4. If you were in a position at a university where the program was illegally giving money to players, how would you go about handling the situation?
5. What is your overall career goal in college athletics?
6. For which sports have you fitted equipment? With which do you feel most comfortable?
7. If a player came to you complaining that equipment hindered movement, how would you handle this?
8. Describe the procedure for fitting a football helmet?
9. What is the most important job of the equipment manager?
10. Do you know the recommended maintenance/replacement schedule for football equipment, helmets in particular?
11. Why do you enjoy coaching?
12. What "style" of coaching do you use?
13. At what level would you like to ultimately coach?
14. What goal would you like to achieve in coaching?
15. What do you consider success in coaching?
16. What if your top quarterback was considering transferring to another top university and one of our biggest alums decided to buy him a brand new Porsche. The deal was totally "under the table" and nobody found out. What would be your feelings on this situation as an assistant coach? What would you do?
17. What is your position on Title IX?

18. What type of things would you suggest to increase attendance?
19. Football is a big revenue sport at _____. However, women's soccer is an important part of the women's program and does not receive as much funding. As an athletic director, if there was extra money in the budget and both programs were requesting money, to which program would you allocate the money? Why?
20. What would you do if another university had an away game and didn't show up? How would you handle it?
21. Have you taken care of athletic equipment before?
22. Why do you want to be an equipment manager?
23. Do you plan to stay in college promotions?
24. How are you going to handle the drug testing policy? What penalties would you like to see enforced?
25. How would you get students more involved in college athletics?
26. Why should we hire you as a graduate assistant for our athletic department?
27. How did you get involved in compliance?
28. What is your experience with Division _____ compliance rules?
29. What do you perceive to be the main difference between the NAIA and the NCAA?
30. At your previous university where you interned, what did you learn about their operations when they moved from NAIA to NCAA? From Division II to Division I?
31. Coaches are expected to fulfill other roles in their off season? What can you contribute?
32. Do you have any teaching experience? Would you be willing to teach at our university?
33. What makes a college coach an effective classroom teacher?
34. Have you ever failed a compliance test given by your athletic department?
35. As a graduate assistant, what were your coaching responsibilities?
36. How did your graduate assistantship prepare you for this position?
37. With what statistical programs do you have experience regarding sports information?
38. What is your favorite statistical program to use for sports information?
39. How good are you at developing web-sites to keep our athletic department's webpage up-to-date?
40. What do you know about the position of a Senior Woman Administrator?

PROFESSIONAL SPORT MANAGEMENT QUESTIONS

1. What would be a promotional plan that you could come up with while doing your internship?

2. Why do you want to be a marketing promoter for NASCAR?
3. If you were put in a position where there was a new race track (NASCAR) being built, how would you be able to promote the track to the surrounding area and fans?
4. In what area of professional sport are you most interested in building a career?
5. What is your career goal in professional sport management?
6. If you could make three (3) changes in the _____ league, what would they be?
7. How would you handle a coaching change after a popular coach has been fired?
8. If your team has had a bad attendance year, what would you do to make sure this improved next year?
9. How would you promote your star player in order to raise the popularity of the rest of the team?
10. NASCAR has grown in terms of popularity. What would you do to continue this trend?
11. NASCAR has an image with some people of being entertainment for old-fashioned country boys. How would you change this perception or do you think a change is necessary?
12. How would you promote a motorsport event after a bad accident has occurred and is fresh on the fans' minds?
13. What is your outlook on pro-sports and sports equipment industries for the future? Positive or negative?
14. Do you have any ideas about new & different activities you might plan for a professional golf/tennis tournament that would raise more money for our community's charities?
15. What does marketing and promotions mean to you? (in your own words)
16. What do you know about the Super Bowl as an event? World Series? World Soccer Cup? Master's?
17. Have you had any promotions experience? Concessions/field maintenance?
18. Describe your golf background and experience and how it pertains to this job.
19. Do you feel pro sports salaries for players are too high?
20. Explain your job duties and projects you may have developed with other professional teams.
21. What do you think is the main problem in professional sports and what would you do to solve this problem?
22. Where do you see yourself ten years from now if you stay in professional sports?
23. What would be your top organizational goal for this professional sport organization?

24. How can we overtake the _____ as the number one team in the NFL in the area of merchandising sales?
25. What is your view on teams moving elsewhere to new locations and leaving their fans behind?
26. Why did you choose a minor league team opposed to a major league team? Why did you choose baseball?
27. If you are hired, give me an example of how you would market our team to boost attendance?
28. Why did you choose to apply to our organization for your internship?
29. What do you know about baseball?
30. What is your goal in professional baseball? Other sport?
31. How can your experience relate to minor league baseball?
32. Are you willing to put in 60+ hours during the season?
33. What do you know about our organization?
34. Where do you see professional baseball 10–15 yrs down the road? How do you fit in that scenario?
35. What changes would you lobby for in major league baseball? Other sport?
36. What experience have you had in the administration of our sport?
37. What is your position on the steroid issue?
38. When you hear our team name, what is the first thing that comes to your mind?
39. What suggestions do you have for getting more people to leave the TV and come to the games?
40. At this entry-level position you will be required to work in several different aspects of the organization such as tickets, concessions, promotions, etc. You will be working long hours and will see very little or none of the games or players. Since you grew up as a fan of this sport, would this present a problem for you?
41. One of your players has just been arrested for possession of marijuana. S/he is your franchise player and has won numerous MVP awards. S/he is one of your position players. How would you handle this?
42. Professional lacrosse is beginning to take hold and there are rumblings that our city wants to attract a team? Is the leisure spending of our citizens such that you believe there is still enough to support the existing pro teams?
43. What do you feel is the role of community relations in a professional sport organization?
44. Our website has a lot of information about our community relations department. What do you know about it?
45. Why do you want a career in player development? What scouting experience do you have?

RECREATIONAL SPORT MANAGEMENT

1. Why do you want to be an intramural director?
2. What experience do you have in working with intramurals? Family or youth programming?
3. How would you get more students involvement in intramurals?
4. Title IX impacts collegiate recreational sport. Do you feel it is important to have as many opportunities for women as you do for men in the intramural program?
5. Since students serve as program supervisors, what type of staff training would you develop to assure the liability is decreased and program quality is enhanced?
6. What do you see as some of the most important issues facing the recreation field in the future?
7. How do you feel about working in several areas of the recreation field?
8. Where do you see yourself in recreation ten years from now?
9. How would you start an ultimate Frisbee league?
10. How would you approach the current generation of college students in your attempts to get them to participate?
11. How would you deal with underage drinking and drugs on campus, especially when you find an incident occurred resulting from a recreational sport program you sponsored?
12. What are your career goals in recreation management?
13. If you obtain this job, what do you feel you can contribute to our campus recreation organization?
14. What are your major strengths and weaknesses in the area of recreation?
15. What type of experience have you had working with campus recreation? Any branch of recreation?
16. Why do you choose to work in the recreation field?
17. Have you ever had experience in planning recreation programs on your own?
18. We run family programs on our campus. Do you enjoy working with children?
19. How do you believe children benefit from recreational sport programming?
20. How would you promote summer sport camps?
21. Let's say one of your programs reached its capacity and a parent was irate because her child couldn't be enrolled. What would you do?
22. What do you know about sport clubs? Instructional programs housed in our department?
23. This is a golf community and our largest enrolled class for children is

golf. However, most of our kids hate golf. How would you teach the class to make it fun?

24. You have a plan to initiate a new sport for our community. What would it be and how would you sell it?
25. What would be your "first" project as a new assistant director?
26. Can you give me any ideas which you think might improve how the YMCAs are run?
27. What referee experience do you have?
28. Do you feel you could revamp our referee training program?
29. Do you have experience with starting/sponsoring an official's club to promote professionalism?
30. Do you know how to set-up different types of tournaments including single and double elimination, round robin, and ladder tournaments?
31. Explain a situation you have observed or have had to manage when you had a large tournament bracket set up and a team did not show up but did not give any notice? What did you do?
32. We would like to build a climbing wall. What experience do you have with managing this type of facility?
33. We want to improve our programming for the physically challenged student. What ideas do you have?
34. Do you believe young children (under age 8) should be exposed to competitive sports?
35. Wellness programming should be a big part of any campus recreation facility? How would you go about starting such a program?
36. We plan on building a new wellness facility. With your recreation background, what experience do you have in designing such a facility? What would you include?
37. Do you believe in hiring students to staff a campus recreation wellness facility? If so, what credentials would you require?
38. College students do not have very good diets and sometimes do not make very good choices when it comes to wellness behaviors. Describe a program you could institute that would assist them in making better choices? Would you need to hire additional staff?
39. Describe one situation where you feel recreational/wellness programming turned around a young person's life?
40. Why should we hire you as a graduate assistant for aquatic programming? Sport club programming?

SPORT SALES/MARKETING

1. What experience do you have in sales?
2. What qualifications do you have that would increase ticket sales for our organization? Group sales?
3. How do your communication skills complement this sales position?

4. Tell us about some of the sales programs with which you have been involved?
5. How do you think this experience will aid you in selling sporting goods?
6. Do you want to own a sports store or actually be a sales person?
7. About what types of sport merchandise are you most knowledgeable?
8. What are your views on company travel with regard to the sales staff budget?
9. What salary/commissions do you expect?
10. We need to know about your product knowledge. Convince us that you can sell our products?
11. How would you advertise our product line?
12. Give an example of sales goals you have set in the past for yourself.
13. If I were in your pro shop looking for a new wedge or tennis racket, how would you persuade me to buy your new state of the art equipment?
14. How have your past sales experiences prepared you for this position?
15. With what clientele are you most comfortable?
16. Explain a new product, and tell us how you would sell it?
17. What different sales techniques would you use in selling to the 30–40 age group vs. the 15–21 age group?
18. In what aspects of marketing are you most interested?
19. Are you good with people? In the field of marketing, a lot of one-on-one sales must be done. Describe the first thing you would do when contacting a potential sponsor.
20. How do you perceive your career path in sales?
21. How would you deal with an interested buyer that is not completely sold on the product?
22. What approach would you use on a skeptical buyer?
23. How many times would a consumer have to say "no" before you would give up?
24. In what branch of athletic apparel would you like to work?
25. In what area of sales would you like to work for our team?
26. How will you continue to innovate the product lines in which you are specializing?
27. Within our company, which main sporting goods product do you feel is on the rise and will create much revenue, as well as success for the company? Which product is on the decline and you feel we should drop?
28. What new product idea would you like our company to consider bringing to market?
29. You are in charge of advertising and want to promote your product the best by allowing a sport celebrity to promote that certain product. How would you go about finding that celebrity, getting him or her to

endorse the product, and what will you do to make sure that product sells successfully?

30. Shoes are the most poorly fitted item of athletic clothing. For which sports can you fit shoes properly?

31. What type of clothing would you recommend for running in cold weather?

32. I am 6 ft and weigh 245 lbs; how much longer than a standard length club should I use?

33. What is the significance of the number of dimples on a golf ball?

34. What marketing and previous sales experience have you had in an area other than golf? Tennis? Bowling?

35. Would you consider yourself a reasonably good golfer? If so, would you use the product you sell even if the product was different than what you are presently using?

36. Can you analyze a golf swing and recommend equipment that would help improve that swing?

37. What is your perception of the major colleges across the USA that have our logo on their jersey? Do you think it's fair to the smaller schools that we are more interested in making deals with larger schools?

38. What is your previous experience in the area of marketing?

39. Can you sell yourself to me?

40. We are currently involved in marketing a tennis racket the pro tour has ruled as too big. How would you market this racquet?

41. Tell me the qualities of a successful sales person.

42. How do you handle customers who aren't satisfied with our product and want their money back—especially if you can tell the product has been used?

43. There is an old saying, "The customer is always right." Is this always true? Why or why not?

44. If you are not doing well in sales for a particular month, how would you motivate yourself to do better?

45. How do you feel about our company—size, industry, and competitive position?

46. What are your views on customer relations?

47. Give me an example of a marketing research project in which you have taken part.

48. Our team just suffered a terrible season. Obviously, sponsorships are going to be harder to get and season tickets will be harder to sell at the price they were last year. How will you go about getting those sponsorships from the companies that supported the team last year as well as gaining new sponsorships?

49. What other majors (if any) did you consider in college and why was sport marketing your final decision? What influenced these decisions?

50. Where do you see the professional sports market in 15–20 years? Do you think that fan involvement will continue to increase or do you think fans will get fed up with high salaries?
51. Do you think promotions at games take away from the enjoyment of the fans?
52. Do you have a portfolio of any marketing projects you've done in college or any other time?
53. Describe your hands-on experiences in the field of marketing? What was your role?
54. Given the task to come up with a slogan to try and attract fans to our games, what would it be and why?
55. How would you compare sponsorship in college with professional teams?
56. If given the opportunity to change the team name, what would it be and why would the fans like it?'
57. Have you ever written any promotional ads?
58. Have you ever helped in the promotional aspect of any event?
59. Have you ever conducted or participated in any sport marketing research studies?
60. What does sport marketing involve? Define it.
61. What effective marketing ideas have you seen persuade the buyer? The spectator?
62. How would you market an event that would need contributions from the public to get established?
63. What do you believe to be of great importance in the marketing of our organization? Product?
64. You are a new sponsorship account executive. An alcoholic beverage company wants to give you a large account, but we have typically shied away from these. However, we might be willing to consider it if it is structured properly and family friendly. It's the largest account you have ever been offered. You work on commission? What would you do?
65. You are in charge of the family section of our stadium? Tell us about your sales/marketing ideas?

SPECIAL EVENTS/FACILITY MANAGEMENT

1. In what type of facility do you wish to work?
2. What experience do you have with facility management?
3. In your opinion, what is the MOST important aspect of facility management?
4. What types of research do you need to perform to promote a show?
5. What types of programs could you use to sell your facility?
6. What classes did you take in school which may have helped you the most to enter event/facility management?

7. Why did you choose facility management as a career field?
8. How do you feel you can help manage this facility?
9. If you are having an event in this facility, do you feel it is necessary to have a liability plan?
10. How would you train your staff and all employees in risk management?
11. Tell us about ANY risk management experience you have?
12. What salary do you expect?
13. Are you a "people" person?
14. What do you know about our facility?
15. How would you market our facility?
16. How would you pack our arena for a basketball game?
17. How would you promote a business convention in our arena?
18. Why did you choose our facility?
19. Are you willing to work in other areas within the organization?
20. We have a lot of down time and want to bring in more events to our facility. What types of events do you feel would be good for our community or clientele?
21. What do you feel is the most important characteristic an event/facility manager needs to be effective?
22. Why do you prefer a pro facility in comparison to a collegiate facility?
23. What are your goals in event/facility management?
24. If you were put in charge of an event with 50,000 people and there was a person who sustained a major injury, what would be one of the first forms of action you would take beyond medical care?
25. How important is advance risk management planning to the operation of an event or facility?
26. Have you developed a risk management plan for a facility or event?
27. Can you describe the necessary components of a successful risk management plan that would help us prevent injury to our spectators?
28. Do you have any experience in designing any type of facility even if it was a class project?
29. Have you ever participated in a feasibility study?
30. What professional memberships do you hold with any sport related facility management organization?
31. Did you purchase a student membership with any facility management organization?
32. As an intern, what will be your first contribution to our facility management staff?
33. What experience do you possess in attracting major events to a sport facility?
34. Did you run any tournaments as part of a class in college? If so, tell us about it.
35. We want to improve our recreation facilities? After your tour of our

physical plant, do you have any ideas on what would be the first facility you believe we need?

FITNESS/WELLNESS MANAGEMENT/DIRECTOR/ STRENGTH & CONDITIONING COACH

1. What are your salary expectations as a manager of the fitness club?
2. This is a large fitness facility. How will you keep everyone working together cohesively?
3. What will you do to increase the number of clients without sacrificing quality of their experience in this facility?
4. What will you do to ensure the clients are satisfied?
5. How will you review the performance of your certified fitness trainers?
6. What is your philosophy of requiring certifications for fitness trainers and what certifications do you prefer?
7. What type of experience have you had in working at a health and fitness club?
8. A fitness club manager should have a strong background in management and exercise science. Explain how your background fits this position.
9. What training have you had working as a wellness director?
10. While working as a wellness director, what would be the most IMPORTANT programs you would implement? Which ones would you focus on the most in helping your members?
11. What have you already done and what will you do in the future to benefit other people's health through your work as a wellness director?
12. What certifications would you require your employees to possess if hired as manager of our club?
13. Explain your personal training experience and the type of client with whom you most prefer to work.
14. Have you encountered a serious health situation with a member in which you have had to help rehabilitate (e.g., Paralysis, heart attack, broken bone)? If you encountered this or another type of serious situation, how would you go about rehabilitating the patient?
15. Have you ever run a cardiac rehabilitation program in concert with physicians? What ideas might you have for workouts? What kind of safety procedures do you think should be used? How might you motivate them to stay with their rehabilitation program?
16. What do you think is the best way to keep customers safe?
17. How would you deal with someone who is not adhering to fitness club rules?
18. How important is it to enforce safety rules?
19. What should a fitness center/weight room contain?
20. Do you have experience with the elderly?

21. How would you motivate a person who is out-of-shape and doesn't like physical activity to begin to enjoy an exercise program?

22. With what brands of equipment are you familiar? Weights? Cardio-vascular? Stress tests or computer programs dealing with nutrition or fitness?

23. Have you ever conducted any classes or workshops on nutrition or fitness?

24. In your opinion, what is the ideal fitness club?

25. How do you assist your client who has difficulty in communicating with you in a foreign language?

26. Let's assume that it is 15 minutes before closing time and your client visits you to have some kind of assistance? What will you tell this client?

27. Describe to us what you believe should be included in a wellness program?

28. What aspects of your character will enable you to become a successful strength coach?

29. A team strength and conditioning coach must be a leader. What type of leader are you?

30. What is your position on supplements in the strength and conditioning of young players?

31. You have been the strength and conditioning coach of this team for _____ years? As a new head coach, why should I retain you on my staff?

32. Explain a typical individual workout for a certain position player on the team?

33. What is your philosophy on strength and conditioning of baseball players? Track athletes? Swimmers?

34. You have a pure strength and conditioning background but no educational background in management. Explain how this makes you an effective coach.

35. You have a bachelor's degree and good experience? Would you be against getting an advanced degree to assist you in management philosophy while serving as a strength and conditioning coach full-time?

36. Explain your experience in maintaining an injured player's conditioning status.

37. Risk management in a strength and conditioning facility is paramount. Explain basic safety rules.

38. We would like our new strength and conditioning coach to also assist in the development of programs for the recreational athlete. What experience do you have with this and how would you fit into your daily schedule?

39. Describe your greatest success in conditioning an injured athlete.

40. Why should we hire you as a graduate assistant in our fitness center?

GENERAL QUESTIONS

1. What are some of your qualities on which you need to improve?
2. What are your strengths? Weaknesses? How would you evaluate yourself?
3. Who could I talk with about your work ethic?
4. What one college class has MOST prepared you for this type of work? Why?
5. How would you handle a conflict between yourself and your co-workers, supervisors, or customers?
6. What makes you different from the other applicants?
7. What would you like to learn during your internship and how will you apply it in the job setting?
8. What were your responsibilities during your internship?
9. What was the most significant contribution you made to the company during your internship?
10. This is an unpaid internship. How will you support yourself over the next three months?
11. What is your definition of success? Failure?
12. Are you willing to relocate?
13. What are your short and long range goals for your career? How do you plan to achieve them?
14. How would you describe yourself?
15. What two or three things are most important to you in your career?
16. Describe your concept of the ideal career position.
17. Are there any questions you would like to ask me?
18. What classes at school were most useful to you for this position?
19. What courses in ethics did you take in college? How have they helped to shape your perspective of sport ethics?
20. Tell me the special qualities you possess and how they will help you with this position.
21. Tell me about a project you initiated.
22. What can we expect from you if you get this job?
23. What were your major responsibilities at your previous job?
24. What kind of supervisory experience have you had?
25. With what kind of people do you dislike working?
26. Do you find yourself to be a self-motivated worker?
27. What do you want to achieve as an employee here?
28. As an intern, how do you feel you can contribute to our organization?
29. Is there anything important that you haven't had the chance to tell me?
30. How does your educational background pertain to this job?
31. Have you ever been disciplined for any performance related problems?

32. Can you explain your working relationships with peers and supervisors?
33. Describe yourself as an individual and as an employee.
34. What makes you the best candidate?
35. In what community activities do you participate?
36. What two or three things are most important to you in choosing a position?
37. How would you motivate people?
38. Tell me a situation where you had to persuade another person of your point of view.
39. Give an example of a problem you solved and the process used?
40. Describe a project that best demonstrates your analytical skills.
41. Why did you choose this career?
42. Which is more important to you, the money or the job?
43. In what kind of work environment do you think you would excel?
44. What personal accomplishments did you have in your previous assignments?
45. What do you see yourself doing next year? In ten years?
46. What benefits are important to you in your career?
47. What do you want out of a career?
48. How do you feel about traveling on the job?
49. What sets you apart from everyone else?
50. What types of character traits do you possess that make you unique for this position?
51. Are you better working alone or as part of a team?
52. How do you handle pressure situations?
53. What are your hobbies and interests?
54. Why is this internship good for you?
55. What is your ideal job?
56. What are some of your goals?
57. What made you decide to go into this field?
58. Do you have any computer experience? If so, please explain.
59. What determines a winner?
60. What brought you to our organization? Where did you learn of this organization?
61. Why do you deserve this position?
62. How do you think this organization will benefit by hiring you?
63. Would you consider yourself more of a leader, follower, or a person who just gets (stays) out of the way?
64. What did you do with your spare time during the four years you were in college?
65. On a scale of 1 to 10 (10 highest), how would you rate yourself on dependability and the ability to work with others?

66. At any given point in time, did you ever think about giving up on receiving a college diploma? If so, what made you stick with it?

67. What would you be doing right now if you were not out on this interview?

68. How would you handle being placed in charge of a group of 10–15 employees that were all twice your age?

69. If you saw an employee stealing money who had been with the company for a long time and never caused any trouble, would you report the incident? Why or why not?

70. My theory is the more people you empower, the more room there is for a mistake. Do you agree or disagree?

71. My theory is the more people you empower, the better the organization. Explain what you believe this means.

72. Would you prefer to do everything yourself or delegate important tasks to others.

73. What do you know about our company? Why do you want a position with us?

74. Do you have a role model? Who & why?

75. Do you prefer to work with an individual or a group?

76. With what aspects of the industry are you looking to get involved?

77. How do you feel about changing your plans with little notice?

78. Why did you choose to attend the college(s) you attended?

79. What do you look for in a boss or supervisor?

80. Show me how creative you are.

81. Tell me about a time when you had to make a decision but didn't have all the information you needed.

82. What is the biggest mistake you've made in your work and how did you recover from it?

83. Give me a specific example of something you did that helped build enthusiasm in others.

84. Give me an example of a time you had to persuade other people to take action. Were you successful?

85. Tell me about a time you had to handle multiple responsibilities. How did you organize these responsibilities?

86. As of right now, our organization is running perfectly fine without you. We do not need you as much as you need us. So from our viewpoint, we have nothing to offer you. Tell us what you have to offer us.

87. There are larger schools and other schools that can offer you more in internships. So, other than the fact that we are in close proximity to where you live, why do you want to do your internship here?

88. Describe your fantasy job, its benefits and salary, where it is, and how long you plan to be on that job.

89. We see on your résumé that you interned the same place you

worked as an apprentice. Why did you decide to do this vs. learning new ways of doings things by selecting a different organization?

90. What two or three things are most important to you in your career?
91. If you could pick a position, any position anywhere in the U.S., where would you like the position to be?
92. Tell me about any group work experience you have that would be relevant to this position?
93. Where do you see this program in five years?
94. What do you feel qualifies you for this position and why do you feel you should be hired?
95. Have you done any volunteer work in this field?
96. What qualifications do you have that make you more marketable for this position?
97. What past experience, person, or information led you into this field?
98. What new insights can you bring to our organization?
99. How would you rate, from 1–10, your public speaking and communication skills?
100. What is the most self-fulfilling thing that you have done in your life regarding the sport management field?
101. Are you more of a leader or follower?
102. What is the one main new idea you would bring to our organization?
103. Will you be able to work weekends and evenings?
104. What previous experience do you have that makes you more qualified for this position?
105. Is money a strong motivator for you?
106. In what type of work environment are you most comfortable?
107. How long could we count on you staying with us?
108. When can you start if given this position?
109. Would you mind working in any geographic location if we do hire you?
110. How long do you think it would be before you could make a contribution to our company?
111. Could you handle taking instructions and orders from your supervisor? A female supervisor? A younger supervisor?
112. What qualifications do you have to be successful?
113. How will you review the performance of your employees?
114. You've never supervised anyone. What makes you believe you will be a good supervisor?
115. We like to hire interns into full-time positions. At the end of this internship, why will we hire you?

COLLEGE PROFESSOR/INSTRUCTOR

1. You have not finished your dissertation. How will you handle this with a full-time teaching position especially when your first year is very time demanding with the development of classes?

2. As a new professor, how do you plan on progressing toward promotion and tenure?
3. What will be your area of research?
4. Do you prefer teaching or research?
5. What experience do you have in academic advising?
6. Describe to us the role of an academic advisor?
7. You will be starting a new sport management program? What is your first order of business?
8. Have you ever hired faculty?
9. How do you feel about committee work?
10. Have you ever served on a committee or chaired a committee?
11. How good are your time management skills?
12. Describe your most creative teaching methodology?
13. How do you get a student who is underperforming in your class to improve?
14. We get quite a few athletes in our major. What is your attendance policy and how lenient are you with students missing classes?
15. How are you a good fit for our institution?
16. Our typical class load is four courses per semester? How do you feel about that?
17. In your graduate assistantship, what duties did you perform for your professors?
18. How did your graduate assistantship prepare you for teaching?
19. Explain the administrative responsibilities you had in sport management as a graduate assistant.
20. What responsibilities did you have as a graduate assistant that would enhance our sport management program?
21. How do you feel you will work with graduate students since you just finished your degree?
22. How in depth are your research skills? Do you feel you could teach research courses?
23. Tell us about your thesis/dissertation and what were your results?
24. What do you consider your teaching specialty? If someone already teaches this, what other courses do you feel capable of teaching?
25. What different courses do you feel you can teach in sport management?

GENERAL QUESTIONS AN APPLICANT COULD ASK IN AN INTERVIEW

1. Is there any chance of advancement in this position?
2. What will be the duties for this position?
3. What is a typical work schedule for individuals in the off season?
4. What is your strategic planning process?
5. Does everyone get to participate in strategic planning?

6. I could not find a mission or vision on your website. What is your mission and vision?
7. Where does management see this organization in five years? Ten years?
8. What is your timeline for making the final hiring decision and making an offer to someone?
9. I noticed you have a generous benefits package. Could you explain a little more about your dental/vision/medical plan?
10. I noticed your sales staff works on commission. What is the typical commission for selling a group plan? Sponsorship signage?
11. I am anxious to contribute 100% in this internship. Will I get to participate in the sales of sponsorship signage?
12. I am passionate about tournament scheduling. Will I be able to set up any tournament schedules in this internship?
13. I noticed there are several vacancies on the sales staff? Is there a particular reason for this?
14. How are sales staff members evaluated? How will I be evaluated if hired?
15. How does the organization use ticket sales to evaluate their marketing efforts?
16. What is the history of returning sponsors with this organization?
17. I noticed the organization has several foundations. As an employee, would I get to participate in fundraising for these foundations?
18. How involved is the staff in the community?
19. With the new facility opening in _____, what is the plan for the selection and hiring of new staff members to staff the facility?
20. I noticed an extensive event schedule on your website. Who is responsible for establishing the schedule or selecting events?
21. What is your anticipated salary range for this position? Have you decided on an exact starting salary?
22. I've noticed that many individuals have been with this organization quite awhile based on their bios on your webpage. Why do people like working here? Why would I like working here?
23. I am passionate about safe activities and facilities? Is there a risk management plan in place? If not, will I be able to develop one that is supported at all levels?
24. Is your staff open to me bringing in a new strength and conditioning program for your athletes?
25. I believe in a team self-scheduling system for intramural programs where teams self-select a day and time slot for all of their regular season contests? How do you think the students would adjust to this type of system?

Appendix D

Recommended Readings

Bolles, R. N. (Updated Annually). *What color is your parachute?* Berkeley, CA: Ten Speed Press.

Bynum, M. (2003, March 1). Grooming habits: How is the rec industry preparing its young professionals to be tomorrow's leaders? *Athletic Business.* Retrieved from http://www.athleticbusiness.com/articles/article.aspx?articleid=437&zoneid=10

Bynum, M. (2005, July 1). Sowing seeds: A handful of universities are disseminating essential knowledge to today's sports turf professionals and preparing the field for tomorrow's caretakers. *Athletic Business.* Retrieved from http://www.athleticbusiness.com/articles/article.aspx?articleid=1076&zoneid=24

Bynum, M. (2007, March 1). Getting to know you: With a new national program, NRPA aims to identify, qualify and train all recreation volunteers. *Athletic Business.* Retrieved from http://www.athleticbusiness.com/articles/article.aspx?articleid=1458&zoneid=38

Cameron, S. (2006). Classes dismissed. *Amusement Business, 118*(5), 10.

Chantiri, E. (2009, August, 20). Lifecycle: New fields. *BRW, 31*(33), 52.

Cohen, A. (2006, July 1). Winning personalities: Successful programs and successful program managers are everywhere you look these days, but the qualities that make true leaders are in shorter supply. *Athletic Business.* Retrieved from http://www.athleticbusiness.com/articles/article.aspx?articleid=1219&zoneid=39

Daily Telegraph, The (Sydney), (2009, September 26). Elite stars need new skills for life off the field. Careers in sport and recreation: A special advertising report.

Elfman, L. (2008). A love of sports and leading the way. *Diverse: Issues in Higher Education, 25*(17), 35.

Farr, J. M. (2002). *Getting the job you really want. A step-by-step guide to finding a good job in less time* (4th ed.). Indianapolis, IN: JIST Publishing.

Gleason, J. R. (2008). More than a game: The business of sports. *Techniques: Connecting Education and Careers, 83*(5), 20–25.

Hardin, M. (2009). Token responses to gendered newsrooms. *Journalism, 10*(5), 627–646.

Huddleston, E. (2001, September 1). A strategic move: A career in military recreation can provide extensive travel opportunities and experience. *Athletic Business*. Retrieved from http://www.athleticbusiness.com/articles /article.aspx?articleid=236&zoneid=11

Kaplan, R. M. (2002). *How to say it in your job search: Choice words, phrases, sentences and paragraphs for résumés, cover letters and interviews.* Upper Saddle River, NJ: Prentice Hall.

Matthes, F. J., & Matthews, J. M. (2008). Charting a new course. *Diverse: Issues in Higher Education, 25*(8), 32–34.

Miller, S. (2008, June 9). John Lasker: He's inventing ESPN's digital world. *Broadcasting and Cable, 138*(23), 28.

Mornell, P. (2000). *Games companies play: The job hunter's guide to playing smart and winning big in the high-stakes hiring game.* Berkeley, CA: Ten Speed Press.

Nobel, D. F. (2001). *Gallery of best résumés: A collection of quality résumés by professional résumé writers* (2nd ed.). Indianapolis, IN: JIST Publishing.

Steinbach, P. (2003, April 1). An active job market: Amid a sluggish economy and competition from the municipal sector, career opportunities in campus recreation are attracting widespread interest. *Athletic Business*. Retrieved from http://www.athleticbusiness.com/articles/article.aspx?article id=454&zoneid=39

Steinbach, P. (2007, May). Kevin Fringer: Money man Kevin Fringer paints a financial picture of the modern-day athletic department. *Athletic Business*. Retrieved from http://www.athleticbusiness.com/articles/article .aspx?articleid=1537&zoneid=36

Triola, T. N. (2008). Under representation of female athletic director at the secondary level: Thirty-five years later. PhD dissertation, Widener University. Retrieved from Dissertation Abstracts International, 2008-99190-111.

Verner, E. (2004). Internship search, selection, and solidification strategies. *The Journal of Physical Education, Recreation & Dance, 75*(1), 25–27.

Votik, J. (2009). The analysis of chosen characteristics of alumni who studied the program physical education and sport at the University of West Bohemia in Pilsen. *Human Movement, 10*(1), 67–74.

Walker, I. (2009). African American women athletics administrators: Pathways to leadership positions in the NCAA—A qualitative analysis. PhD dissertation, North Carolina State University. Retrieved from Dissertation Abstracts International, AAI3329361.

Weber, K., & Kaplan, R. (2001). *The insider's guide to writing the perfect résumé*. Lawrenceville, NJ: Peterson.

Weidlich, J. (2008). Learning sports and entertainment marketing: 'Apprentice' style. *Techniques: Connecting Education and Careers, 83*(5), 26–27.

Yates, M. J. (2000). *Résumés that knock 'em dead* (4th ed.). Boston: Adams Media.

Yates, S. M. (2008). The career development of a senior woman athletic administrator. PhD dissertation, North Carolina State University. Retrieved from Dissertation Abstracts International, AAI3306662.

Index

About the Authors

 **Susan Brown Foster**, PhD, is a former department chair and a professor in the Department of Sport Business and International Tourism in the School of Business at Saint Leo University. Since 1985, she has supervised more than 800 students in their field experiences at both the undergraduate and graduate levels. She considers her teaching specialties to be legal issues, risk management, event and facility management, recreational sport management, strategic planning, and senior seminar/pre-internship courses. Academic advising is also a passion of Foster's.

Her academic degrees are from Florida State University, Eastern Illinois University, and a PhD in sport management from Ohio State University. Foster has been elected three times to *Who's Who Among America's Teachers*, having been nominated by students in her programs. In 2006, she received the Sport and Recreation Law Association (SRLA) Honor Award for support of undergraduate student legal research and three of her students have won the outstanding undergraduate legal research award sponsored by SRLA. She has also been honored with the prestigious National Intramural-Recreational Sports Association service award for her contributions to the writing of the Certified Recreational Sports Specialist national certification exam. She has delivered more than 50 presentations from the state to the international levels and has authored 10 book chapters in leading sport management textbooks. Her journal articles have been published in the *Journal of Sport Management*, the *Journal of the Legal Aspects of Sport*, the *International Journal of Sport Management*, *Sport Marketing Quarterly*, the *NIRSA Journal*, and the *Journal of Physical Education, Recreation, and Dance*. Throughout her career, she has served on the editorial boards of four different professional journals. In 2009, she received Saint Leo University's Lifetime Publication Award.

At all three institutions where Foster has taught full-time, she was appointed to and has served a combined nine years on President/Chancellor Strategic Planning Committees. While also serving on numerous professional and institutional committees, she has chaired faculty athletic, internal and external affairs, institutional effectiveness, and curriculum committees, and was an elected member of the Faculty Senate at Western Carolina University.

Foster was elected as the chair of the Sport Management Program Review Council for five years, when she guided the national approval program for sport management curriculum at the undergraduate, master's, and doctoral levels. As chair, she conducted annual workshops for institutions preparing portfolios and individuals wishing to serve as portfolio reviewers. She currently serves on the advisory board for the Rockledge High School Sport, Entertainment, and Tourism Academy in Rockledge, Florida.

In 2009, she activated her own business, Sport Business Consulting, Inc., where she conducts consulting projects for sport organizations and assists individuals in designing their own strategies for finding employment in the sport business industry.

 **John E. Dollar**, PhD, is an associate professor in the sport administration graduate program and department head for Health and Human Performance at Northwestern State University in Natchitoches, Louisiana, his master's alma mater. He completed his undergraduate degree at the University of Central Arkansas in Conway, Arkansas, where he was a four-year letterman in track. Prior to his appointment at NSU, Dollar was a visiting assistant professor, interim program coordinator, and internship coordinator for the sport management program at Texas A&M University, where he also received his doctorate.

Dollar's publications have appeared in *Sport Marketing Quarterly*, *Athletic Business*, the *International Journal of Sport Management*, and in the online publication *Sociology of Sport*. He has co-authored abstracts that appear in several conference proceedings including the Annual Conference on Girl's and Women's Physical Activity in Sport; the Louisiana Alliance for Health Physical Education, Recreation, and Dance; and the National Association for Girls and Women in Sport. He also has a published abstract of completed research in the *Research Quarterly for Exercise and Sport*. He has presented at state, regional, national, and international workshops and conferences. Included among his publications and presentations are 19 topics involving mentoring, experiential learning, internships and supervision, service learning, career development, and curriculum development in sport management. He has also served on numerous doctoral dissertation and master's theses committees.

Institutionally, Dollar has served on numerous committees and councils including graduate council, faculty senate, standards, academic advising, scholarship, distance learning, and faculty guidelines. He received the Advisor of the Year Award in 2007 at NSU and has been nominated for the same award on multiple occasions. He was also a finalist on three occasions for the Emil Mamaliga Award, an outstanding teaching award at Texas A&M University. In 2006, he received the Peacemaker of the Year Award, a domestic violence victim's service award from D.O.V.E.S in Natchitoches, Louisiana.

Dollar has taught courses in sport law, ethics and sport governance, human resource management, recreational sport management, research in sport, and, of course, has supervised more than 1,000 experiential learning experiences for his students at both the undergraduate and graduate levels. He also possesses lifetime teaching certificates in Texas and Louisiana.